Samuel Beckett

John Pilling

Department of English Language and Literature
University of Reading

Samuel
Beckett

Routledge & Kegan Paul
London, Henley and Boston

First published in 1976
by Routledge & Kegan Paul Ltd
76 Carter Lane,
London EC4V 5EL,
Reading Road,
Henley-on-Thames,
Oxon RG9 1EN
and 9 Park Street,
Boston, Mass. 02108, USA
Set in Monotype Baskerville
and printed in Great Britain by
Ebenezer Baylis and Son Ltd,
The Trinity Press
Worcester, and London

ISBN 0 7100 8323 8

To my Mother and Father

Contents

Preface and acknowledgments

Beckett's writing has not lacked commentators in recent years, and some explanation is obviously needed to justify another full-length account of his work. The first, and perhaps best, reason is that I was dissatisfied with all the other available accounts, which, however helpful they were in one area, seemed misleading, or insensitive, in others. The second, and supplementary, reason is that a full-length account of Beckett's complete work to date, based on Beckett's own aesthetic thinking, and on the intellectual, historical and literary tradition and milieu that had sustained it, seemed to offer the best opportunity of redressing the imbalances I felt to exist. The picture of Beckett which emerges is no doubt as coloured and as partial as any other, but as long as nothing written here actually prevents or inhibits a reader's enjoyment of Beckett, no damage will have been done. Hopefully the following paragraph, together with the select bibliography, will do something to mitigate the arrogance of the dissatisfaction registered above.

I have been fortunate enough to be helped, from the early days of studying Beckett, by those who have done most to make serious criticism possible: Professor John Fletcher, of the University of East Anglia; Professor Raymond Federman, of the State University of New York at Buffalo; Professor Lawrence E. Harvey, of Dartmouth College, New York; and Dr J. R. Knowlson, of the Department of French Studies in my own university. It was conversations with Professors Alice and Kenneth Hamilton, of the University of Winnipeg, which first suggested how important Gnosticism was as a background to Beckett. The kindness of Samuel Beckett himself, in answering queries by correspondence and in conversation, permitting quotation from his work, and in making available, through the Beckett Archive in the Library of the University of Reading (Archivist: Mr J. A. Edwards), material otherwise difficult or

impossible of access, is not something one can easily repay. I have
been saved from bibliographical error by Mr G. Roe and Mr D.
Chambers, and from all the linguistic disabilities that Mrs M.-M.
Gervais, Dr R. Bruni and Mr A. B. J. Grenville could reasonably
have hoped to cure me of. The intelligent interest of my colleagues
has been much appreciated, and I am grateful to M. Jérôme
Lindon and his staff of the Éditions de Minuit for the kindnesses
shown me in Paris in 1970. It is a great pleasure to thank Professor
J. Chalker, of Westfield College, London University, for many hours
of his time, and the University of Reading Research Board for
assistance with travel. Mrs M. Quinlan and Mrs S. Waygood
typed a difficult manuscript with great patience and skill. The
errors of fact, and failures of interpretation, are my portion.

Acknowledgments are due to the following for permission to print
extracts from Beckett's works: Calder and Boyars Ltd and Grove
Press Inc. for *Proust and Three Dialogues with Georges Duthuit, No's
Knife, Three Novels (Molloy, Malone Dies, The Unnamable), Watt,
Poems in English*; Curtis Brown Ltd for *All That Fall*; Les Éditions
de Minuit for *Poémes*, the *Foirades, Esquisse radiophonique, Fragment de
théâtre*; Faber & Faber Ltd and Grove Press Inc. for *Play and Two
Short Pieces for Radio, Krapp's Last Tape and Embers*; Faber & Faber
Ltd and New Directions Publishing Corporation for *Our Exagmina-
tion round his Factification for Incamination of Work in Progress*; Grove
Press Inc. for *More Pricks than Kicks*.

Acknowledgments are also due to the following for use of quota-
tions from the works shown: Bucknell University Press for *Murphy's
Bed* by Sighle Kennedy; Cambridge University Press for *Mauthner's
Critique of Language* by Gershon Weiler; Gerald Duckworth & Co.
for *Joseph Conrad: a Personal Remembrance* by F. M. Ford; Faber &
Faber Ltd and Cornell University Press for *My Brother's Keeper* by
Stanislaus Joyce; Faber & Faber Ltd and E. P. Dutton Inc. for
Yeats: the Man and the Masks by Richard Ellmann; The New
American Library for *Hyperion* by F. Hölderlin, trans. W. Trask;
New York University Press for *Jacques the Fatalist and his Master* by
D. Diderot, trans. J. R. Loy; Miss M. Playter for *The Enjoyment of
Literature* by J. C. Powys; Yale University Press for *Existential
Thought and Fictional Structure: Kierkegaard, Sartre, Beckett* by E. Kern.

All translations appended to works quoted in French are by the
present author.

The University   J.P.
Reading

1 Biographical

The author is never interesting.   (Samuel Beckett)

True lives do not tolerate this excess of circumstance.
                                                    (*Malone Dies*)

others knowing of my life only what they could glean
by public records hearsay   (*How it is*)[1]

The hearsay, as one would expect, reveals little of value. The public records reveal that Beckett was born on 13 April 1906 (appropriately enough for this God-haunted man a Good Friday), the second son of a quantity surveyor who married a nurse. 'You might say I had a happy childhood,' Beckett has said, 'although I had little talent for happiness.'[2] It was, however, perfectly normal on the surface: he went running, played cricket and rugby with his brother Frank, and went fishing with his father. His parents were Protestants in Catholic Ireland and he was brought up 'almost a Quaker'.[3] He is still proud today of the fact that the Becketts spring from Huguenot stock.

At Ida Elsner's Academy, a kindergarten he attended at Still-organ, and later at Earlsfort House prep school in Dublin, where he first learned French,[4] Beckett began to reveal the scholastic ability that later led to a university teaching post. Hand-in-hand with this went a developing sensitivity to suffering. He gave up eating lobsters when he discovered they were boiled alive (a theme dramatized in 'Dante and the Lobster'), drew pictures of tramps, and suffered from a fear of heights that seems to have been brought on by his father giving him diving lessons.[5] The sight of Dublin blazing in Easter Week 1916, as he and his father looked on from the hills above the city, has remained deeply impressed on his mind. The deaths from tuberculosis of members of his family was a cause of great sadness in the early years; the death of a girl cousin he was particularly close to was perhaps the most crucial of all.[6]

At the age of 14, during the Easter term, he joined his brother as a boarder at Portora Royal School, a well-known public school at Enniskillen, near the Republic. Here he showed considerable ability at French, Latin, Classics and English, swam distance races and sprints, boxed, and continued to play his favourite games – rugby and cricket. His juvenilia seem, mercifully, to have disappeared; while they would no doubt offer a fascinating insight into what he had been reading, they could only have been derivative and lightweight.[7] A more important consideration is the kind of distinctively Irish environment in which he was growing up, marvellously summarized by Joyce's brother, Stanislaus:

> there is properly speaking no national tradition. Nothing is stable in the country; nothing is stable in the minds of the people. When the Irish artist begins to write, he has to create his moral world from chaos by himself, for himself . . . [it] proves to be an enormous advantage for men of original genius.[8]

Another enormous advantage for men of original genius in Ireland is the existence of Trinity College, one of the great places of learning since its foundation in 1591. It was here, in 1923, three years after going to Portora, that Beckett began to read for a degree in Modern Languages (French and Italian). His tutor was A. A. Luce, the editor of Berkeley; his professor, T. B. Rudmose-Brown, was a poet, and editor of Marivaux, Racine and Corneille. Beckett very largely inherited the enthusiasms of these two men; his first play, little more than a skit, was subtitled 'a Cornellian nightmare', and when he lectured on *Andromaque* years later as a don, he analysed the play as characters chasing each other in a circle[9] – which may tell us more about the future author of *Murphy* than about Racine. After a good, and then an indifferent year, he got the best First of his year and was elected in 1926 to a Foundation Scholarship. In his leisure moments, he went to the Abbey Theatre, where both the acting and the plays were as good as anything to be seen at the time.

Further academic success followed. He was awarded the Large Gold Medal in Modern Literature during the Michaelmas term of 1927, and his Bachelor of Arts in the December of that year. He went as a teacher to Belfast ('a terrible place', he told me, 'full of bigotry'), spent two terms at Campbell College and then, in October 1928, went to the École Normale Supérieure in Paris, which counted Sartre and Simone Weil among its students.[10] He had been abroad before this: in 1926, with an American friend, he had cycled through the Loire Valley; in 1927, he had gone to Florence, with its wealth of Renaissance paintings (often referred to in his later art criticism). The move to Paris nevertheless represented a major change in his life: it was his first important job, his first considerable period abroad, a release from the Irish parochialism so memorably satirized in *More Pricks than Kicks* and, most important of all, it led (thanks to Thomas MacGreevy) to him meeting James Joyce and the group of intellectuals and helpers he had gathered round him during his long quest for recognition. With Joyce he shared a liking for arcane facts and figures, a love-hate relationship with Ireland, an interest in experimental literary forms, and a strong affection for alcohol. At the same time Beckett renewed his friendship with Alfred Péron, who had taught at Trinity by the same exchange agreement that had allowed Beckett to come to Paris. The friendship with Péron brought him face to face with danger in later life, the relationship with Joyce (with whom friendship was difficult) led to a complete change of direction.

'Paris in the twenties', he told me, 'was a good place for a young man to be.' Since then, in countless books of memoirs, it has been all things to all the artists and writers who made it the intellectual centre of Europe: a moveable feast,[11] a whore,[12] a mistress,[13] the City of the Sun,[14] 'a great machine for stimulating the nerves and sharpening the senses',[15] 'exciting and peaceful'.[16] For Beckett it may have been any or none of these; it was, at any rate, financially a good place to be, and intellectually the most exciting city in the world at that time. France, 'the most intellectually sensitive of modern nations',[17] and its culture, delicately poised between classical and romantic affiliations, had dominated European literature since the eighteenth century, and at the end of the nineteenth century, after a curiously brief and in some ways half-hearted flirtation with Romanticism proper, it was from France, and specifically from Paris, that the first stirrings of what has come to be called 'modernism' began to be heard. No mere rehearsal of names and ideas could possibly do justice to this period of experimentation and achievement, which sustained French writers and artists through the First World War, encouraged *émigrés* from America, Ireland, Germany and England in the *entre deux guerres* period, and provided a solid basis for the survival of French culture after the fall of France. It is less a matter of 'the great tradition' than most Englishmen might care for, and much more a sometimes indefinable atmosphere which has nothing to do with the merely picturesque. Since the middle of the seventeenth century, through a bewildering number of social and political changes, France has offered a soil in which the most advanced artistic ideas can come to fruition and flourish, without necessarily succumbing to the idols of the marketplace. The 'banquet years' came and went,[18] just as the Magny dinners had done,[19] but the cuisine, for those not suffering the traditional English *pudeur*, remained, for over a hundred years, one of great range and richness.

Beckett's Paris preserved features of 'la belle époque'. But a change, much more dramatic than that experienced in England, or in Ireland by Yeats, came with the First World War, most sensitively analysed in the second chapter of the last volume of Proust's great novel, as the sirens and aeroplanes threaten, though they cannot crush, the epicureanism his narrator has been a part of for so long.[20] The culture of the salons is momentarily revealed, through the afternoon party at the house of the Princesse de Guermantes, in a flash more devastating than even the German aeroplanes can inflict. The new dispensation, into which Beckett found himself thrown, was once again dominated by women, by the Americans Gertrude Stein, Sylvia Beach and Peggy Guggenheim, by Adrienne Monnier, and by the English upper classes in the shape of Nancy Cunard. It was moneyed without being aristocratic; the patron was much more intimately involved in what she patronized, and the greater dependence on personal, even idiosyncratic, taste was an inevitable result of the chaos of values that the First World War had brought into being. An excellent exchange rate, a beautiful city, the chance to develop an independent way of life, and the opportunity of working in close contact with Joyce, must be one of the more powerful seductions circumstance has ever exerted on a writer whose academic commitment was tenuous enough to be severed within three years.

Between teaching duties, Beckett worked on two projects in the library of the École. The first was a study of Descartes towards which a £50 prize had been given by Trinity; the second was a study of the Unanimiste group of poets led by Jules Romains and Pierre-Jean Jouve. The influence of Descartes on his subsequent writing can hardly be overestimated. He liked Romains's concrete imagery and met Jouve, but the meeting was a disappointment to him, and although Jouve was 'deeply haunted' by 'the Nada theme, the theme of absence',[21] Beckett's interest in him lapsed with his religious verse. The Unanimistes were clearly a passing enthusiasm only, although in 1934 he was still speaking highly of Romains.[22]

During this period Beckett was obviously engaged in reading everything he could lay his hands on, free from the constrictions of his university syllabus. The bulk of his attention, as is natural with any writer of talent, must have been given over to his contemporaries and associates, but he seems to have had more time for the writers of earlier periods – no doubt partly as a result of his scholarly training – than is perhaps usual in a modern writer. The 'wonderful memory' which he appears to have had as a young man[23] is everywhere in evidence in his early writing, which constantly alludes to what he has been reading, renowned or remote. 'Dream' in particular shows clearly that he was afflicted, much more than a less well-educated writer would have been, by the compulsion to see life in terms of literature, through the spectacles of others, before he could actually respond to it, or use it as material for fiction, in a truly exploratory way. As he developed as a writer, he realized more and more that the horror and pain of living could not be domesticated and tamed by the culture he had acquired, and the realization that his creative gift could only be satisfied by the expression of his own innate feelings must, whenever it came, have diminished all other cultural activity (with the exception of Joyce's, which was as much a moral as a fictional model)[24] to a greater or lesser degree. The plunge into philosophy may conceivably have been conducted in a spirit of escape from precisely such activity, but there are indications, in his earliest published essay, that mere philosophy was no more use to him than mere literature. The play of ideas, the fascination with the way they reappeared in startlingly different contexts and in ever more complex configurations, would ultimately have to be abandoned in the face of a force that he had already recognized, in 'Assumption', as irresistible and decisive.

At the same time more amusing events were taking place. After the famous dinner of 27 June 1929, at the Hotel Léopold near Versailles, held to celebrate (belatedly) the French translation of *Ulysses* and the anniversary of Bloomsday, Beckett's desire for alcohol provoked Joyce to leave him behind, as Joyce put it, 'at one of those palaces . . . inseparably associated with the Emperor Vespasian'.[25] More eccentrically, he would sit up half the night in his room at the École playing the flute, 'an instrument of which he was far from being a master'.[26] Beckett has always had a profound interest in music – he is an accomplished pianist and is married to a musician – but this anecdote also suggests that he cared little for the traditional pieties, or for his colleagues' sensibilities. His growing disaffection for the scholarly life is reflected in the fact that he did little research while in Paris; 'I slept through the École', he told me recently.

In this same year, 1929, his first published work, a learned, intellectually exhibitionist account of the background to Joyce's 'work in progress', *Finnegans Wake*, was published in the little magazine *transition*, run by Eugène Jolas. The history of *transition*, which survived through different formats until 1950, still requires to be written, but above and beyond the inherently romantic story of the little magazine and the big fish (Joyce), it is important to realize how necessary Jolas was to the unknown writer in the 1930s and 1940s. The distinguished figures to be found in the files of *transition*, made available to the intellectual public for a relatively cheap outlay, with occasional printing vagaries not even a surrealist could have dreamed up, were given the chance to express themselves in a way that might turn out to be more ephemeral than a book, but which also might enable them to translate their experimentalism into something of permanent value.[27] Joyce, as acknowledged leader of the *avant-garde*, had no difficulty (and sometimes little scruple) in persuading his friends to help him in any way they could. The peculiarly synthetic quality of the text – the fact that it was to be written in an entirely new polyvalent language appreciable at several levels – together with Joyce's gradual blindness, meant that Joyce needed considerable help from members of his circle. Beckett and others based essays on these discussions, apparently written under fairly close surveillance from Joyce himself. Beckett's independence of mind survived this, but as an explanation of what Joyce was up to, the essay is too self-indulgent to be completely satisfactory. Beckett's critical journalism during the 1930s in London – upon which he often depended for survival – shares the same faults: an over-allusive approach bred of distaste for the task and uncertainty as to his own direction in life. His first creative work of any importance, a short story called 'Assumption', shares many of the same faults, but from our point in time it marks out where his real interest lay. Jolas, who was a friend of Beckett's until his death in 1952, was followed as editor by Georges Duthuit, who was discerning enough to suggest that Beckett make public his ostensibly absurd views on art. The quality of the contributions to post-war *transition* is sometimes a little disappointing because Duthuit's policy was less adventurous than Jolas's, but Duthuit at least continued Jolas's policy of publishing extracts from works in progress; and it was in *transition* that extracts from *Molloy* first reached the public. The real death of *transition* had nothing to do with quality and everything to do with the inexorable murderers of the little magazine, lack of money and lack of interest.

During this period in Paris Beckett briefly met Ezra Pound, but although his interest in medieval literature was something he shared with Pound, neither then nor later did the two men become friends, though Pound regretted this in later life.[28] While assisting Péron and others in the immensely difficult task of translating part of Joyce's 'Work in Progress' into French, a more interesting project came his way. As a result of a recommendation by Richard Aldington[29] (who, with Nancy Cunard, had helped to found the Hours Press and published his poem *Whoroscope*), Beckett wrote a critical study of Proust's massive novel *A la Recherche du temps perdu*. He gave up (as he still rather ruefully phrases it) his long vacation to reading the sixteen volumes of the 'abominable' NRF edition[30] *twice*. After such concentrated activity and after becoming emotionally involved with Joyce's schizophrenic daughter Lucia[31] (which later led to a temporary estrangement from Joyce) it is hardly surprising that, when he returned to Ireland in the summer of 1930, to take up a post as Lecturer in French at Trinity, his mother was shocked to see how thin and ill he looked. After a few sporadic literary efforts, the groves of academe seemed to have claimed him for good.

Back in Ireland he read the philosophers Geulincx, Kant and Schopenhauer,[32] of whom the first and last particularly interested him. Schopenhauer is still a figure likely to call forth from Beckett such terms as 'wonderful' or 'extraordinary', and he always stresses how fine his *writing* is. He lectured on the poets Alfred de Vigny and Alfred de Musset, on the great nineteenth-century novelists Balzac, Flaubert and Stendhal, on Racine, and on the philosopher Bergson. At about this time he met Jack B. Yeats, the painter brother of the more famous poet and Nobel prizewinner W. B. Yeats. Increasingly, his teaching duties became more and more irksome. After a few terms he resigned his post, leaving in Easter 1932: 'I saw that in teaching I was talking of something I knew little about, to people who cared nothing about it. So I behaved very badly; I ran away to the Continent, and resigned from a distance.'[33] It is characteristic of his rigorous humility that this manifestly brilliant man can admit that 'he could not bear the indignity of teaching to others what he did not know himself'.[34] It is also characteristic that his guilt at resigning in mid-session, and from the safety of the continent, should still so haunt him in the 1950s that he should wish to order all royalties from his play *Krapp's Last Tape* to be presented to his old university.[35] It is further characteristic of the kind of courage he later showed in both his life and his art that he gave up the safe and cloistered academic world for the altogether more uncertain and difficult life of creative writing.

He returned to Ireland, having given up his first attempt at a full-length novel, 'Dream of Fair to Middling Women'. Its best passages he used again for a collection of stories, *More Pricks than Kicks*, which sold very poorly and was a 'fiasco' (as he calls it), though it is now a rare collector's item. During this period he wrote a number of poems, one of the most affecting of which is a poem on the sudden death of his father in 1933, from a heart attack. 'What am I to do now', he wrote to a German friend, 'but follow his tracks over the fields and hedges?'[36] It is no surprise to learn that, following this, the two years in London (1933-5) were 'bad in every way – financially, psychologically'.[37] He was looked after by an Irish landlady in comfortable lodgings in the World's End area of Chelsea, and was often in contact with the artists and writers connected with the great Surrealist Exhibition of 1936. But it was most of all the depressing landscape of the poorer parts of Chelsea, leading down to the Embankment, ruled over by Lots Road and its power station, that dominated his imagination. They compose the background for the opening of his novel *Murphy* (begun in 1935 and recommended to Routledge by Herbert Read),[38] and one can perhaps be forgiven for finding the conjunction of arbitrary divine justice (in the story of Lot) and the World's End strangely prophetic of his later interests. The novel also celebrates a hospital for the mentally ill at which one of his friends was a doctor, and at which Beckett worked, for a while, as an orderly.[39] His sympathy for the sick and incurable had been crystallized by the deaths of members of his own family, and in the environment of the hospital he became consumed with sadness at the human condition in general. His feelings of helplessness were reflected in his addiction to silence. It was apparently in the company of Joyce, who was also addicted to silence, that one of the main differences between the two men became clear, Joyce being mainly troubled about himself, and Beckett about the world in general.[40]

A period of 'lostness . . . apathy and lethargy'[41] followed. In November 1935 he left England for Germany, moving from town to town, concentrating on the art galleries and museums. The large number of places he visited suggests how restless he was: Hamburg, Lübeck, Lüneburg, Brunswick, Leipzig, Halle, Nuremberg, Weimar, Würzburg, Regensburg, Hanover, Munich, Berlin, Dresden.[42] These last three cities were particular favourites, but it was in Dresden that he first heard the voice of Hitler over the radio. His close relationship with such Jewish intellectuals as Willi Grohmann (whose work on Kandinsky he later praised, and whose job had been taken away from him by the National Socialists) helps to explain his later behaviour after the fall of France. He lived a very solitary life at this time, reading much German literature, but made the acquaintance of such artists as Ernst Barlach and Karl Schmidt-Rottluff, famous for his work in originating the Brücke group. It was at this time that he first read Fontane's *Effi Briest* and the 'magnificent' poems of Hölderlin.

He returned briefly to London, and then left England for good in the October of 1936, taking a hotel room in Montparnasse. He had to return to Ireland in the autumn to give evidence in a libel case centring on Joyce's old acquaintance Gogarty, in which he enjoyed a brief celebrity in the Dublin newspapers as 'the Atheist from Paris', despite his disclaimer that he was nothing of the kind.[43] In the spring of the following year he moved to a seventh-floor flat off the rue de Vaugirard, where he remained until 1961. At 6, rue des Favorites, the novel trilogy, *Waiting for Godot* and the other works of Beckett's most concentrated period were written. They were written in French, a language Beckett apparently used only for poems in the early years of his residence in France. Beckett began writing in French primarily out of dissatisfaction with English; in 1929 he had written, 'No language is so sophisticated as English. It is abstracted to death.'[44] He had at first been tempted to adopt an escape route which his countryman W. B. Yeats had recommended: 'Our common English', wrote Yeats, 'needs such sifting that he [who] would write it vigorously must write it like a learned language.'[45] *Murphy* convinced him this was no solution. When he came to write that extraordinary rationalization of the irrational, *Watt*, it was particularly important that words should become hard-edged, without any vaporizing on the periphery. According to Ford Madox Ford, Joseph Conrad had been troubled by similar problems:

> He used to declare that English was a language in which it was impossible to write a direct statement . . . no English word is a word . . . all English words are instruments for exciting blurred emotions. 'Oaken' in French means 'made of oak wood' – nothing more. 'Oaken' in English connotes innumerable moral attributes. . . . Conrad desired to write a prose of extreme limpidity.[46]

Certainly a prose of extreme limpidity – much more limpid than Conrad's ever was – was the primary effect of the change, although there are moments in *Watt* which suggests he might have been able to achieve this in English as well. The change to French was clearly more than simply a question of technique; it involved him in a linguistic alienation more emotionally important even than the geographical alienation he had already undergone.

'Anyone who wishes to excel as a poet', wrote Vico, 'must unlearn all his native language, and return to the pristine beggary of words.'[47] Writing in French enabled Beckett to do precisely this. Although in one sense it was much more an act of will than leaving England, it was an act of will that made things difficult as well as easy. There was to be no easy intellectualizing in the manner of *More Pricks than Kicks*; style could no longer be exhibitionist, it must

9

be so functional that it would appear to disappear. He 'couldn't help writing poetry' in English;[48] in French he could write 'without style. . . . Perhaps only the French can do it'.[49] It became Beckett's aim to prove that an Irishman could do it as well.

Beckett has spoken of coming to live in Paris permanently as being in some sense like coming home. It was not, however, in any sense, an unalloyed homecoming. After only a year there, he was gratuitously stabbed in the back by a *clochard* on the avenue d'Orléans.[50] Joyce was especially upset and anxious, and visited him in hospital. The knife had narrowly missed his lung, and he was fortunate to live. It is reported that his assailant visited him in hospital, that Beckett asked him why he had done it, and that the man replied, 'Je ne sais pas, monsieur', with the helpless ignorance of one of Beckett's heroes.[51] Another important visitor at this time was the French woman he later married.

The surface of day-to-day living, mildly affected by the heartening news that *Murphy* had received one or two favourable reviews in the London press, was shattered again eighteen months later, in June 1940, when Beckett was among those forced to leave Paris in the general exodus before the conquering German army. He went to Vichy, where he met Joyce for the last time, then went south, first on foot, then by train to Toulouse, and on to Cahors and Arcachon. In October of that year he returned to Paris, but in January of the next year he was heartbroken to read of Joyce's death in a Paris evening newspaper. He made contact with his old friend Alfred Péron, and through him joined a Resistance network centred on the secret agent (and translator of Melville) Armel Guerne. Information on troop movements was classified by Beckett, translated, typed out and prepared for microfilm. This 'boy-scout stuff', as he calls it,[52] ended in disaster. A member of the network 'blew' the group after torture, and Péron was arrested. (He was taken to a concentration camp, and died at the end of the war.) Péron's wife sent a cryptic telegram to Beckett, which he received at 11 o'clock on the morning of 15 August 1942. Four hours later he was gone, one of the thirty who escaped from a network of eighty. Once again he was on the move: Vichy once again, Avignon, and finally the small village of Rousillon in the Vaucluse above Avignon, whose connection with Petrarch must have seemed, at the time, a relic of civilization[53] amid so much barbarism. While on the run he disguised himself as a French peasant; safe in the Vaucluse he became, to all intents and purposes, exactly that, working as a farm labourer and odd-job man during the day. In the evenings he would talk with the painter Henri Hayden (in later life a very close friend), listen to Henry Crowder's music played on the old upright piano,[54] and compose his second novel *Watt*, 'to get away from the holocaust of war and occupation'.[55] The novel remained unpublished until 1953, by which time his novel trilogy in French from the post-war years had been published.

In August 1945, as the war ended, Beckett, at the suggestion of a close friend who was a doctor (whose death is the subject of the fine poem in French 'Mort de A.D.'), applied for a post as interpreter at the Irish Red Cross Hospital at Saint-Lô in Normandy. He also helped with supplies, unloading on the Dublin wharves, and co-ordinating materials coming from Cherbourg and Dieppe. After six months, at the beginning of 1946, he returned to Paris, to find his old apartment, miraculously, still available.

The *vita activa* was followed by years of contemplation. For the next six years, before success burst in upon him, he lived a life of great seclusion, writing a succession of works that publishers chose to ignore. His wife Suzanne indefatigably hawked his manuscripts round from one firm to another, while Beckett himself remained characteristically helpless and resigned to his fate.[56] Through the foresight and sensitivity of Jérôme Lindon of the Éditions de Minuit, these works finally saw the light of day. In 1951 Lindon read the opening sentences of *Molloy* ('It was like taking a walk', Beckett told me, when he spoke of the comparative ease he had in writing *Molloy*), and instinctively knew he was confronted with something unique. Lindon deserves praise and credit for accepting a work that he must have felt was a certain commercial disaster, even after the sensitive early reviews. *Molloy* is now, ironically enough, estimated to be one of the largest-selling Minuit publications, and it is fair to say that the fortunes of the publishing house most often associated with the *nouveau roman* were very largely revived, from an apparently irretrievable position, by the interest in Beckett's writing.

Beckett is primarily known, however, for his play *Waiting for Godot*, which was produced in Paris in 1952, and in London in 1955. Beckett had, in the late 1940s, seen a rehearsal of Strindberg's play *The Ghost Sonata* and decided that the producer, Roger Blin, who had been a friend of Artaud, was the right man to produce *Godot*.[57] Blin apparently thought just as highly of the still unpublished 'Eleuthéria', but ultimately chose *Godot* because it only required five actors and funds were low. The play proved such a puzzle to theatre-goers and critics that such inauspicious beginnings soon ceased to matter. The columns of the august *Times Literary Supplement*, on which Molloy found not even farts could make an impression,[58] burned with all the white-hot indignation of a *cause célèbre*. Although Beckett had forecast (and perhaps secretly hoped) that it would play to empty houses,[59] *Waiting for Godot* was an immense popular success. It was the popular success of *Godot* and the critical praise lavished on his subsequent drama that gave Beckett financial security for the first time in his life, and enabled him to buy, in the French manner, a house in the country and a new flat in Montparnasse, on the street from which pilgrims used to begin the journey to Santiago de Compostella – the irony is doubtless not lost on him. The years of hardship and deprivation have been such that they could not be simply shrugged off, and the blandishments of the mass media have proved to be nothing more than a torment to a man whose reticence is not characteristic of his profession. The man who contrived not to appear on the photograph of Joyce's Bloomsday celebrations, and who in 1948 refused to deal seriously with even a *transition* interviewer,[60] has been more than a match for newspaper reporters who have realized what good copy the extremity of his reticence can make. 'Success and failure on the public level never mattered much to me, in fact I feel much more at home with the latter, having breathed deep of its vivifying air all my writing life, up to the last two years.'[61] The less vivifying air of personal bereavement brought him back to Ireland in 1950 and 1954 for his mother's and brother's deaths,[62] and in 1959 he received an honorary degree from his old university.

His flat commands a view across Paris that many would envy, which short-sightedness does not allow him to enjoy. It also provides an unrivalled view of the Santé prison as a constant reminder of human suffering, in an area of Paris that has recorded public executions in living memory. The packed bookshelves of a man who once took pride in bookishness are now secondary since, as he says, 'I must keep my eyes for my work'. He writes in a condition of absence so extreme that he can remember very little of what he has written.[63] He is known to despise fame and fortune, although the Prix Formentor in 1961 and the Nobel Prize in 1969 were marks of public recognition he had no wish to avoid, and was grateful for. As writing has become more and more difficult, he has turned more and more to the minutiae of production. He has become, like Stravinsky, his own interpreter. He retires to work in his 'hole in the Marne mud',[64] when not supervising productions in Berlin, Paris or London. Two walls keep away unwanted visitors and the view from the house makes no concession to the picturesque. As time allows, he works in the garden, following Candide's advice, 'to keep himself from thinking'.[65]

2 Writings on literature and art

A testimony to the intimate and ineffable nature of
an art that is perfectly intelligible and perfectly
inexplicable.
                                                    (*Proust*)[1]

The most important neglected part of Beckett's total *oeuvre* to date is
undoubtedly his criticism, which he himself repeatedly disparages
and which remains uncollected. It is no part of my intention to
examine it as criticism, though it is only fair to point out that the
Proust book (1931) and the *Our Exagmination* essay (1929), especially
the former, are both a good deal more than Beckett prophetically
outlining the course he in fact followed for the next forty years.
These essays, and his other scattered writings, are, in fact, an
essential prerequisite to a full understanding of Beckett, and if at
times they are difficult to understand – Beckett's range of reference
is very large and his style bizarre – he is rarely less than stimulating
and always exciting. Behind the erudition is an intense interest in
the theory and practice of art in general and his own art in particular.

Tracing the development of Beckett's aesthetic thinking involves
extracting from his scattered reviews those passages where Beckett is
unmistakably speaking in his own voice. The task is complicated
by the fact that Beckett's *literary* criticism is actually quite sparse,
most of his critical corpus consisting of art criticism, 'best forgotten'
in Beckett's opinion.[2] Furthermore, it is almost entirely called forth
by the fact that the painter under discussion is one of Beckett's
personal friends, who has either been unjustly neglected or unjustly
criticized. This is the case with his article on Henri Hayden and his
frequent essays on the van Velde brothers; it is also the case in his
reviews of poems by Thomas MacGreevy and Denis Devlin.[3]
Beckett has remained constant in his interests: he wrote five separate
pieces on the van Velde brothers between 1938 and 1961, and three
on Jack B. Yeats between 1936 and 1954.[4] Appropriately enough,

the three paintings hanging in his Paris flat are by Bram van Velde, Henri Hayden and Jack B. Yeats.

Joyce was also a personal friend, and it was to defend his 'Work in Progress' that he wrote *Dante . . . Bruno. Vico. . Joyce* at the age of 23. Among the more interesting contents of this earliest performance are a warning: 'The danger is in the neatness of identifications. . . . Literary criticism is not book-keeping',[5] and a surprisingly violent attack on such book-keepers:

> if you don't understand it, Ladies and Gentlemen, it is because you are too decadent to receive it. You are not satisfied unless form is so strictly divorced from content that you can comprehend the one almost without bothering to read the other. This instinctive skimming and absorption of the scant cream of sense is made possible by what I may call a continuous process of copious intellectual salivation. The form that is an independent and arbitrary phenomenon can fulfil no higher function than that of a stimulus for a tertiary or quaternary conditioned reflex of dribbling comprehension. . . . Here form *is* content, content *is* form.[6]

The conclusion is less impressive than what builds up to it; the crude wrath was an indulgence Beckett did not allow himself when he came to write *Proust* – though he described it to me as an 'angry book' – written largely in a café near the École Normale Supérieure where he taught between 1928 and 1930. This brief essay, commissioned by Richard Aldington, is easily the high-water-mark of his criticism, though he refuses to translate it into French. Although he gave over his university long vacation to reading the 'abominable sixteen-volume edition' twice, and still regards it as more about Proust than himself,[7] the aesthetic beliefs behind it strike one immediately as having great relevance to Beckett's own practice as a writer. From behind a pseudo-metaphysic of time – split into its component parts of habit and memory – comments on technique occupy the centre of the discussion, notably in the surreptitious introduction of his basic premise in the second paragraph: 'He is aware of the many concessions required of the literary artist by the shortcomings of the literary convention. As a writer he is not altogether at liberty to detach effect from cause.'[8] Only much later does he reiterate and expand this anti-logical stance, praising Proust for his 'fine Dostoyevskian contempt for the vulgarity of a plausible concatenation'[9] and for the way he has grasped the implications of such an alogical procedure: 'he understands the meaning of Baudelaire's definition of reality as "the adequate union of subject and object" and more clearly than ever the grotesque fallacy of a realistic art – "the miserable statement of line and surface", and the penny-a-line-vulgarity of a literature of notations.'[10] The book-keepers are again taken to task; Beckett never names names but he seems to be thinking of the naturalists, Wells, Bennett, Zola, *et al.* What is clear is that a complete way of looking at the world – and the concomitant way of reproducing it as art – is being outlined; the reality of the 'realists' is no more real than that of the 'impressionists', among whom he numbers Proust. He is careful to define precisely what he means by this term: 'By his impressionism I mean his non-logical statement of phenomena, in the order and exactitude of their perception, before they have been distorted into intelligibility in order to be forced into a chain of cause and effect.'[11] Once again logical form is attacked, and the method of this impressionism is revealed: 'The copiable he does not see. He searches for a relation, a common factor, substrata. Thus he is less interested in what is said than in the way in which it is said.'[12] Leaving on one side for a moment the concern with style, it is clear that this assertion of substrata, of an internal form, has been necessitated by the removal of external form, 'the chain of cause and effect'. Beckett harks back to Baudelaire again to explain the double form of the creative process, the perception of reality by the artistic mind and the reproduction of it in art by the workman:

> The work of art [is] neither created nor chosen, but discovered, uncovered, excavated, pre-existing within the artist, a law of his nature. The only reality is provided by the hieroglyphs traced by inspired perception [identification of subject and object] . . . for the artist, the only possible hierarchy in the world of objective phenomena is represented by a table of their respective coefficients of penetration, that is to say, in terms of the subject. (Another sneer at the realists.) The artist has acquired his text: the artisan translates it. 'The duty and task of a writer (not an artist, a writer) are those of a translator.'[13]

The double process described here in oblique terms is only made clearer when he returns to the implications for style, left on one side after his assertion that Proust is more interested in manner than matter. When he turns to discuss Proust's style, Beckett repeats the indivisibility of form and content that he had earlier found in Joyce:

> style is more a question of vision than of technique . . . he makes no attempt to dissociate form and content. The one is a

15

concretion of the other, the revelation of a world. The
Proustian world is expressed metaphorically by the artisan
because it is apprehended metaphorically by the artist: the
indirect and comparative expression of indirect and comparative
perception.[14]

Proust's double 'impressionism' is here clearly stated and placed
alongside the non-logical statement of 'substrata'. Although the
'substrata' are very much part of Proust's project, related to the
excavation mentioned earlier, on two occasions Beckett seems to
read rather more into *A la Recherche du temps perdu* than is actually
there, giving us the tantalizing glimpse of a writer unknowingly
prophesying his own course:

> The only possible spiritual development is in the sense of
> depth. The artistic tendency is not expansive, but a contraction.
> And art is the apotheosis of solitude. There is no
> communication because there are no vehicles of
> communication. . . . The only fertile research is excavatory,
> immersive, a contraction of the spirit, a descent. The artist is
> active, but negatively, shrinking from the nullity of
> extracircumferential phenomena, drawn into the core of the
> eddy.[15]

The disappearance of the artist by total immersion is not an
original idea – Flaubert's *style indirecte libre* and Joyce's God behind
the handiwork had already propounded this notion – but these two
passages are nevertheless original in their suggestion of a sinking
circular structure at the centre of which the artist may be found,
solitary, uncommunicating. The 'core of the eddy' recalls 'the ideal
core of the onion'; both are symbols of Beckett's idea that 'the only
world that has value and significance' is 'the world of our own latent
consciousness'.[16] This is to be Beckett's own territory; he will go on
excavating and contracting, only to find the centre of the circle does
not exist. And if the ideas on communication are not new – Eliot and
Hulme, to name only two, had anticipated these – the horrifyingly
logical pronouncement that 'There is no communication because
there are no vehicles of communication'[17] is an astonishingly
accurate forecast of the struggles he will later wage, and indicate
how near we are to the nihilism of the surrealists Beckett knew.
Unconsciously perhaps – he admitted to me: 'Perhaps I overstated
Proust's pessimism a little' – Beckett has placed his Proust just where
Edmund Wilson (in the same year, 1931, in *Axel's Castle*) places
him, on the main thoroughfare from symbolism to surrealism.

The implications of this final necessity – we move from premise to process to product to audience – are not elaborated in *Proust*. But in 1932 he wrote his first full-length novel 'Dream of Fair to Middling Women', and certain implications become very much clearer. It is cast in so loose a mould that there is ample space for Beckett to develop his opinions on every conceivable matter, but uppermost among his aims is a desire to formulate for himself (in the uncannily prophetic manner of the *Proust* monograph) an aesthetic in which he can put his faith. It contains a passionately mandarin account of the mechanics of creation:

> The night firmament is abstract density of music, symphony without end, illumination without end, yet emptier, more sparsely lit, than the most succinct constellations of genius. . . . The ecstatic mind achieving creation . . . rises to the shaft-heads of its statement, its recondite relations of emergal, from a labour and a weariness of deep castings that brook no schema. The mind suddenly entombed, then active in an anger and a rhapsody of energy . . . such is the ultimate mode and factor of the creative integrity, its proton, incommunicable; but there, insistent, invisible rat, fidgeting behind the astral incoherence of the art surface.[18]

Beckett's desire is that we should 'school ourselves . . . from the desire to bind for ever in imperishable relation the object to its representation'[19] and he is concerned enough to hypothesize an ideal response: 'The experience of my reader shall be between the phrases, in the silence, communicated by the intervals, not the terms.'[20] He has accepted that the absolute absence of absolutes commits one to a median position: 'for me the one real thing is to be found in the relation.'[21]

Even more importantly, it commits one to passivity in relation to one's material; only in this way can one avoid falsifying the relationship. The right kind of passivity is hedged round with a number of courses masquerading as ideal. There is the studied randomness, reminiscent of Surrealism: 'one can always organise a collision. . . . But how . . . could it be anything but the fruit of a congruence of enormous improbability?'[22] There is the consolation of the undifferentiated picaresque: but 'fake *blasé* . . . is a vulgarity that I cannot tolerate'.[23] Nothing merely auto-destructive will do: 'How could the will be abolished in its own tension? . . . The will and nill cannot suicide.'[24] Two solutions offer themselves: the first is the 'incoherent continuum' that he associates with Rimbaud (and, rather more eccentrically, with Beethoven),[25] the second is the 'perpendicular, *diamanté*' styleless writing of Racine and Malherbe, writing of great clarity that is not ashamed to show the materials, 'the flints and pebbles . . . humble tags and commonplaces' of which it is composed.[26] As yet Beckett can see no way to bring these two together and collapse them into one another, but a considerable amount of dead wood has been cleared away. And the subject-matter, at least, is situated. The 'dark gulf', with the 'glare' of the will expunged, has been seen, and seen clearly. Now only the means to reproduce a place 'where there was no conflict of flight and flow . . . without axis or contour' are lacking.[27]

In the next six years he wrote several reviews, but none of them reveals a significant development in his thinking. Much of his most profound thinking was obviously done in private, and in a letter to a German friend, Axel Kaun, in 1937, he revealed how difficult a solution would be: 'Grammar and style. They appear to me to have become . . . obsolete. . . . A mask.'[28] His area of concern is much more obviously technique than in the earlier published works and the very basis of literary expression, language, comes in for a startling attack. Beckett's aim is a 'literature of the Unword' where language is eroded 'until that which lurks behind it . . . begins to trickle through.'[29] What he later (in 1962) called a 'syntax of weakness'[30] is even outlined in detail in the letter: 'Is there any reason why that terribly arbitrary materiality of the word's surface should not be dissolved . . . so that for pages at a time we cannot perceive [the tonal surface] other than . . . as a vertiginous path of sounds connecting unfathomable abysses of silence.'[31] This desire for an erosion of language is a natural step from the assumption in *Proust* that there are no vehicles for communication, but in a contemporaneous essay on the poet Denis Devlin, Beckett develops one of the more important implications of this as far as the audience of art is concerned:

> Art has always been this – pure interrogation, rhetorical question less the rhetoric. . . . The time is not perhaps altogether too green for the vile suggestion that art has nothing to do with clarity, does not dabble in the clear, and does not make clear, any more than the light of day (or night) make the subsolar, – lunar and – stellar excrement.[32]

Here he states bluntly that the task of art is to contemplate and not to solve problems. The laboratory novel of the naturalists, the social novel of the 1930s, the *engagé* work of any period, all this, Beckett would claim, manifests a 'morbid dread of sphinxes, solution clapped on problem like a snuffer on a candle'.[33] There is a respectable ancestry for this theory that art does not explain, but only contemplates. Chekhov for example wrote: 'you confuse two conceptions: the solution of a question and the correct setting of a question. The latter alone is obligatory for the artist.'[34] Flaubert also said: 'The stupidity consists in wanting to arrive at conclusions.'[35] Less respectable, and rather more verbose, is the similar claim of the surrealistically orientated 1932 manifesto *Poetry is Vertical*, among whose signatures Beckett's name appears, and among whose ideas is the idea of loss of self developed in the *Proust* essay:

> The final disintegration of the 'I' in the creative act is made possible by the use of language which is a mantic instrument, and which does not hesitate to adopt a revolutionary attitude towards word and syntax, going even so far as to invent a hermetic language, if necessary.[36]

The 1938 distaste for clarity is clearly an extension of this but, for all Beckett's despair about the possibilities of words, he is not yet in anything like an extreme position with regard to expression.

It is in his first major article on the van Veldes, of 1945, that the insufficiency of the word becomes critical: 'each time that one wishes to make words do a true work of transference, each time one wishes to make them express something other than words, they align themselves in such a way as to cancel each other out.'[37] The crucially important idea of 'cancelling out' is new, even if the sneers at the realists' 'stories of objectivity and things seen'[38] are not. The idea of translation first propounded in connection with Proust's 'impressionism' is retained, but in a slightly modified, slightly vaguer form:

> There is no painting. There is only pictures. These, not being sausages, are neither good nor bad. All that one can say about them is that they translate, with more or less loss, absurd and mysterious compulsions towards the image, that they are more or less adequate oppositions of obscure internal tensions.[39]

The procedure is no longer so clear-cut: the compulsions are 'mysterious', the tensions 'obscure', the results only approximate. The need to reflect ordinary phenomenal reality has effectively been removed altogether, and the practice of art has been made much more difficult:

> To force the deep-seated invisibility of exterior things, to the point where invisibility itself becomes a thing . . . that is a

labour of diabolic complexity, which requires a framework of
suppleness and extreme lightness, a framework which insinuates
more than it asserts.[40]

While this outline of internal form is an elaboration of elements that
can be found in *Proust*, artistic composition is now seen as inherently
much more problematic, in fact 'a labour of diabolic complexity'.
Beckett briefly toys with the idea of impossibility which figures so
importantly in the *Three Dialogues* four years later: 'For the painter,
the thing is impossible. It is moreover, in representing this impossibility that modern painting has extracted its greatest effects.'[41]
With this state of affairs now prevailing, it is hardly surprising to
find criticism dismissed as 'hysterectomies with a trowel'[42] and to
learn that 'the work considered as pure creation, whose function
stops with its genesis, is consecrated to the void'.[43]

His second major article on the van Veldes, of 1948, is largely a
repetition and consolidation of already stated views. Having decided
in the first article, that 'the static thing in the void' is 'finally ... the
visible thing, the pure object',[44] he again praises these painters for a
totally new approach to the old question of subject and object,
reality and representation. They are the trail-blazers in what he
calls 'the first assault on the object grasped independently of its
qualities, in its indifference, its inertia, its latency',[45] and their
particular brilliance lies in 'glimpsing in the absence of relation and
in the absence of object the new relation and the new object'.[46]
Form, it must be stressed, is still retained, but it will be a form unlike
anything ever seen before, and the content which it shapes, and
which shapes it, will be equally new, since the process of perception
and representation has been fundamentally altered. The artist's aim
and the realization of that aim stand now in an essentially problematic relation to one another.

On the thesis that the problematic and impossible are the essence
of modern art, no more subtle analysis than the *Three Dialogues with
Georges Duthuit* exists. These highly stylized arguments were born
from actual conversations Beckett had with the then editor of
transition, and were re-worked and published on Duthuit's suggestion
that Beckett make his views more generally known. As an introduction to the three painters dealt with they are perhaps only marginally
enlightening, but as brief, brilliantly constructed vignettes (full of
incidental Beckettian humour) clearly outlining Beckett's theories,
they are of extreme interest and importance to the reader. In the
first, on Tal Coat, Beckett replies to Duthuit's description of pure
abstraction as the liberation all artists have longed for by question-

ing whether a real revolution has taken place on even the most basic level. For him, Matisse and Tal Coat have only 'enlarge[d] the statement of a compromise' by remaining 'on the plane of the feasible'.[47] Tal Coat is only doing what has always been done; 'thrusting towards a more adequate expression of natural experience'.[48] Duthuit common-sensibly asks, 'What other plane can there be for the maker?' Beckett's reply is that logically there can be none, but accepted ideas of logic are something he had been combating since 1931. This does not prevent the final development of that 1931 position being a massive paradox: 'The expression that there is nothing to express, nothing with which to express, nothing from which to express, no power to express, no desire to express, together with the obligation to express.'[49] But what other conclusion can there be to a situation in which there is no communication and no vehicles of communication? Most important of all perhaps is Beckett's emphasis, no doubt due to the experience of the trilogy, on the fact that the artist is no longer in control:[50] he is, by an ambiguous force of whose origin he is ignorant, somehow compelled to express despite the total obstacles to expression. Logic has been replaced by conditions of paradox and impossibility which, in the second dialogue, Beckett admits may only be a dream: 'my dream of an art unresentful of its insuperable indigence and too proud for the farce of giving and receiving.'[51] And yet to anyone who finds remaining 'on the plane of the feasible' a good thing, Beckett asks: 'What is the good of passing from one untenable position to another, of seeking justification always on the same plane?'[52] The dialogue on Bram van Velde is designed to show precisely how his friend has gone one step further than anyone else: 'Others have felt that art is not necessarily expression . . . van Velde is the first whose painting is bereft . . . of occasion in every shape and form . . . and the first whose hands have not been tied by the certitude that expression is an impossible act.'[53] The 'impossibility' is dramatically formulated in Beckett's parallel statements concerning van Velde's situation and what he does with it: 'The situation is that of him who is helpless, cannot act, in the event cannot paint, since he is obliged to paint. The act is of him who, helpless, unable to act, acts, in the event paints, since he is obliged to paint.'[54] When Duthuit squarely faces for the first time the 'obligation' Beckett spoke of in the first dialogue, his question, 'Why is he obliged to paint?' only receives the reply, 'I don't know.' His second query, 'Why is he helpless to paint?', prompts Beckett to a simpler statement of his idea in the first dialogue: 'Because there is nothing to paint and nothing to paint with.'[55] Thus, with the logic he affects to despise, Beckett demonstrates that if it is an art of the impossible, it must also necessarily be an art of failure. In Beckett's own words: 'To be an artist is to fail, as no other dare fail.'[56] This accounts for the 'impasse' he encountered to the writing of the trilogy,[57] the subject and object united by Baudelaire are now always threatening to cease to exist. He has moved from the position of language being problematic to that of the whole of existence being problematic. Everything becomes a paradox. As Beckett said to Roger Blin, 'I have nothing to say but I can only say to what extent I have nothing to say.'[58]

In these scattered essays Beckett is demonstrably more concerned with the genesis of a work of art and the conditions in which and out of which it comes to exist; only occasionally is he concerned with formal categories. And yet as well as a gradual erosion of language in the ever-contracting excavation inwards, which gives a general direction to Beckett's work as a whole, there is also the necessity from Beckett's point of view, for pattern in the separate works that make up the corpus, works with a form much like that he found in Bram van Velde's paintings: 'a framework of suppleness and extreme lightness, a framework which insinuates more than it asserts.'[59] The question of form dominates the 1961 interview with Tom F. Driver. Beckett first of all distinguished his work from Kafka's, in one of his most brilliant and accurate self-analyses: 'Kafka's form is classic, it goes on like a steam-roller, almost serene. It seems to be threatened all the time – but the consternation is in the form. In my work there is consternation behind the form, not in the form.'[60] The new, 'un-classic' form is elaborated in detail, when Beckett talks, as he often does, of 'the mess':

> The confusion is not my invention. . . . It is all around us and our only chance now is to let it in. The only chance of renovation is to open our eyes and see the mess . . . there will be new form, and . . . this form will be of such a type that it admits the chaos and does not try to say that the chaos is really something else.[61]

In a 1962 conversation with Lawrence E. Harvey, Beckett made quite clear what it is that causes 'consternation' – it is the artist's self: 'Being is constantly putting form in danger. . . . I know of no form that does not violate the nature of Being in the most unbearable manner.'[62] But he went on to say, using almost the same terms as those of the Driver interview, 'If anything new and exciting is going on today, it is the attempt to let Being into art.'[63] The implicit equation, Being = Chaos, is, of course, felt everywhere in Beckett's fiction, and it is the equation of a man who can say,

'I'm not interested in any system . . . I can't see any trace of any system anywhere'[64] and who can nevertheless write prose fiction with as fine a sense of form as anyone now writing.

Since there has been a 'rupture of the lines of communication between subject and object'[65] ('Recent Irish Poetry', 1934), both the artist and the occasion have become unstable terms of relation. 'All that should concern us', therefore, 'is the acute and increasing anxiety of the relation itself.'[66] By 1945 Beckett was convinced that this was what would constitute the new relation, but in 1949, talking to Duthuit, he was unable to prove it to his own satisfaction. In the *Three Dialogues*, his most severe formulation, he reasserts the absence of occasion, and yet postulates a kind of imprisoned freedom for the painter Bram van Velde, less free than Masson's and more dearly bought, but more impressive in so far as it is operating in an entirely different set of conditions, beyond 'the plane of the feasible'.

Van Velde is 'free' because of his helplessness; he does not know what he wants to do, and he is incapable of achieving it anyway: desire and potency are dead. Yet he is only paradoxically free, for certain areas have inevitably been ruled out altogether in moving beyond the plane of the feasible. His freedom is so limited that it is quite remarkable that he paints at all. Van Velde's struggle is, consequently, of a much higher order than Masson's 'wriggling',[67] or the 'fidgets' of Rilke he had complained of fifteen years before.[68] Leonardo's *disfazione* (destruction) (which fascinated Beckett as early as the *Proust* volume)[69] masks a basic possessiveness inherent in him;[70] van Velde's *disfazione* is genuinely contingent, unwilled and uncontrollable. Van Velde is an artist who remains in the domain of the particular, with his eye on the object but who nevertheless achieves, by some magic that Beckett does not discuss, a form that can be generally appreciated. Beckett's analysis of his own work in 1961 is strikingly similar and, incidentally, a model of lucidity: 'The form and the chaos remain separate. The latter is not reduced to the former. That is why the form itself becomes a preoccupation, because it exists as a problem separate from the material it accommodates.'[71] A formulation like this helps to explain his difficulty in coming to terms with Surrealism. He knew many of the leading surrealists and praised it in 1934 as 'celebrat[ing] the cold comforts of apperception'[72] but by 1945 he found its 'dérèglement . . . de tous les sens' too rationally (and hence wilfully) based, describing it (via Lautréamont, whom the surrealists revered) as 'a sewing-machine on an operating table'.[73] The phrase nicely catches the mechanical qualities he finds in Surrealism at the same time as summoning up a fantastic surreal image. Beckett admits that such

B

painting can produce masterpieces, but temperamentally he prefers work like Jack B. Yeats's who 'brings light, as only the great dare bring light, to the issueless predicament of existence',[74] or that of the van Veldes' that 'state[s] the space that intervenes'[75] as a result of the sundering of subject and object. In a text written to accompany the catalogue for an exhibition of Avigdor Arikha's work (1966) Beckett both describes and embodies his predicament. Through an imagery of battle ('siege', 'wound', 'truce') Beckett develops the idea that the 'without' is 'impregnable', 'unseeable', 'unmakeable'. Expressing oneself is still possible, but expression is severely reduced in scope. The painter's job, like the writer's, is to record the 'marks of what it is to be and be in face of', the latter part of which phrase emphasizes once again that a symbiosis is unavoidable, and that the object cannot simply be ignored.[76] We have travelled from Baudelaire, whose aesthetic formed the basis of the *Proust* volume, and who turned the book of nature into a 'dictionnaire hiéroglyphique'[77] through Joyce, whose 'Work in Progress' had the 'savage economy of hieroglyphics';[78] to Bram van Velde, who intuits hieroglyphs without the wherewithal or the desire to translate them into more accepted language-codes. Van Velde – and, more importantly, Beckett – achieves a generalized particularity which becomes an ebony tower rather than the more familiar ivory variety.

Despite this last sleight-of-hand – this recommendation of the 'tour d'ébène'[79] – it is sometimes difficult not to feel that Beckett's criticism reveals an acutely enervated aestheticism peering from behind a somewhat quixotic rationalism. Judged by his own high standards of excellence, he is clearly no Valéry. But there is a very genuine honesty (bred of helplessness) in the confusions and evasions, and a manifest intelligence (residue of the failure of the Faustian intellect) at work in these writings. Furthermore, by post-dating the practice, the theory helps to make it more accessible, without having to enter the work (as Joyce's did) to do so. He rejects unequivocally symbolism, satire, Prometheanism, misanthropy, sensationalism and pot-boiling, and rests his case on a qualified humanism. This humanism has been variously described as 'defensive', 'quietist' and 'graveyard' and should at all times be distinguished from the tragic variety exemplified by Camus.[80] It is, nevertheless, determinedly humanistic because Beckett's aim is a literature that is 'the passive receptacle for a self entirely independent of literary inventiveness'.[81] He realizes it is impossible of attainment. 'You realise the absurdity of what you advance?' says Duthuit. To which Beckett replies, 'I hope I do.'[82]

3 The prose fiction

It is not a question of saying what has not yet been said,
but of repeating . . . what has already been said.

('Peintres de l'empêchement')[1]

There are unquestionably a number of special problems for the
reader approaching Beckett's fiction seriously for the first time. It is
only occasionally difficult to catch the tone of voice, and not difficult to grasp his vision. But it is sometimes difficult to bring the
two things together. This is especially true if we think of his works
as wholes rather than brilliant fragments with desultory linking
narratives. One-man shows and gramophone records of excerpts
have inevitably pushed Arsene's 'short statement' from *Watt* and
Molloy's stone-sucking into the limelight, but they are really only
parts – admittedly very brilliant parts – of works conceived and
executed as wholes.

The plots of his novels (such as they are) do not lend themselves
to paraphrase and paraphrase is likely to leave the reader in the
state of fascinated puzzlement in which he began. A more sensitive
method is needed, a method which does not separate out story and
meaning as if they were independent. Accordingly, in the first part
of this chapter my discussion centres on the structure of events
in the world of Beckett's fiction, and the second part supplements
this with detailed consideration of some of the special techniques by
which the events become fixed in our minds. Before doing either of
these things, a general survey of the bases on which Beckett's fiction
is built is essential. And it is built, like all fiction, on language above
all.

'Language', wrote the German philosopher Cassirer, 'harbours the
curse of mediacy, and is bound to conceal what it seeks to reveal.'[2]
Mauthner (the logical positivist from whose work Beckett read

aloud to the blind Joyce in the early 1930s) also stressed the epistemological implications of this curse of language:

> If the 'I' – consciousness, if individuality, is seen to be but
> deception, then the very ground whereon we stand trembles
> and our last hope for even a trace of world knowledge
> collapses. . . . The subject disappears behind an object and we no
> longer detect any difference between the philosophic endeavour
> of eons of humanity and the dream existence of an amoeba.
> Even the concept of individuality has become verbal abstraction
> without representational content. . . . Then there is nothing but
> words in the 'I'.[3]

Perhaps we no longer even need such learned authorities as these to testify to the peculiarly contemporary obsession with the inaccuracy of language as an instrument; it is designed to express, but, almost actively, refuses to do so. Our deepest insights remain incommunicado. Our most pressing concerns are dissipated by truisms and made to seem trivial and absurd. The whole of Beckett's work stems from this realization, and the realization has two prongs: rage that things should be so, and resigned acceptance that things must be so. Between these two poles, passing through a number of intermediate zones, the narrator, Beckett's *alter ego*, his representative in the work, oscillates.

For Beckett, the universe is made of silence; silence existed before man came, and silence will supervene when he goes. Every word uttered (and by extension every word written and sent to the publishers) is somehow an impertinence, a needless addition to a state in which, if admittedly nothing is said, at least nothing can be misunderstood. In his plays, he has allowed the silence that *Krapp's Last Tape* fades off into to become the very substance of a work like *Breath*; in his prose work such a drastic step has proved completely resistant to the medium; 'you must say words as long as there are any' the Unnamable realizes.[4]

In recent years, however, in exploring the landscape of the mind, he has unveiled a land in which signs can hardly be interpreted, where the act of interpretation is bedevilled by the compulsion to express, and where expression is reduced to a denuded, occasionally hermetic language. The long wrestle with language ends with something uncommonly like language winning, and the words that one has mathematically controlled conveying only the abstraction of mathematics. But the struggle, in its remorselessness and in its courage, compels one's admiration.

At the same time Beckett has always known how to write well by traditional standards, and his so-called 'preciosity' has even seemed, to some, out of key with his professed aims.[5] But his lyricism (felt particularly in the Celia scenes of *Murphy*) can be overstressed, and it is often not simple wish-fulfilment so much as a deft and even desperate attempt to see if precision of a different kind can be attained. Hence even the most recent work has its lyricism. The anthropomorphic outlet of landscape may be cut off: 'Islands, waters, azure, verdure, one glimpse and vanished, endlessly, omit', as it says in *Imagination Dead Imagine*.[6] But the quiet tone and the cadenced rhythm often betray traces of nostalgia, of resignation not quite dead: 'Rediscovered miraculously after what absence in perfect voids it is no longer quite the same, from this point of view, but there is no other. . . . But go in and now briefer lulls and never twice the same storm. . . . No, life ends, and no, there is nothing elsewhere.'[7] Even *Ping* has its 'eye unlustrous black and white half closed', even *The Lost Ones* its moments of union, while *Enough* is, throughout, suppressing behind its blandness an emotion that would spill if not restrained. In avoiding pathetic fallacy, the early prose seeks scientific objectivity. The 'tesserae of small fields' that compose 'Fingal' in *More Pricks than Kicks*[8] may seem precious to some, but the attempt at accurate clear-sightedness, plus the fact that Belacqua has impetigo, effectively squashes any consoling lyricism. In the same way, the 'g' of Molloy's Mag does yeoman service in destroying his notion of his mother:

> I called her Mag because for me, without my knowing why,
> the letter g abolished the syllable Ma, and as it were spat on it,
> better than any other would have done. And at the same time it
> satisfied a deep and doubtless unacknowledged need, the need
> to have a Ma, that is a mother, and to proclaim it audibly.[9]

This is Beckett's disarming doubleness at its best. It involves no more fence-sitting than Johnson's deep moral explorations in *Rasselas*; it is the balance of tragi-comedy, the largeness of vision that takes in both real and ideal, the philosophically serious and the ludicrously absurd.

Such doubleness does, however, naturally give rise to uncertainty, and uncertainty gives way to crippling doubt. Beckett himself has itemized 'perhaps' as the key word in his work[10] and occasionally (as in the Unnamable's 'Dim intermittent lights suggest a kind of distance')[11] doubt is so thoroughgoing as to almost annul the words that are said. Although Beckett is perfectly familiar with the technical rhetorical term for what Descartes elevated into a method – 'aporia'[12] – it is not always Beckett's method; the fatalism of

Murphy ('So all things limp together for the only possible')[13] to some extent precludes it. But even there the notion of swings and roundabouts elevated to sonorous paradoxes ('Nothing to lose. . . . Therefore nothing to gain'; 'Humanity is a well with two buckets.')[14] has something aporetic about it. Aporia pure and simple, as the Unnamable realizes, runs the risk of tedium; even the second possibility he entertains, 'affirmations and negations invalidated as uttered', fail, and when they fail, 'other shifts' must be tried, approaches of greater sensitivity.[15] All, however (as the word 'shifts' suggests), involve jolting us out of our usual quotidian certainties and complacencies; and constantly trying other ways of solving the problems.

Now since language is a system doomed to failure, it is only natural that, in the human need for order, other systems should be turned to; this is, in itself, a matter for despair because for a writer, the need to believe in his primary system of language is obviously crucial. Broadly speaking, the other systems in which comfort can be sought are either scientific and rational, or aesthetic and intuitional. Mathematics and astronomy (the latter explored in *Murphy* especially) are offshoots of the first; religion is one of the forms of the latter. In *How it is*, in which the narrator semi-nostalgically recalls his past abilities, scientific systems predominate: natural sciences, anatomy, geography and arithmetic are among those mentioned. Of these it is, as many commentators have pointed out, arithmetic that fascinates Beckett most. It can be a solace in itself; Murphy's biscuits may get eaten by Miss Dew's dog, but at least he can arrange them to his satisfaction. By contrast, the opening words of 'The Expelled' reveal that the ostensibly simple act of counting steps is in fact attended with crippling difficulties; this is the first really serious erosion of the certainty of mathematics. Molloy's sucking stones prove much more difficult to arrange (and much less satisfying when arranged) than Murphy's biscuits; this is one of the low points of the arithmetical escape-route. By the time of *How it is*, however, things arithmetical have taken an upward turn. After innumerable repeated claims that there is 'something wrong there', it is momentarily comforting, in the middle of part three, to find that something is 'correct', not just once, but five times,[16] in each case accompanying a piece of mathematical computation worthy of a school-teacher. Later, it is true, the system comes briefly under threat ('something wrong there' soon returns) but nevertheless the important statements of the section get stated. In the most recent work, where language has proved less and less helpful, the narrators have taken refuge in the geometry and arithmetic necessary to chart the position of bodies in cylinders (*Imagina-*

tion Dead Imagine), or in calculating how large groups of 'vanquished ones' can circulate in a cylinder (*The Lost Ones*). The fascination with cylindrical shapes is itself new; in the days when numbers seemed a doubtful escape-route, such forms as the circle (*Watt* and *Molloy*) and the ellipse (*The Unnamable*) were Beckett's favourite shapes. The increased solidity of cylindrical forms is certainly appropriate to the increasingly abstract and allegorical writing of Beckett's recent period, whereas trudging round the perimeter of an endless and immaterial circle or ellipse is an image that, while not exclusive to the trilogy, is particularly appropriate to it. Whatever form is adopted, by the time of *How it is* arithmetic has not been totally vindicated. 'I always loved arithmetic it has paid me back in full'[17] says the narrator, with a special fury, precisely because it had seemed to offer a genuine alternative to language which it cannot really provide. Only in *Imagination Dead Imagine* and *Enough* ('We took flight in arithmetic')[18] is the discipline finally adopted, and the prose begins to approach ultimate circumscription. In *Enough* the repetition of all the possible hypotheses in a given permutation is only one paragraph long, but *Ping* and *Lessness* are in permutative form throughout.

Permutation depends on both repetition and reduction; a field is marked out and arrangements are reiterated. In Beckett's prose reduction is first of all evident in his subject-matter. Beckett's own, very familiar, description of his interests is perhaps the clearest: 'I'm dealing with something other artists have rejected as being by definition outside the realm of art . . . the zone of being.'[19] However, the zone of being, as the philosophers of the Enlightenment discovered when they turned their attention to it, is an area the location of which may be difficult: propositions about the self are unverifiable and ultimately meaningless because, as Beckett puts it in *Proust*, 'the observer infects the observed'[20] precisely because of the specially privileged position that ideally ought to make for acute vision. At this point repetition (or as Beckett would call it 'habit') enters the lists; for while it is of no earthly use repeating something that cannot possibly be true, it is only human ('a lobster couldn't do it',[21] as the Unnamable says) to believe that the ultimate and most relevant truths (even or perhaps especially in the deflated wisdom of clichés) have been much the same for all times and for all people. Equally, man being what he is, he has always had similar imaginative flights; religious writers from Zoroaster to Milton and beyond have persistently spoken of light paradises and dark hells.[22] It is even arguable, in a doubtful situation, when all is flux and nothing makes much sense, that what the mind and senses repeatedly think and feel *must be* the answer to the problem. And, in any case, great satisfaction can obviously be obtained from hurling one's defiantly held opinions into the face of an apparently hostile or indifferent universe, and so repetition can provide solace of a rather more negative kind.

The question of repetition is bound up with the question of time. Beckett's people are repeatedly placed in a condition very similar to Augustine's: they know well enough what time is, provided no one asks them or they are not compelled to ask themselves. When either of these conditions do apply, they are baffled. The narrator of *Murphy* knows perfectly well what time is, but then for him time is linear and seems like a succession of points on a line drawn into eternity, and even he gets his time-scheme confused and tangled till about half-way through, at which point he can forget about his characters' diversity in space, and concentrate on their coincidence in time. For Watt, Molloy, Moran, Malone, time has become more of a continuum, a kind of vacuum in which incidents occasionally happen, but so rarely that they cannot be satisfactorily related one to another. It is as if time has been lengthened; events of accepted importance happen with greater infrequency, throwing emphasis on events of lesser importance. Only seasonal markers (summer, autumn, winter, spring) and religious festivals (St John the Baptist's day, the Assumption, the Annunciation) remain: seasons are vague indicators, and feasts are moveable. It is hardly surprising therefore that Beckett's narrators adopt the 'One day. . . .' form of narration popular among storytellers from the earliest times; it is, for the most part, all they have to go on. When, after a while, time ceases to be linear and end-stopped and is seen to be circular and eternal, the merely individual occurrence is swamped. It is unpleasantly like Fortune's Wheel in fact, though without the prospect of death as a way out. For the unpalatable truth that circular time forces on Malone and the Unnamable (since Molloy and Moran remain almost unscathed) is that death will never come, any more than Godot will ever arrive or (to use an example Beckett is fond of) Zeno will ever halve his heaps. And if the only paradise is the paradise that has been lost (as Beckett says in *Proust*),[23] so that it is only time and not paradise that can be regained (Proust's vision rather than Milton's),[24] then the triadic vision of Dante that so appealed to Beckett (hell, purgatory, paradise) has to be replaced by a kind of monadic condition[25] which, for Beckett, is purgatorial. And purgatory is a concept that can apply to Beckett's work from his first published essay to his latest published fiction.

Repetition, or habit, is a partly volitional kind of thing when it is a matter of utterances and images; but time cannot be regarded in the same light. 'He that runs against time has an antagonist not subject to casualties.'[26] Time (as revolutionizers of narrative have recognized from Sterne onwards) is an antagonist no narrator can afford to take lightly. It is of the very essence of narrative; a story in the past tense must by definition have already taken place in some reality. It is all very well to say that the reality concerned is fictional; the past tense none the less confers reality on fictional events in such a way that (as numerous examples attest) readers often forget which is which. Now for the novelist intent on recording the reality of the present moment (and in his present writing someone else's past), this is clearly a problem which is only partially eased by the adoption of a stream-of-consciousness technique. And for the novelist unsure of his actual existence in the present moment, the position is even more desperate, for the stream is subject to drying up. Beckett's solution is characteristically imaginative. He adopts (and surely this is one reason for his change to French) a tense that is neither present nor past: the imperfect. And he does this under the tutelage of Proust, whose novel doubtless crystallized his thoughts on time in the first place. Proust called the imperfect a 'cruel tense, which presents life to us as something at the same time cruel and passive, which in the very act of retracing our actions turns them into illusion', and said that it 'always remained for me an in-exhaustible source of mystery and sadness'.[27] In Cassirer's terms, it is the tense *par excellence* to harbour the curse of mediacy, but Beckett's people are in a median position, and it suits them admirably.

The end result of being in this median position is that Beckett's narrators return again and again to clearly marked points of or-ganization. It can be a system with which we are familiar and in which we can place external credence, such as the astronomical or linear time systems of *Murphy*, or the mathematical permutations of the later work; or it can be a system with which we are unfamiliar, which is in fact only created by the work we are reading, such as the images of sea in *Malone Dies*. In each case it is repetition which fixes the system in our minds, amplifies it, gives it body and relevance. From the narrator's point of view it guarantees the form he feels is necessary for art, 'without trying to pretend that the mess is other than it is'. It is this which explains the extraordinary need felt by every narrator from Murphy onwards to repeat often the most trivial material over increasingly wide areas of text. One parallel pair of relatively unimportant phrases in *The Unnamable*, for instance, need to be linked up over twenty-three pages of unparagraphed and turbid prose.[28] Obviously, the more the repeated elements operate on the surface, the more comforting they are; the quasi-Dickensian narrator of *Murphy* with an eye for the joke relies on this being true. But it is equally true for the nameless narrator of the permutative texts: the blankness and opaqueness provide him with a refuge which ordinary language denies his invented character. It provides him, in fact, with a text he can disappear into. It is precisely in those texts that most often discuss the need for calm ('The Calmative', *Malone Dies*) that calm seems farthest away, and tenses change rapidly, and repetitions seem least likely to happen. And it is only when repetitions occur (as the Unnamable shows in his exordium) that one can relate the fragmentary atoms of one's environment. Thus the man who gives Molloy money comes every week, the woman who fills Malone's dish and empties his pot comes every day, and the Unnamable notices that Malone is a frequent visitor and the pseudo-couple Mercier–Camier an infrequent one. 'A and C I never saw again', says Molloy boldly, only to find that the denial of recurrence leads to problems: 'But perhaps I shall see them again. But shall I be able to recognise them? And am I sure I never saw them again?'[29] Most readers have felt that he does meet at least one of them again, during his peregrinations through the forest. But, in the same way as both acts of *Godot* repeat each other with slight differences, in Beckett's fiction events may only be said to almost repeat, as if the fact of repetition were both a comfort (since it provides a criterion for ordering experience) and a torment (since it suggests that cyclic flux will always dominate). Thus Watt's departure from Mr Knott's house (forecast by Arsene) means not only the failure of his quest and the harsh return to the world of everyday, but also the fulfilment of a predetermined pattern (once again we recall Molloy's half-serious account of Leibniz's pre-established harmony)[30] that has provided for him the solace of the lunatic asylum and the 'companionship' of Sam.

Repetition as a device is also of particular importance when we think of Beckett's imagery, through which much of his meaning is conveyed. Inevitably, his images, as befits a writer whose plots can be so easily assimilated into myths, are the most frequently used images of the past: light and dark, sound and silence, desert and sea. In *The Unnamable* and *Texts for Nothing* the 'penny-a-line vulgarity' Beckett spoke of in *Proust* has been left far behind, and manifestly unreal situations (situations which are themselves merely images, approximate projections of events in the phenomenal world) are tested out against the coherent minutiae that comprise reality. In his most recent work he is doing something else again, treating the image as the real and ending up somewhere near allegory, which as a form he had castigated in no uncertain terms in *Proust*.[31] Speaking of Addison's *Vision of Mirza* Beckett said that good allegory is flat writing. *The Lost Ones* sometimes seems perilously close to being good allegory, but flat writing.

When we look at the structure of events we see the way all these considerations get dramatized. The point that Molloy comes back to is always his mother; Moran returns always to the question of Molloy; Mercier and Camier return to the comfort of Hélène's. Departure is usually attended with difficulties. The most striking examples of the obscure need to return before finally departing occur in *Murphy*, where Murphy returns before leaving for good, and where Wylie returns to assault Miss Counihan. Scarcely less notable is Arsene's return in *Watt* before he vanishes, and Watt's return later in the book when he comes to leave Knott's house.

'All roads were right for me, a wrong road was an event for me', Molloy says; Mercier agrees.[32] It is not simply that the myth of the journey dominates their minds; it is more a matter of feeling that every action is determined. They feel threatened from without, like centres a prey to circumferences. Murphy, seeking himself, is sought by others. Even though their quest is not successful (only Celia sees him alive of those who need him, and Miss Dew and Ticklepenny and Endon don't need him), he is much more in demand than any later Beckett hero. The hero of 'The End' is only an exhibit in a Marxist orator's argument; but the medians 'or whatever the hell they are' of the *Murphy* world meet ('outside us' as Neary carefully notes)[33] in Murphy and nowhere else. The place Murphy ends up at may be a more ironic version of the earthly paradise than Sam and Watt's garden in *Watt*, but it is the only meaningful centre any character achieves. The others remain helplessly scattered on the circumference, unable (or unwilling) to change state. Celia goes back on the game, and will always dream of Ireland in preference to pursuing her inner self, Bom Clinch (like any caricature) will always act the same whatever situation presents itself. With the exception of Celia (who briefly tries to achieve Murphy's second zone), the secondary characters are both peripheral to the plot and only peripherally alive. But even Murphy's quest for the mystically timeless is destroyed by what historians of religion would call the fall into time, the restitution of history that death brings into being.[34] Death is truly the great leveller; the old butler and Mr Kelly, neither of whom have mystical pretensions, finish up in much the same way as Murphy. And yet Murphy's quest, though a failure, is much more successful than the quests of his successors. He can construct in his mind the conditions necessary for calm, and find a niche for himself in the external world that mirrors these conditions as nearly as possible. The calm of flux may seem paradoxical, but the mental hospital is obviously a satisfying external projection of the internal need for a hermetic situation, the 'closed system' of Neary's horse-dealer's daughter from Proverbs.[35]

Watt's quest also fails, but his end is eternally deferred. The structural displacement of his journey to the asylum being placed in the narrative after his arrival there throws the weight on the asininely sentimental remarks of the group on the station: 'And they say there is no God, said Mr Case. / All three laughed heartily at this extravagance.'[36] There is for them no conflict between self and world, but Watt is taking refuge in the asylum precisely because, in his quest for the absolute, he has found that conditions cannot suit his temperament. His excessively rationalist approach is really only happy detailing (a) what did not happen, and (b) what could have happened but did not – the negative and the hypothetical. Faced with what actually did happen (especially if it only happened once), Watt's system breaks down. Faced with the inexplicable, the almost invisible Mr Knott, he finds the situation as genuinely ineffable as a practising Christian (which Watt is not) could wish. But Watt is not so much concerned with what is lawful, only with what is feasible. The broken, backward-talking figure of the end is the same genuine figure of pathos he was at the beginning. But there may be some confusion in Beckett's working out of the plot here. The quest for God having failed, the earthly paradise of the asylum seems fairly easy to achieve. Perhaps the very struggle of the first militates against its success (the true mystical experience being spontaneous and intuitional); perhaps the very ease of the second contributes to its attractiveness. The fatalism seems less oppressive than Hardy's because the character persists in inquiry. In the later novels, all inquiry is doomed and resignation supervenes. And the expulsion from home is more critical – actively bringing about the suffering that follows and constituting the first event the recording consciousness feels drawn to discuss. There is no asylum to go to; in this respect they are, reluctantly, freer than their forbears.

Murphy's emotions are in excess of the facts as they appear; the avoidance of sexual involvement (Celia) and personal and monetary involvement (the Neary group) is described in a gutsy Dickensian way that makes life seem preferable to death. The celebration of Celia especially contributes to this. Watt's sufferings are more real, but his expression of them is mediated by the neutralizing force of Sam, who reduces everything to the same level, and when Arsene and Arthur become narrators, things liven up considerably. Paradoxically, Watt's sensitivity is so extreme that it can seem insensitive, and his psychology is really as conditioned in reflex as any Pavlovian could wish. There is a suggestion here of what Beckett castigated in others when speaking of 'the morbid dread of sphinxes'; Watt's rationalism is really 'solution clapped on problem like a snuffer on a candle':[37] the book suffers from being too clear, too allegorical; far from there being 'no symbols where none intended', there are symbols everywhere inviting us, like Watt, to explain and exorcize.

In the *Nouvelles* a freer psychology is at work. The quest is narrower; it is no longer for a house and a head, but simply for a home. The hero of 'The End' goes into the mountains to look for one; the hero of 'The Expelled' makes do with a stable. Molloy has found a home, though he doesn't know how. In writing his story, it is really the owner of his home (his mother) that he seeks. But his quest is less successful than Watt's: he finds his mother's room but not his mother. Moran's is less successful still; he can't find Molloy, loses the joy of his home, and is unaware that he has found himself. Malone seeks to chart the stages of his quest, but the quest proves resistant to this. The fiction-telling satisfies his desire for play, but brings him no nearer to an understanding of himself; the sections of 'récit'[38] and the sections of fiction are studiously kept apart until half-way through, where they threaten to get conflated. Malone's agonizing clearly derives from his inability to marry the real and the fictional as exhibited in the plainly self-deluded remark: 'nothing is less like me than this boy' (Sapo),[39] who is obviously one aspect of his childhood. But it is important that the Proustian idea of fiction as a means of discovering the past should be finally exposed for the snare and delusion it is.

The Unnamable's quest is as much for the preconditions of selfhood (a tense – 'When now?'; a place – 'Where now?') as for selfhood itself ('Who now?'). The quest is bedevilled by the very things it seeks to find; the *now* only defines itself in relation to a *then* which, in requiring examination, throws the emphasis on to the wrong place; the *where* is both external (the 'island' of Ireland, the streets of Paris) and also a very private place like the inside of a skull. None of his quests, though approached from an astonishing diversity of angles, succeed; *How it is* continues the inquiry into tense and location for that very reason, the *Texts* having only multiplied the angles and also failed. But there are in *The Unnamable* some magnificent failures; much of the work is Beckett at his best.

In *How it is* and the following works, the circumscription of the problems creates conditions propitious for their solution. Bom's quest for Bem is in no danger of being unsuccessful; the cyclical time and the struggle imposed by the mud guarantee periodic encounters. The irony is that the encounters increase rather than relieve the pain. Location ceases to be such a problem; although the narrator remembers the racecourse and his home, there is no chance now of getting them back, much less chance than Celia has of seeing again the Ireland she remembers. Belacqua's constant movement gets its come-uppance here, for movement is almost impossible. Tense, however, is still a problem, because memory is still possible. Only in *Ping* are active verbs left out, because there is hardly any remembering left ('that much memory almost never' says the voice). Perception is made easier by the adoption of a scientific notation, and the postulating of a severely circumscribed space; the question of fiction and reality is decided squarely in favour of fiction (*The Lost Ones*). The quests become successful by the abandonment of questing.

The situations are frustrating in the extreme; remorselessness gives rise to despair, and despair bites remorselessly. It is a climate of violence, violence turned inwards, suicidally orientated. In such circumstances, it is hardly surprising that the suppressed violence occasionally turns homicidally outwards towards others. Molloy kills a charcoal-burner. Moran batters the head of one inquirer to pulp. The individual elements that make up these worlds are straining apart; the macrocosm is as fragmented as the microcosm. Loneliness, however, is at least assuaged. Encounters do at least take place, and assume considerable importance. They are almost all chance meetings, random and tangential collisions, but some last longer than others. Molloy stays with Lousse for about a year; the narrator of 'The Expelled' makes much of the fact that the cabman stays with him for an afternoon. More often, however, the encounter only serves as a prelude to further alienation: the dialogue between Molloy and the police-sergeant generates intense emotion but no solution, and Moran's verbal assaults on his son lead to nothing. Moran, when left on his own, is strangely prone to encounters. He meets first an unidentified farmer he says he knew, then a figure in many respects resembling Molloy, then finally 'a dim man, dim of face and dim of body' whom he gratuitously kills.[40] Here, as with Lemuel's actions at the end of *Malone Dies*, we are faced with something analogous to Gide's *acte gratuit* as most celebratedly described in *Les Caves du Vatican*. But the connection is only tenuous; there is little desire to *épater le bourgeois* in Beckett, and the gratuitousness is in the service of a completely different vision.[41] Moran's whole section on the murder is of particular interest:

I do not know what happened then. But a little later, perhaps a
long time later, I found him stretched on the ground,
his head in a pulp. I am sorry to say I cannot indicate more
clearly how this result was obtained, it would have been
something worth reading. But it is not at this late stage of my
relation that I intend to give way to literature. . . . I bent over
him. As I did so I realized my leg was bending normally.
He no longer resembled me.[42]

Apart from the characteristic snipe at psychological literature's
comprehensiveness, the two most important results of this gratuitous
murder are that it is (a) curative, if only briefly, of physical ills,
and (b) enables the murderer to be more discriminating about his
own individual entity. In the first case, the homicidal act's origin
is clearly in agreement with the documented findings of modern
psychiatry; in the second, there is mythic and individual confirmation in Jungian and Yeatsian notions of the anti-self. He is
saying that encounters are necessary constitutents of any narrative,
however unrealistic, but that other people, especially the created
character, rob one of one's own identity, and need to be eliminated
(if only fictionally) if one is to maintain a truly solipsistic position.
Hell is, in this view, as much oneself as other people, with other
people only making one's own isolation more painful. The fact that
the beneficent effects of the murder are only temporary tends to
confuse the issue slightly, but in itself alerts one to the issues involved.
For it is the penalty of being born that such solace can only be temporary, and although Beckett's is a world of strangers, familial
killings are consequently the most crucial of all: 'My father, did I
kill him too as well as my mother, perhaps in a way I did.'[43] Killing
one's parents, however, is like shutting the stable door after the horse
has bolted: being born may be a curse but killing one's parents
won't expiate it. Some consolation can be found in the fact that the
same mistakes need not be made again. The curse of generation
(another idea Beckett may have got from Yeats)[44] can at least be
eased by having no more children. And killing has at least the
advantage of saving the sufferer an old age of pain: 'If I don't kill
that rat he'll die' (*Endgame*).[45]

All Beckett's people abjure sexual involvement absolutely. Love,
for Proust (according to Beckett), is 'a desert of loneliness and re-
crimination'. Friendship, while it is 'the negation of that remediable
solitude to which every human being is condemned', is only a 'social
expedient' of 'no spiritual significance'.[46] It is of all things the
affection most alien to the needs of the artist, who 'has no brothers'

as Beckett in his 'Homage to Jack Yeats' puts it.[47] Beckett's heroes conform to this pattern; but their feeling for community and fellowship is subject to sudden resurrection. Encounters may not be very fruitful occurrences in Beckett's world, but there is nevertheless an extraordinary preponderance of couples. The couple characteristically involves an increase rather than a decrease in tension. The narrator of Text One puts his finger on it when, in another connection, he says 'we're fond of one another, we're sorry for one another, but there it is, there's nothing we can do for one another'.[48] Affection and sympathy go hand in hand with helplessness, and helplessness leads ultimately to disaffection and hatred. Only the dialogue keeps Clov where he is (and his ignorance of the combination of the larder), Estragon refuses to return the ball when asked, Moran speaks to no one more harshly than his son. Even the relatively placid relationships of Mercier and Camier or Sam and Watt are subject to misconstructions, wrangles and unpleasantness. It is noticeable that in the writers Beckett particularly admires (Cervantes, for example, or Diderot) similar conditions apply: Lui needs Moi in *Rameau's Nephew*, Quixote needs Sancho, Jacques needs his master, and Hic (to take an example from Yeats) needs Ille.[49]

Encounters, then, prove of dubious usefulness. Since they are usually the result of movement (which in the Beckett universe is a very dubious accomplishment), this is only to be expected. Beckett's first important hero Belacqua puts his trust in movement: 'My sometime friend Belacqua enlivened the last phase of his solipsism by thinking . . . that the best thing he could do was to move constantly from place to place.'[50] But, as Byron recognized, 'mobility' can be 'a most painful and unhappy attribute'.[51] However much one moves, one is still *there*: 'being there' – and Vladimir and Estragon take particular exception to people reminding them by saying 'There you are' – is unavoidable. So one might as well keep still. Movement causes more problems than it solves. 'Once and for all, do not ask me to speak and move at the same time', says Mr Rooney in *All That Fall*.[52] The 'absurd mishap' that prevented Molloy from heading for his mother's house[53] (and resulted in his year or so with Lousse) was the direct result of movement out of control. 'I did nothing but go to and fro', says Moran,[54] like a latter-day Belacqua. But this only cloaks his vacancy and later, when he has slowed down, he will see more clearly. Stasis, however, does not have everything its own way; since it is one of the preconditions of the void so ardently desired, it is also something of which to be afraid. Or as the narrator of *How it is* puts it – 'must keep busy otherwise death'.[55] Much of *The Lost Ones* is concerned with the need for (and problems of) movement. Beckett's final opinion seems to be that there must be movement somewhere, but that the 'predicament of existence' is 'issueless'.[56] The serenity of *The Lost Ones* comes from there being no exit. The voice of *Ping* is as desperate in looking for a way out as the voice of Text Nine, but it is *huis clos* indeed. As Rasselas found out, an exit leads somewhere, to a painful confrontation with reality. A utopia is a hermetic microcosm containing certainties, but issues outside of it that have not been experienced can be only provisionally answered. In this respect, existence is both issueless in the sense of having no exit, and issueless in the sense of not having any real issues that can be solved. In a utopia everything would be as ordered and structured as Clov's dream in *Endgame*: 'Raise your eyes, and look at all that beauty, that order.'[57]

Beckett's ironic perception of how impossible that state of order is to achieve largely accounts for Winnie quoting Verlaine's famous lines in *Oh! les beaux jours*: 'Le ciel est, par-dessus le toit, / Si bleu, si calme.'[58] The calmness and the blueness (the Baudelairean variety of which figured in *Proust*)[59] have always been Beckett's concern. In *How it is* the scenes of 'life above in the light' are scenes of blue sky and peace and quiet. *Ping* also is a text that can remember scenes of 'blue and white in the wind'. The very title 'The Calmative' announces its main topic, but sedatives are not adequate. Only complete loss of being above and beyond death can guarantee ultimate calm, all things for ever at rest at last. And for that only the restitution of the womb will do. The possibility of attaining womb-like situations in real life is never discounted. The locations in the most recent texts are the culmination of Beckett's obsession with life in the womb from at least as early as *Murphy* onwards. The shuddering lights and variable temperatures mean that the structures are curiously imbued with a sense of pulse that makes the voice unwilling to relinquish this idea, and peculiarly sensitive to the need to discriminate. *Ping* attempts to sophisticate the notion of movement by breaking it into two parts: *Bing* in the French text indicating a mental movement, *hop* a physical one. But the English text blurs a distinction that is actually of dubious value because it is never fully articulated.

Beckett's uncertainty is reflected very dramatically in his changing narratorial approach. In realistic fiction the narrator is usually felt to be omniscient, arranging coincidences behind the scenes and generally, as Sartre said of Mauriac, 'playing God'.[60] The artifice of this method often makes for interesting outbursts, Jane Austen suddenly leaping to the defence of the novel as a form in *Northanger Abbey*, or D. H. Lawrence doing much the same in one of the many harangues in *Lady Chatterley's Lover*.[61] This obviously breaks our willing suspension of disbelief and what had seemed like disinterested descriptions suddenly become occasions for letting off steam. In the twentieth century it has generally been believed that the author should always be felt, but always appear to disappear, and claims have even been made for Dickens in this respect.[62] At the start of his career, Beckett makes no bones about it, and appears on his own stage: 'thank you Mr. Beckett' says one of the characters in 'Dream of Fair to Middling Women'. But then 'Dream' is a mélange of autobiography, literary criticism, art appreciation, aesthetic theory, Joycean neologisms, eighteenth-century 'characters', travelogues, and occasionally almost incomprehensible narrative. It is hardly a 'fiction' at all. *More Pricks than Kicks* is all of this, too, but more fictional, in so far as control seems to be imposed from outside by a non-participating personality, a projection of Beckett but not simply Beckett himself, an implied author or second-self. As a result, some of the worst audacities of 'Dream' (of which it is a rewriting) are sloughed off (though others remain), and many of the addresses to the reader are left behind. Addresses to the reader are toned down even further in *Murphy*, and relegated to the appendix in *Watt*. Since it is in *Watt* that the peculiarly problematic nature of narration begins to receive close attention, it is perhaps helpful to look at the structure of that novel in rather more detail.

Watt is definitely fragmentary. Its central narrative, outlining Watt's adventures in quest of Mr Knott's house, is flanked by an introductory section of great brilliance and an addenda at the end of great obscurity. The calm surface of the main narrative is further undermined by three passages that seem to grow out of all proportion to the rest of the book – Arsene's 'short statement', the story of the Lynch family and the Louit interpolation. These passages are by general consent the most enjoyable in the novel, which may come as a pleasant surprise to those who have found that Rabelais, Cervantes, Fielding and Sterne contain *longueurs* that distract our attention from the main story. Beckett's use of interpolations may be eighteenth century in origin, just as his use of the 'character' (for example, Madden in chapter 3 of *Mercier and Camier*) is very reminiscent of that period. But it is eighteenth-century with a difference. In the picaresque novel and its offshoots the interpolated story did three things. It was, first of all, a useful way of providing a new character with a background, and defining his individuality in a context where many characters had already come to life; secondly, as in the romance from which it sprang, it added a pleasant complication to the plot, which could be used either to promote further complexities or to unravel those already established; thirdly, it allowed the narrator–author a 'breather', a relaxation from the pressures of his story, and a chance to illustrate some moral speedily and elegantly. It is characteristic of Beckett that his interpolated stories never quite do any of these things. In the case of the first, Arsene's 'short statement' of sixteen pages, we may say that, far from clarifying the issues of the book, it in fact confuses them. The joke about the shortness of the statement is waggish, and may seem little more; but this disparity between promise and performance is actually one of the most dramatic ways of alerting us to the metaphysical implications of a narrator who is out of control. The second interpolation, the Lynch episode, certainly provides light relief, since it is an hilarious comment on human aspiration and absurdity, but it also complicates the structure of the book, since by being an absurd story within an absurd story, it gives a Chinese-box effect to the whole. It is intended as an explanation of the background to Mr Knott's mealtime system, but the link is so tenuous, the concentration so intense, that we soon forget its *raison d'être*. This applies even more strongly to what is really the most extraordinary passage in the book, the story of Louit and Mr Nackybal. Once again a link-up is attempted: 'I shall better illustrate what I mean', says Arthur to Mr Graves the gardener, who has complained of the sudden onset of impotence, 'if I tell you what happened to a friend of mine, a Mr. Ernest Louit.'[63] From this apparently harmless beginning springs the outrageous tale of Louit's examination of the Mathematical Intuitions of the Visicelts, to satisfy the requirements of the Ph.D. degree. The story, like other Beckett stories, is told in immense detail. The detail is itself so amusing that it drowns our critical faculties, we are content to see the trees rather than the wood, and before we know where we are we have forgotten that the story was intended as an example or illustration.[64] It is only at the end, when the Chinese-box structure is again strongly felt, when another collection of confusing and contradictory events needs to be interpreted, that we realize that, far from tightening the structure and making it coherent, as it promised to do, it has in fact weakened it further, and left it in an almost hopeless state.

This erosion of structural certainty and clarity is also carried out, in a more direct manner, in the refusal to narrate chronologically. Sterne was particularly fond of this device and the complexities of his time-scheme in *Tristram Shandy* are really startling.[65] Beckett does something much simpler: he writes a four-part story with the third and fourth parts swapped round. The result of such a rearrangement is to throw special emphasis on the section that is out of place, and in *Watt* this is because most of the clues necessary to understanding the work are in the third section. For instance, anyone faced by Watt on page 126 saying 'Ruse a by', is entitled to puzzlement; but only the third section reveals how eccentric Watt's linguistic habits are. Equally, Watt is revealed as the source of all the incidents that happened to him in Knott's house; the narrator had not in fact been with him – as his bland, distanced unflurried tone has already suggested. Most important of all perhaps, the narrator himself is revealed as a 'real' person, a character in his own right called Sam. It is not surprising that the proximity of his name to that of his creator has tended to make critics conflate the two; but he is really only a persona for Beckett himself, an analogue, a creator like himself. For, though Watt is our source of knowledge where his adventures are concerned, Sam is our only guide. The situation as Sam describes it, is already at one remove, because he wasn't there; but it is in fact at two removes, because Sam is a lunatic.

The question of structure is also at the heart of *Molloy*. Molloy's quest for the mother whose room he is inhabiting when the novel opens can be interpreted in Freudian terms as a desire to return to the womb, and Beckett's own claim to remember what such an existence was like (which he passes on to Murphy) helps to enforce this identification. But it is, in fact, equally possible to see it in Jungian terms, as an example of unconscious identity between parent and child deriving from the *anima*, the female element in the unconscious man. 'An inherited collective image of woman exists in a man's unconscious', Jung writes in *Two Essays on Analytical Psychology* (paragraph 301), 'with the help of which he apprehends the nature of woman'.[66] Molloy, of course, tends to equate all the women he has ever known, Lousse, Ruth–Edith, his mother, as if he genuinely hoped to do this. But nothing the narrator himself says necessitates these parallels being accepted. No Freudian, or Jungian, key will unlock *Molloy*. 'Here', as Moran says of the bees, 'is something I can study all my life, and never understand.'[67]

Molloy's quest is less obviously circular than Moran's. At the end of his narrative he is in a ditch, with help on its way, while at the beginning (later in time) he is, thanks to an ambulance or vehicle of some kind, in his mother's room; Malone's arrival in his room is equally problematic for him. Beckett does not leave a gap in the transmitted information, as he does in *Watt*, but one takes place none the less. The pattern however is very clear: out and back, leaving and returning home, as with the narrator of 'From an Abandoned Work'. At the same time, different elements occur in the two quests of Molloy and Moran; the landscapes are similar, but the signposts aren't quite the same. Molloy's internal voice tells him 'you have never left [your region] and you never shall',[68] while Moran's internal voice speaks sagely of the differences between the regions of Turdy, Turdyba and Turdybaba. Molloy speaks of a swamp, Moran of a strangled creek; Molloy attacks a charcoal-burner, Moran attacks a hazy figure. On the other hand, nothing in Moran's experience is similar to Molloy's poignant description of how A and C met, of how one returned and one went on; equally, nothing in Molloy's experience is as cosy or amusing as Moran's extraordinary dialogue with Father Ambrose. The manic, almost mesmeric repetitions in the dialogues between Molloy and the police-sergeant, and Moran and his son Jacques, are obviously similar. But in the first, Molloy is, as usual on the receiving end, while in the second Moran is characteristically dealing out punishment. It is not possible to confuse the hesitant, resigned, passive, constantly wavering Molloy with the officious, socially accepted, over-cautious Moran. But they are clearly complementary figures. Moran obeys some higher command which, for all its vagueness, he believes in; Molloy speaks constantly of a voice that is telling him what to do. Just as Molloy has a shifting conception of his mother, so Moran has a shifting conception of Molloy. He devotes four and a half pages to describing what he knows of Molloy, but he is never sure of the name, and much of what he says is as true of himself as it is of Molloy. It is no accident that his account of Molloy follows immediately upon his account of his onanistic activities: Molloy is like some sperm he has ejected that will never find an egg. In the same way as Watt, Arsene and Arthur may be creations of narrator Sam, Molloy may be a creation of Moran's. 'Between the Molloy I stalked within me thus and the true Molloy', he admits, 'the resemblance cannot have been great.'[69] Molloy's obsession, his mother, is a much more tangible figure than Moran's Molloy, and the unforgettable description of their method of communication supplies at the beginning of Molloy's narrative the climactic meeting that will be missing at the end. Nevertheless, despite her solidity, she is easily assimilated into the female stereotype, just as Lulu can become Anna in *First Love*,[70] and the narrator never decides between Marguerite and Madeleine in *The Unnamable*.[71] Molloy's mother, the object of his quest, may well be imaginary. Aspects of Moran's quest, by the same token, also seem strangely self-imposed. He has 'never seen any other messenger than Gaber nor any other agent than myself'.[72] Later, he tantalizingly tells us, 'sometimes I was asked for a report';[73] at two other points he bad-temperedly interrupts

43

other business – and in so doing draws special attention to his interruption – to say 'He wanted a report he'll get a report'.[74] But from the evidence we have, this is simply an assumption on his part, as much of a self-imposed task as his quest for Molloy. Furthermore, the fact that the first words of his report ('It is midnight. The rain is beating on the windows') are also the first words of his narrative, suggests that the narrative is the report. And if the report is false (as the last words of the novel reveal) the narrative is false, and Beckett's desire for a self-destroying, self-cancelling void has been achieved. Moran's approach at the start is very far from the emotional approach of Molloy. It is, in fact, deadpan, objective, blunt, the language of a report: 'I am calm. All is sleeping . . . my name is Moran, Jacques. That is the name I am known by. . . . My son too.'[75] What we have in *Molloy*, then, is another acknowledgment to the power of the fiction-making impulse, that inner compulsion towards self-expression doomed to failure by the form it must take and the words it must use. It is a more indirect statement than *Watt*; it suggests the tasks are self-imposed and, in their working out, self-gratifying. 'Perhaps I shall not finish it', says Moran, and yet his narrative makes an admirable ending to the 'beginning' Molloy makes so much of.

The dual structure of *Molloy* becomes centralized in one figure in *Malone Dies*: the resulting analysis of what is true and false, real and fictional, is consequently immensely confused, much more confused than in *Molloy* or *Watt*. Occasionally the confusion impugns the (often very considerable) value of the insights into the relation of fiction and life, and the confusion is only ironed out in *The Unnamable*, where a totally new form accommodates a new vision. In the later work the confessional approach is adopted, but it is as if the work writes itself, as if the narrator is so fragmented that to all intents and purposes he does not exist. This is a general trend of all Beckett's later work, and it is a paradox that must give Beckett pleasure, that the more computerized his utterances become the more eccentrically individual and personal they become. In *The Unnamable*, we are faced with a situation in which, with a constantly displaced end that seems ever more remote, more and more means are generated to fill up the space. And after the thirteen *Texts for Nothing*, the problem of narration is not faced again until *How it is*.

There is a child-like clarity of incident in *How it is*. The three parts concern themselves with 'before Pim with Pim after Pim', or in another formulation, 'the journey the couple the abandon'. But from the start this simplicity is threatened: the circularity of time and the inaccuracy of language mean that the narrator must constantly make modifications and precise discriminations if he is to express his deepest intuitions. Repeatedly he comments 'something wrong there' as if an item originally intended for a later section has cropped up in his consciousness, and his faithfulness to veracity has forced him to express it right away. Equally, in part one, the memories of a former existence ('life above in the light') and specifically two or three incidents from it (praying at his mother's knee, falling unconscious at the table, walking with a young girl and a dog, visiting a woman in hospital), press so powerfully on him that utterance, for the sake almost of exorcism, is necessary. In the same way, in part two he constantly recalls part one, and in part three he constantly recalls the other two parts. But this 'farewell to incompetence' is spurious;[76] the narrator keeps to his programme only a little better than Malone. It is in the third section that the frightfully median position of man, suspended between memory and hope, strikes most powerfully. A massive self-destructive *volte-face* destroys the reality so sedulously constituted. While this has been repeatedly attempted by the innumerable comments 'I quote' or 'end of quotation', they are nothing in comparison with the ultimate inquisition. Part two ends with 'noes' and 'yesses' held in suspension, but part three ends with an accumulation of 'yesses' of immense force. If Molly Bloom's celebrated 'yes' at the end of *Ulysses* indicates acceptance, this narrator's 'yes' signifies nothing less than an unqualified rejection, and Beckett's distinctness from Joyce is perhaps nowhere more marked than here. It is in part three that he discovers and squarely faces the fact that only a fourth part could give a comprehensive account of things; the four parts of *Watt* have elegance and symmetry. As it stands, 'of our total life [*How it is*] states only three-quarters'.[77]

'I quote' and 'I say it as I hear it' indicate how far we have moved from Molloy, Moran and Malone, who were in control of their narratives at least to the extent that they could decide when to omit, rearrange, emphasize or select aspects of their experience. To begin with, the Unnamable seems in control, but as sentences lengthen and structure becomes more repetitive, and as he stresses the ubiquity of 'they', it is plain that his narrative powers have been usurped. Text Thirteen ends with the suggestion that a nameless, inhuman agent is now controlling speech; the last words 'it says, it murmurs' jolt us with their sudden distancing.[78] Since *How it is* the discourse has become increasingly dictated, inexorably imposed on the human consciousness from without.

How it is is really the apotheosis of the anti-novel, in so far as it is

the fullest and most passionate working out of the implications involved in thinking of the book rather than the experience as the
primary fact. Swift's *Tale of a Tub* is the best dramatized account
of a failed book,[79] a book that mocks itself and distorts itself by
including the things that it cannot contain (lacunae, footnotes,
contradictory information). But a mixture of Sterne's deftness and
lightness of touch with Swift's deeper emotional insecurity, his
'spiritual haemophilia' as it has been well called, combines in Beckett
to produce the ultimate non-realistic realism – *How it is*, the self-
advertising book.

How it is provides its own commentary on itself, a commentary
that is often acute: 'deterioration of the sense of humour'[80] is a
strikingly accurate description of Beckett's development. On occasions it even asks the very questions some critics would like to ask:
'the idea of three books set aside where's the greatness'.[81] In this
respect it is ultimately more valuable than the trickle of texts that
have succeeded it; it creates the taste by which it is to be enjoyed.
In the late texts, by contrast, the insistence on a limited repertory
of items becomes a source of confusion. The style is so idiosyncratic
that one's attention is drawn to everything; as in Joyce's *Finnegans
Wake* the Jamesian idea of total relevance seems to have been taken
about as far as it can go. Yet, in being drawn to everything, we tend
to lose the sense of bas-relief; one detail may seem much like another,
one perception merely a pendent to another. The repetitive technique carries within it a separating as well as a combining factor
since, at the same time as it insistently thrusts forward words and
phrases, it effectively thrusts them into the background the more
they are allowed to dominate the discourse. But it is undeniable that
the more this happens, the more dispensable much of the text
becomes. It is as if the text, in being uttered, swallows itself, as a
black hole swallows matter. The serpent with the tail in its mouth
is, in these works, actually able to finish the job completely. The
question marks and lacunae of *Watt*, and the sudden oblivion in
which Moran kills the dim figure in *Molloy*, finally receive expression in words. It is the ultimate paradox of a spoken silence, a void
that is also a plenum.[82]

The key incident in Moran's account, the fatal blow, is carefully
left out, just as Gaber leaves out any reference to a report, and even
what to do with Molloy when he is found (this last an increasingly
obsessive matter for Moran). Similarly, Moran arbitrarily decides
to omit from his account 'the obstacles we had to surmount, the
fiends we had to circumvent', the 'fiends in human shape and the
phantoms of the dead that tried to prevent me getting home'.[83]

This amusing criticism of the conventions of the quest novel (and by extension the adventure story generally) is placed in relief by the events that actually *are* included: two questionnaires (one a very funny theological one), a dialogue with Gaber, and a few rambling reflections (as damning an indirect attack on traditional novel practice as anything directly uttered in *Proust*). Like Sterne and Diderot before him, the Beckett narrator *creates* what is important, outside the received tradition. And it is the trivial that is most often important. The style tends to elevate or to reduce everything to the same level of importance, rather as Defoe was wont to do. A strange blandness invests everything with equal value. Paradoxically, the special bluntness of most of the dialogues (Moran uses almost nothing but imperatives to his son, at one point even catching himself doing so) – together with the fact that they are contained within the paragraph rather than typographically set apart as in normal practice – adds to this feeling of uniformity. One item follows another desultorily, with only tenuous connection. Consequently the tone veers from the absurdly funny: 'Damp, I said. Tut tut, he said, how annoying. The words tut tut seemed to me the maddest I had heard', to the resonantly serious: 'Animals never laugh, he said. . . . Christ never laughed either, he said, so far as we know. He looked at me. Can you wonder? I said.'[84] Such a change can take place within two paragraphs. The persistent blank repetition of the simplest kind of descriptive precision ('I said', 'he said', etc.) is both maddening and strangely soothing, insistent and yet dully remote. It draws attention to the spoken words in the same way as the opening tableau of *Watt*, where each speaker is religiously noted, in pursuance of an absurd theory postulated in the first footnote. Dialogues are more common in *Molloy* than in the companion novels and though the dialogues are often violent, part of the book's less fraught atmosphere doubtless derives from this. But the fact that circularity is almost achieved – Molloy does finally end in his mother's room, Moran still has the hope of meeting Molloy, and his last words almost echo his first – is another factor which contributes to the peculiarity of tone in *Molloy*.

Such brisk tonal changes make for tragi-comedy, but they also seem to have been adopted by the narrator as a means of expressing a more comprehensive view of reality. It is particularly characteristic of Beckett and his pre-trilogy people that Sam in *Watt* should attempt to describe the occasions on which he and Watt came nearest to God by an exhaustion of aspects that is entirely negative in basis: 'Of flowers there was no trace. . . . Of vegetables there was no sign. . . . Of seats, on which to sit down, and rest, there was not the slightest vestige. Shrubs and bushes, properly so called, were absent from the scene.'[85] For long periods, the novel proceeds only by regressing, only by negative definition. Later heroes are more hesitant: 'To say I did so with satisfaction would be stretching the truth'; 'Without perhaps having exactly won her heart it was clear I did not leave her indifferent.'[86] Certainties are not to be expected in an emotional state where everything is in continual change. In each case, as Beckett develops, the problems become harder to solve, because questions that ought to have made things easier of solution have in fact helped only to reveal deeper, more fundamental, more unanswerable questions underneath. It is perversely appropriate, threfore, that certain characters should recommend a more general approach. Mr Kelly in *Murphy* complains violently about the 'demented particulars'[87] of Celia's narrative; 'True lives', Malone says, 'do not tolerate this excess of circumstance.'[88] It is the same feeling that leads Moran, in a manner very reminiscent of Gulliver at the end of his voyages, to say 'I am not giving this duet in full. Just the main themes.'[89] Beckett spoke in *Proust* of 'the vulgarity of a plausible concatenation', and for Beckett it is all too simple to add up the details and get a result. It is, in fact, 'answer clapped on problem like snuffer on a candle'. And yet of course, Beckett, like Joyce, is fascinated by detail. The description of Belacqua with his toast at the beginning of *More Pricks than Kicks*, like that of Murphy setting up his garret, is one seen at close range, a vision of tangible solidity, of a fully visualized reality. This is an art the narrator of *Imagination Dead Imagine* thirty years later has not completely forgotten, even if his desperate position only permits sketchiness: 'Islands, waters, azure, verdure, one glimpse and vanished.'[90] In the early work background material, especially in relation to characters, and the device of flashback which is often an inseparable accompaniment to it, are elements in the traditional armoury of realism. Such Dickensian grotesques as Hairy Quin, for example, though eccentric, are always plausible.

But Beckett's impulse towards satire, especially in the early work, does not always allow such closeness and concentration of detail. Satire as a genre traditionally requires a more distanced and impersonal approach. But it thrives on sheer malice. In *More Pricks*, this is often seen most clearly in the highlighted scene (for example, the wedding of Thelma and Belacqua), and in the *aperçu* (for example, 'she had at least the anagram of a good face', said of Thelma and borrowed from Donne).[91] At such points Beckett's early work is reminiscent of the eighteenth-century novel; Otto Olaf, referring his wife 'to that portion of himself which he never desired any person to kick nor volunteered to kiss in another', or Walter, being given the run of Otto Olaf's house 'where, as formerly he had abused that privilege in the bed of his host, so now he did out of his decanter', have a balance and elaborateness of phrase that one might find in Fielding.[92] It is not necessary to recognize the origin in Donne of the description of Thelma's face; it is a biting remark whether one knows its origin or not. Elsewhere the erudition seems unnecessarily self-conscious and exhibitionist, and all too often irrelevant to the matter in hand. In Beckett's first published story, 'Assumption', the references to Browning (whom he had studied), the Unanimistes (whom he was in the process of studying) and Michelangelo's tomb in Santa Croce (which he had visited three years before, in 1926) seem altogether too discursive for what is, after all, a fairly short and intimate story. His unpublished novel 'Dream of Fair to Middling Women' errs even more dramatically in this respect. As well as referring to the mythical figures Phoebus, Daphne, Narcissus and Echo (Daphne recurs in *Watt*, and Ovid's story in *Metamorphoses* of Narcissus and Echo fascinated him enough for him to use it in the title of his first volume of poems), Beckett refers to (among others) Shelley, Rimbaud, Pisanello, Botticelli, Blake, Rousseau, 'George Bernard Pygmalion' and even quotes Hamlet's 'springes to catch woodcocks'.[93] Traces of this habit remain in *Murphy*, but the references to such things as the Book of Job, modern psychology, Pythagoras, etc., are less frequent and more amusing. *Watt* represents a further advance: the learned lumber is relegated to the appendix and in the trilogy there are only occasional references of this kind to such figures as Toussaint l'Ouverture, about whom he probably read while working on Nancy Cunard's *Negro* anthology.[94]

Erudition is, however, clearly a cast of mind, and it frequently infects the diction of even Beckett's later work. The ludicrously high-flown and inflated rubs shoulders with the bathetically trivial. Thus Watt and Sam are almost 'obnubilated', while in *The Unnamable* we meet such words as 'aporia', 'ephectic', 'narthex', 'helicoidal', 'manstuprate'.[95] *How it is*, that threnody for the whole Western intellectual tradition, includes such arcane gems as the following: 'speluncar', 'dextrogyre', 'sinistro', 'introrse', 'apostil', 'rowel', 'sparsim', 'deasil', etc.[96] It is noticeable that with Beckett, as with the Johnson he so much admires, the root is often Latin and the total effect grandiloquent. In Beckett such vocabulary does two things: it calls attention to itself (this is especially true in a work like *How it is* where the majority of the work is rather bare and formulaic) and hence mocks itself; but it also makes a specialized, scientifically accurate language seem momentarily possible. As a result, the first mock is often succeeded by a drier, more despairing mock, a *risus purus* indeed.

The language in Beckett's most recent prose has, however, sought more and more to attain consonance between what it is and what it says. *Enough*, a very fine short work from 1966, is written in a resigned style of great simplicity, which is constantly redefining what it is saying. *The Lost Ones* proceeds on a different level, in the unengaged manner of *Imagination Dead Imagine* ('Hold a mirror to their lips, it mists'),[97] but more ethereal: 'Floor and wall are of solid rubber or suchlike. Dash against them foot or fist or head and the sound is scarcely heard. Imagine then the silence of the steps.'[98] Along with this goes a resuscitation of the tendency towards notation found in Malone's final pages, as if the recording consciousness were weary of the effort of writing carefully cadenced sentences: 'Inside a cylinder fifty metres round and eighteen high for the sake of harmony or a total surface of roughly twelve hundred square metres of which eight hundred mural. Not counting the niches and tunnels.'[99] Both *Ping* (a reduction of material from the drafts of *The Lost Ones*) and *Lessness*, the most recent texts of all, take this notational technique to its logical conclusion. Whereas in *The Lost Ones* the sentence could contain material fully explored (even though the lack of subsidiary punctuation tends to test the reader's powers of involvement to the full), the sentence now becomes full of material only half-expressed. Whereas in *The Lost Ones* each subsequent sentence tends to amplify the preceding one (as do the sections), in *Ping* they tend towards uniformity. The sentence 'traces blurs signs no meaning light grey almost white' appears three times, and many of the others are very similar without being exactly the same. At a casual reading, as a result of the repetition, the piece is completely mesmeric. *Lessness* represents only a minimal advance on this, consisting of 120 sentences, the second sixty repeating the first sixty but in a different order. Such extreme simplicity, which may seem crude, is not, of course, adopted without good reason. In *Lessness* it is as if an area is staked out, an area to which (though other experience may have been arbitrarily omitted) some kind of assent is going to be given. But the narrator discovers that even with a severely circumscribed amount of material, problems of order and arrangement are not, and never can be, solved: the possible order of the sentences is so much more infinite than that of Murphy with his six biscuits or Molloy with his sixteen stones. However, this desperate realization has its compensations. By repeating the same material again (as happens also in *Play*) one suggests to the reader (or audience) that this limited amount of material is all that can be said, repeated verbatim (or almost verbatim) *ad infinitum* through time. There is, that is to say, an inbuilt feeling of eternity in the device, which helps to convey Beckett's feeling that we live in a continuum, where past, present and future mix indistinguishably.

In this respect the quest that all the heroes after Watt undertake might be said to be the quest for a tense; since their very existence has become problematic, the present tense 'I am' no longer has any validity. It is particularly in *How it is* that Beckett explores the problem of tense. He summarizes the possibilities open to him: 'present past future and conditional of to be and not to be'.[100] Despairing of one tense alone being correct, he tries putting two together: 'from it I learn from it I learnt what little remained learnt what little remains of how it was . . . how it is'.[101] In the same way he tries to cut across the gap between subjective and objective statements by stating both: 'I'll describe it it will be described . . . I do not say it is not said.'[102] The narrator of *The Unnamable* feels this and often passionately expresses it, but nowhere as intransigently or dramatically as the narrator of *How it is*. Unfortunately, the attempt to be comprehensive can only lead to contradiction. *Both* the perception *and* the subsequent representation of an object are impossible. Equally, for Beckett's personae, the realization that they have no real self (what the Twelfth Text of *Texts for Nothing* calls a 'babble of homeless mes and untenanted hims')[103] leads them to think of their situations as *literally impossible*. Hence they speak of 'this impossible night, this impossible body'.[104] It is both a consolation, and at the same time a sharper jab in the ribs. The Thirteenth Text of *Texts for Nothing* makes the ultimate move in this direction: 'And were there one day to be here, where there are no days, which is no place, born of the impossible voice the unmakable being, and a gleam of light, still all would be silent and empty and dark.'[105] At points like this, the immediate contradiction allows the work to register an unchallenged proposition, and appropriately enough, these are almost the last words of the last text. The impossible, to be uttered, needs to be put in the form of a contradiction, but as Wittgenstein has pointed out (*Tractatus*, 4.464) a contradiction's truth is impossible. The contradiction negates itself; it is the nearest approximation to actual absence that the literary work can support. In *Breath*, the absence of words is compensated for by the elemental gesture of a cry; but between the versets of *How it is*, or in the blank pages of Sterne, the work becomes totally free – we invest the work with what we like. If it remains doubtful that the 'different intensities of silence' Ellmann speaks of in *Giacomo Joyce*[106] were actually

51

Joyce's aim, Beckett's *How it is* suggests that such effects may well be possible.

The blank page of the totally free work is, of course, a dead end. Beckett is interesting in proportion as he keeps the ball in play. But clearly one of the main things to be avoided in the traditional narrative in the past tense (when all the events to be narrated are 'over', and known to the teller) is an overindulgent employment of special knowledge. The 'if I knew then what I know now' method, with its easy elegiac appeal to nostalgia, stales quickly. Molloy avoids it largely by offering us, a little hysterically, his 'beginning'. Moran has more difficulty in avoiding it. Such remarks as 'I added rashly, we are not going into the wilderness'[107] are eminently natural, but occasionally Moran is so heavy-handedly ironic that he is clearly modifying the old story-telling conventions to arouse suspense: 'And yet the affair seems childishly simple, I said.'[108] Childishly simple their trip into the wilderness is not.

This variation in narrative method, like the earlier variations in tone, stems from the narrators' being completely unsure of how to approach the material they are faced with. Sometimes they simply call a halt. 'Let us try and see where these considerations lead', says the narrator of *The Unnamable*,[109] with astonishing detachment, in the middle of a fundamentally important disquisition on the nature of change and the means of perceiving it. In the middle of *How it is*, careless of the desperateness of his position, the speaker muses: 'some reflections none the less while waiting for things to improve on the fragility of euphoria among the different orders of the animal kingdom beginning with the sponges'.[110] Almost invariably, a distanced view like this has the effect of making us more engaged, more moved; like the Latinisms discussed earlier on, the shift in method is really part of a desperate attempt not to weight the scales too heavily on one side or the other, too optimistically or too pessimistically. Expectations, therefore (since they result from looking forward too optimistically), are as invariably defeated as in *Rasselas*: 'I thought I had done with preliminaries' (*The Unnamable*).[111] 'That makes three remarks. I had only anticipated two', says Moran.[112] In the same way, the last is never the last, be it question or answer, statement or counter-statement. 'I wake how much nearer the last' is a repeated query in *How it is*.[113] Early on in *The Unnamable* the voice cries 'A few last questions',[114] and yet questions of increasing despair recur for another hundred pages. 'I shall say I no more', says Malone,[115] but he does so three times more. Doubt affects the most seemingly innocuous and simple questions: 'I am not deaf, of that I am convinced, that is to say half-convinced' – the Unnamable once more,[116] who can turn this into a most telling way of describing his misery: 'I know my eyes are open from the tears that flow from them unceasingly.'[117]

Often, when the most difficult questions have been thrashed out and no answer reached, the mist lifts momentarily, to allow that most useful of literary devices, the summary, to peep through. 'Present state, three stories, inventory, there',[118] says Malone, and later: 'Visit, various remarks, Macmann continued, agony recalled, Macmann continued, then mixture of agony and Macmann as long as possible.'[119] If these expectations prove as vain as the others, at least the Unnamable can utilize the summary to focus our involvement in his plight. At the end of an especially powerful passage, he concludes 'In a word, no change apparently since I have been here, disorder of the lights perhaps an illusion, all change to be feared, incomprehensible uneasiness.'[120] Such a ploy can be particularly powerful when modulated into a shock-tactic that jolts the reader with its intransigence. Moran particularly favours this device: 'I have spoken of a voice giving me orders, or rather advice. It was on the way home I heard it for the first time. I paid no attention to it . . . I had no information as to his face. I assumed it was hirsute, craggy and grimacing. Nothing justified my doing so.'[121] In *The Unnamable*, coherent statements are even broken into two, so that the jolt is more dramatic: 'What makes me weep so? From time to time.'[122] It is, to be sure, the dissatisfaction with one plane of discourse that leads the Beckett narrator to compose on another. *Malone Dies*, for example, is both spiritual autobiography and fictional narrative and though the one is obviously to some extent a mirror-image of the other, a distinction between them is maintained up to the end. In *The Unnamable* this 'double-discourse' effect is achieved by making identity itself inherently more fluid, and by shifting from one name (Mahood) to another (Worm) with bewildering frequency. This is itself seen at the third remove in those passages where the ever-present 'they' narrow down to a single recognizable voice, and a particularly compelling example of this occurs towards the end when a spectator – with all the indifference and lack of sympathy such a term can imply – quotes facts and figures in a bizarrely inappropriate attempt to jolly the hero up. In *How it is* the notion of the double discourse parallels the structure of two existences (above and below) and is advertised in the very typography of the book, often with laughable absurdity, as when, in seeking to clarify identities, it can only conflate them: 'YOU BOM me Bom ME BOM you Bom we Bom.'[123] The upper case necessarily confers importance on certain items, however, and it is startling to observe how many of the really fundamental issues in *How it is* are stated in upper case. In the texts published since 1961, the tendency has been to revert to single discourse because the nature of the terrain to be covered has demanded it. However, the indirect narrative technique of the female speaker of *Enough* – stating, then amplifying, then re-organizing the same material – is a late survival of this approach, and in *The Lost Ones* similar conditions apply. *Lessness* is, in its very structure, double. The old habits die hard.

The double discourse is a more powerful and general application of the technique of counter-statement. In *Malone Dies* the counter-statement takes refuge in literary comment ('What tedium', etc.). In 'From an Abandoned Work' the surface is broken by the abrupt 'awful English this' as the end approaches. In the *Texts for Nothing* and the *Nouvelles*, the exasperation does not seem so resonant as in the works of the trilogy. 'Weakness' says the narrator of 'The Expelled',[124] rather too bluntly; and the speaker in Text One is immediately caught up in a tail-chasing exercise that would depend upon the spoken voice of drama to be fully effective: 'Suddenly, no, at last . . . a mountain, no, a hill . . . I shouldn't have begun, no, I had to begin . . . I'll describe it, no, I can't.'[125] Text Eleven begins in much the same way, with too much undermining in too short a time, but it saves itself at the end by suggesting that the whole pressure of the text has been towards the moment when the initial statement can be completed:

> And that is why, when comes the hour of those who know me, this time it's going to work, it's as though I were among them, that is what I had to say . . . between two parting dreams, knowing none, known of none, that finally is what I had to say, that is all I can have had to say, this evening.[126]

The 'no, that is a foolish thing to say' that comes at the end of 'From an Abandoned Work' is quieter and less nervous, but as a device, the counter-statement, like the cliché, is rather limited, and perhaps better subsumed in an attempt to dramatize the doubleness of discourse.

Isolating imagery has the effect of admitting its importance at the expense of suggesting it has an independent status of its own, but obviously a writer's most characteristic ways of thinking and most unconscious obsessions are revealed by close attention to it, and Beckett's imagery actually shows him at his most various.

Possibly the most often employed analogy of all, by poets, novelists, and thinkers of all types, is that of light and dark. A mystic like

John of the Cross speaks of a dark night of the soul. Milton (whose *Paradise Lost* and *Samson Agonistes* were on the syllabus at Trinity) repeatedly images themes in these terms. Pope in *The Dunciad* (often with specific Miltonic reference), speaks constantly of the universal darkness of duncery snuffing out the light of wit. Beckett's use of the image becomes important in *Murphy*, in the well-known analysis of Murphy's mind.[127] In the first two zones, the light and the half-light, Murphy feels 'sovereign and free'. The first, however, is, for Murphy, little more than wish-fulfilment, and the second, 'the Belacqua bliss', encourages simply contemplation, with none of the sauce of a 'rival initiative'. It is the third zone that he most desires, 'a flux of forms, a perpetual coming together and falling asunder of forms'. This third state is preferable because the first tends merely to rearrange the problems of physical experience, reproducing its complexity with a complexity of its own; as Beckett puts it, 'it contained the docile elements of a new manifold', and is therefore only 'a radiant abstract of the dog's life'. The third zone is also preferable to the second because, though the second is a state of peace, it is never achieved without effort: the Belacqua 'bogged in indolence' at the beginning of 'Dante and the Lobster' is no freer an agent than his namesake in *Purgatorio*, iv. It is also something still formally recognizable, something that can still be described as a 'state'. The extreme charm of the third zone, the dark, resides in it being 'neither elements nor states, nothing but forms becoming and crumbling into the fragments of a new becoming, without love or hate or any intelligible principle of change'. This deepest zone of the mind – which can only be found by burrowing – is 'nothing but commotion and the pure forms of commotion'. Nor does this lead, as might be expected, to perfect freedom. On the contrary. 'Here', Beckett states in sharply precise terms, 'he was not free, but a mote in the dark of absolute freedom.' It is perfect stasis in an environment that has not attained stasis: 'He did not move, he was a point in the ceaseless unconditioned generation and passing away of line.' As often when he is at the heart of the matter, Beckett's images come together: this image from painting is clinched by one from mathematics – Murphy as the 'matrix of surds'. Beckett's respect for analogy (which derives from the problem being difficult to express) often involves such a collection of images. And here, in a final attempt to fix this curious condition in our minds, he resorts to mechanics: 'a missile without provenance or target, caught in a tumult of non-Newtonian motion.' When one observes that this is itself followed by reference to the 'breakers of the world' (equating mental life in the dark with the flux of the sea),[128] and that the whole is imaged as a hospital

c

'bulletin', it is obvious that we are dealing with an extremely complex imagistic approach.

In *Murphy*, for instance, this light–dark contrast leads towards images of puppetry and images of barriers. Mr Kelly's eyes open and shut like a doll's; Miss Counihan (like Celia) looks out on a 'fosse of darkness' with railings 'spurting light'[129] before she closes her eyes; Celia at the end closes her eyes on the 'unction of soft sunless light . . . that was all she remembered of Ireland'.[130] Later in *How it is* this image of acceptance–rejection, of barrier balanced against free access, is made more schematic by contrasting life above in the light and life below in the dark. Yet it is also made much more specific, expressed in terms of a curtain opening and closing, an image doubtless suggested to the narrator by the cord of his sack, or the opening and closing of his mouth. *How it is* is, as a work, so fluid that all these things can be equated without difficulty. But before this kind of freedom can be reached, the whole problem needs to have been comprehensively explored.

'I enjoy a kind of night and day, admittedly', says Malone. But he is unable to be more than tentative. The light in his den is 'bizarre': 'it is never light in this place, never really light.'[131] His mind oscillates between the desire for extinction and the consciousness of continuation. Similarly the boy Sapo, like Celia in the rocking-chair, watches day give way to night: '[light] entered at every moment, renewed from without, entered and died at every moment, devoured by the dark.'[132] Sunset, for Sapo, is tinged with a suggestion that the earth is being burnt up: 'The heap of earth was dwindling, the earth shone strangely in the raking evening light, glowing in patches as though with its own fires, in the fading light.'[133] Malone, too, recognizes the attraction of the pathetic fallacy, of an external world that mirrors his internal struggle:

> From the hills another joy came down, I mean the brief
> scattered lights that sprang up on their slopes at nightfall,
> merging in blurs scarcely brighter than the sky, less bright than
> the stars, and which the palest moon extinguished. They were
> things that scarcely were, on the confines of silence and dark,
> and soon ceased.[134]

But joy, at the very moment of its coming down, is snuffed out. Once again the movement downwards is in evidence. 'What I sought', Malone says, 'was the rapture of vertigo, the letting go, the fall, the gulf, the relapse', all of which are cognate with 'darkness, nothingness', the essential constituents of 'the blessedness of absence'.[135] *Malone Dies* was, at one time, going to be called *L'Absent*. But darkness is a pre-condition of absence, and Malone's is 'a kind of leaden light that makes no shadow'.[136] The Unnamable hopes to solve the problem by plumping for something securely in the middle between light and dark: 'it is grey we need, to begin with, because of what it is, and of what it can do, made of bright and black, able to shed the former, or the latter, and be the latter or the former alone.'[137] But just as Beckett in the *Proust* volume complained 'The observer infects the observed with his own mobility', so the Unnamable euphonically goes on to admit, 'perhaps I am the prey, on the subject of grey, in the grey, to delusions'. By the time of *The Lost Ones* (written 1965) the grey has become yellow; in *Imagination Dead Imagine* (1965), it is white, a composite of all colours. But the business of distinguishing traces of human existence, or the outlines of objects, is not aided by total whiteness any more than it is by total grey. The rotunda is 'all white in the whiteness'; its interior alternates every twenty seconds from light and heat to darkness and freezing-point. While in motion, the Unnamable's grey state is passed through. This is obviously a more complete statement than his, but the vision is harder to maintain. The second sighting is, for this 'eye of prey', 'quite as much a matter of chance', and when it is lost once more, the vision is gone for good; 'no question now of ever finding again that white speck lost in whiteness'.[138] At the time of the second sighting, the bodies are still and the light convulsive, and in the unpredictable future the same situation may obtain. But, equally possibly, the storm may be worse, and the light or the dark may be dominant.

Throughout *Murphy* the world of light is the world of physical experience; day for Celia, in the rocking-chair, is 'a peristalsis of light, worming its way into the dark'.[139] Beckett is aware that his characters' fondness for the dark may seem escapist; one of the most amusing moments of all is Neary's admission: 'We look on the dark side. . . . It is undeniably less trying to the eyes.'[140] The gruesome Miss Counihan is granted a deeper insight: 'It is only in the dark that one can meet.'[141] The real problem in meeting, however, is the eye itself, as the chess game reveals: 'The relation between Mr. Murphy and Mr. Endon could not have been better summed up than by the former's sorrow at seeing himself in the latter's immunity from seeing anything but itself.'[142] This statement (so reminiscent of Joyce's favourite 'Ithaca' section in *Ulysses*, from where Murphy's 'surgical'[143] quality also probably derives) gives way, as other examples have led us to expect, to a restatement: 'Mr. Murphy is a speck in Mr. Endon's unseen'. This recollection of Murphy's third zone 'speck' is a poignant statement of his failure to achieve his original aim: for Mr Endon's unseen of dark, absolute freedom is, unlike absolute freedom, hermetically closed to anything from without. Murphy is more like Mr Kelly's kite, a 'speck in the glades' of reality, and reality is what the last words reaffirm, as the keeper cries 'All out.' But even here an image is lurking, for the words refer, of course, to the end of an innings of cricket, a game Beckett loves.

Meeting is difficult, therefore, because light and dark cannot be harmoniously combined. But one of the ways one can meet is through the 'music' of love. It is especially ironic that Murphy and Endon should fail to meet since Murphy has felt that M.M.M. (the Magdalen Mental Mercyseat) stands for 'music, MUSIC, *MUSIC*'.[144] Just as the nights with Celia were 'serenade, nocturne, albada'[145] when they started their 'new life'.[146] Although their last kiss is 'in Lydian mode',[147] our chances of getting sentimental about this are severely restricted by the knowledge that even a kiss from Wylie can be 'like a breve tied, in a long slow amorous phrase, over bars times its equivalent in demi-semiquavers'.[148] The imagery of music is, in other words, much better integrated than in *More Pricks than Kicks*, where describing the public-house of 'Ding Dong', Beckett writes of 'A great major symphony of supply and demand, effect and cause, fulcrate on the middle C of the counter',[149] where the image is merely an exhibitionist gratification of his love of Schubert. In *Murphy*, by contrast, Celia's blank distress issues in memories of moments of childhood when Mr Kelly used to sing love songs to her, and in the final scenes in the park Celia remembers an earlier visit when she saw a child playing with his kite: 'The child knelt down in the rain . . . wrapped the tails and sticks in the sails and went away, singing. As he passed the shelter, Celia called goodnight. He did not hear her, he was singing.'[150] Compare this with 'A Wet Night' in *More Pricks than Kicks*, where the references range from classical forms ('a simple cantilena in his mind')[151] to popular ditties (Chas invokes the first line of 'Love's Old Sweet Song')[152] and where even the Alba's obscene Spanish song is made much of. The purely illustrative image cannot compete with the deeply felt, genuinely expressive image: the trilogy is justly called by Molloy the 'long sonata of the dead'.[153]

Music is one way of meeting, but meeting is rendered difficult by the uncertainty of whom one is meeting. 'There is more than one apparently',[154] Molloy says to himself, and by the time of *The Unnamable* there can be no doubt about that. The natural desire of the narrator, suffering under an inner compulsion to express, to put the blame on some external agent becomes clearer as the trilogy wears on. Molloy can still maintain a recognizably traditional relationship with his superiors: 'So many pages, so much money'[155] has, in its materialist way, a comforting ring about it. Moran also, as private investigator, is in a relatively traditional position *vis-à-vis* Youdi's men, even if he never sees them. Malone himself is answerable to nothing but dish and pot, but his characters, notably Macmann, are usually in a state of subjection, nowhere more so than in the House of Saint John of God. For the Unnamable, Descartes's imaginary deceiving demon and Quixote's somewhat more comfortable enchanters have become altogether less distinct, a mere 'they', more savage, more unremitting. In the *Texts for Nothing* they are 'apparitions', 'ghouls', most powerfully perhaps (remembering the cells of the House of Saint John of God), 'keepers'.[156] The cell can of course be a place of refuge, a hermitage, a religious retirement, and elements of such a life frequently appear to be the main desire of Beckett's people. But they are all realistic enough to realize that the cell is more often a place of torment, a prison, a compulsory solitude. Nevertheless the 'art of confinement' (Beckett's description of Bram van Velde's painting)[157] has certain advantages: dimensions are measurable, data are quantifiable. From this point of view, the cube in *Ping* represents an ideal. But in *Lessness*, although the tendency towards hermeticism in language is maintained, the genuinely hermetic situation has been replaced by one in which the barriers between internal and external phenomena have broken down. The four walls of *Ping*'s cube are now 'fallen over backward', and in the flux, it is almost impossible to tell the difference between a fragmentary (but nevertheless consolingly hopeful) fiction – 'in the sand he will make it' – and a deeply felt constricting reality – 'little body only upright four walls' – the four walls of what had been a 'true refuge'. Now both the inside and the outside seem equally constricting. The fatalism of *Murphy* ('So all things limp together for the only possible') thus reaches its ultimate point: 'the record', as the Unnamable says, 'is in position from time immemorial'.[158]

Where nothing can be changed, it is inevitable that the ostensible agents of change must come under scrutiny. Malone, for example, is fascinated by the moon, and so is Molloy. Although Molloy devotes a great deal of time to watching it, he at no point makes so bold an equation between himself and it as does Malone, who imagines at one point that he has been on the moon. And though doubtless familiar with the symbolic use made of the moon by such poets as Coleridge and Yeats, Beckett, as befits his anti-romantic disposition, seems more interested in its place in the cosmological scheme of

things. At the same time, fascinated as he is by such arcane speculations about the nature of God as whether he is at the centre or
circumference of the universe – a matter discussed in Medieval and
Renaissance times most notably by Alain de Lille, Bruno, Nicholas
Cusanus, and Pascal[159] – Beckett transfers these problems to the
human realm, in the hope that, by the analogies he has placed his
trust in, what holds for that realm may also hold for the divine.
The recourse to geometric and arithmetic systems in *Murphy* is
familiar, but the more specifically cosmological approach is less so.
The Unnamable, whose position is the most desperate because as
more time has passed, more events have happened to complicate
matters, is the one narrator who consistently thinks in such terms.
To establish his own position in relation to others is almost his first
task: 'Malone is there. Of his mortal liveliness little trace remains.
He passes before me at doubtless regular intervals, unless it is I who
pass before him. No, once and for all, I do not move.'[160] The
Unnamable is therefore unmoved mover, like God, although in his
uncertainty as to whether he is moving or not, he is like the earth,
circled by a moon yet turning imperceptibly slowly on its own axis.
Malone is more unsure of whether he is a divine being or a human
being, creator or created. At one point he says, 'I alone am human
and all the rest divine',[161] but later he defines 'to live' as 'to wander
the last of the living in the depths of an instant without bounds'[162]
which is clearly something like God's eternal boundless present.
The Unnamable's problem is that, although manifestly the 'creator'
of Murphy, Mercier and all the rest, he also appears to be the
'created' of a figure very much like Moran's Youdi (himself a cor-
ruption of Yahweh), who is in charge of the 'they' that give him so
much trouble. 'My master,' he says to himself. 'There is a vein I
must not lose sight of.'[163] But nothing in this vein is ultimately
decisive.

The imagery of centre and circumference is, therefore, no more
decisive than any other: Mahood, approaching a central rotunda,
is moving from circumference to centre; Worm, by contrast, is
moving from centre to circumference. Worm, indeed, cannot figure
much in the narrative because as soon as he does so, he ceases to
be Worm at all. He shades off into Mahood, or some other persona.
Worm, in other words, represents an ideal, a much lower ideal than
most thinkers would allow, but an ideal none the less. But if Worm
is God, we are, as humans, less than worms, food for worms, and
our analysis must be in words, when the only real communication
is ineffable, beyond words, wordless:

It's a lot to expect of one creature, it's a lot to ask, that he
should first behave as if he were not, then as if he were, before
being admitted to that peace where he neither is, nor is not,
and where the language dies that permits of such
expressions.[164]

Which is where Mr Knott comes in, for as Sam says: 'the only way
one can speak of nothing is to speak of it as though it were something just as the only way one can speak of God is to speak of him
as though he were a man, which, to be sure, he was, for a time.'[165]
It is Arsene, in his 'short statement' who first makes clear Mr
Knott's God-like affinities: 'the coming is in the shadow of the going,
and the going is in the shadow of the coming. . . . And yet there is
one who neither comes nor goes . . . but seems to abide in his place
. . . like an oak, an elm, a beech, or an ash.'[166] However, Watt's
final conclusion confirms our worst suspicions about the unchanging
state of God/Knott: nothing is primary: 'nothing changed, in Mr.
Knott's establishment, because nothing remained, and nothing
came or went, because all was a coming and a going.'[167] An even
clearer identification is suggested when he says: 'nothing could be
added to Mr. Knott's establishment, and from it nothing could be
taken away, but . . . as it was now, so it had been in the beginning,
and so it would remain to the end.'[168] Perhaps the clearest indication
of all occurs when the face of God – according to Hebraic tradition
seen only once, by Moses – comes under consideration: 'here all
presence was significant, even though it was impossible to say of
what, proving that presence at all times, or an equivalent presence,
and only the face changing, but perhaps the face ever changing,
even as perhaps Mr. Knott's face ever slowly changed.'[169] While
Watt both fears and ardently desires to see Mr Knott 'face to face',
finally, like Dante's damned, Watt 'abandoned all hope, abandoned
all fear'[170] of this ever happening; he contents himself with glimpses
of the protean character. His final position is one of total ignorance,
ignorance as utter as that laid claim to by Mr Nixon (speaking of
Watt) at the start. This ignorance, strangely, is seen to be an im-
provement: 'What had he learnt? Nothing. What did he know of
Mr. Knott? Nothing. Of his anxiety to improve, of his anxiety to
understand, of his anxiety to get well, what remained? Nothing.
But was not that something?'[171] The supreme stoical state of
apatheia, resignation, has been reached, the state described by
Beckett in his essay on Proust, as 'the wisdom of all the sages, from
Brahma to Leopardi, the wisdom that consists not in the satisfaction
but in the ablation of desire.'[172]

But is Mr Knott a God at all? 'God', says Sam on only the second page, 'is a witness that cannot be sworn'.[173] Mr Knott is peculiarly obsessed by the need to be witnessed, in a curious reversal of accepted biblical theology: 'except one, not to need, and two, a witness to his not needing, Knott needed nothing, as far as Watt could see'.[174] In this respect (as with his not-knowing) Knott's situation is something less ideal than a God's should be. In him 'the ablation of desire' has not been achieved, and Watt scarcely satisfies what needs he has:

> What kind of witness was Watt, weak now of eye, hard of hearing, and with even the more intimate senses greatly below par? A needy witness, an imperfect witness. The better to witness, the worse to witness. That with his need he might witness its absence. That imperfect he might witness it ill. That Mr. Knott might never cease, but ever almost cease.[175]

Mr Knott's tenuous existence is therefore very similar to Malone's lights 'that scarcely were, on the confines of silence and dark, and soon ceased'.[176] He only exists when he is witnessed; he is not Berkeley's God, but very much like an item in Berkeley's scheme of things. He is the centre which the circumference longs for: 'This body homeless. This mind ignoring. These emptied hands. This emptied heart. To him I brought. To the temple. To the teacher. To the source. Of naught.'[177] He is, at any rate, the master, Watt the servant, like Pozzo and Lucky later. But Lucky, like Jacques the fatalist, leads his master in the end, and this Watt never does. Watt's role is to look after the god's dogs.

The God = dog equation may seem a puerile reversal, the substitution of a palindromic language-game for thought of real substance. But if God is a dog, man is a termite; Watt[178] suggests this may be so, and subsequent narrators have confirmed it. The image of the dog is, in fact, one of Beckett's favourites. In his earliest story 'Assumption' man is worse off than the 'meanest mongrel', and in *Murphy* Ticklepenny attains one of his greatest moments only to have it compared to the movements of a 'delighted dog'. Wylie is a 'cur'; Miss Counihan a 'bitch'.[179] Molloy often behaves like a dog, and Moran at one point implicitly equates himself with the dog Zulu.[180] The Unnamable at one point thinks of himself as 'a constipated dog, or one suffering from worms'.[181] Malone remembers, as Beckett does, 'the barking of the dogs, at night, in the clusters of hovels up in the hills, where the stone-cutters lived'.[182] The animal doubtless appeals to Beckett partly because if living really is 'a dog's life',[183] it is a pretty degrading thing. But Beckett also sees animals as suffering under man's inhumanity. Just as it rankled Swift to think of Houyhnhnms cruelly subdued (*Gulliver's Travels*, book 4, chapter 4) when in many respects humanity was much less accomplished, so Beckett concentrates on the image of the slaughterhouse in the trilogy. He sympathizes (in 1938) with 'the four caged owls in Battersea Park, whose joys and sorrows did not begin till dusk'[184] and again (some twelve years later in *The Unnamable*) with the owl 'cooped in the grotto at Battersea Park'.[185] The image reappears in *Proust*,[186] and is used by Dan to describe the train-compartment in *All That Fall*. It is a two-way image; man is like a beast in his behaviour, yet his behaviour (especially his fiction-making) keeps him caged. For full Beckett treatment, only the unending series needs to be added: hence, the Unnamable sees himself as 'a caged beast born of caged beasts born of caged beasts born of caged beasts born in a cage and dead in a cage'.[187]

The images accumulate. Mahood in his jar is like a bird in a cage;[188] the Unnamable is 'dumb' and 'uncomprehending' like a pig.[189] He stares like an owl, dreams of being eaten by a rat, falls like a carthorse, gets caught like a fish, his thoughts are hornets and ants; his whole environment is peopled with animals.[190] Among earlier examples, Miss Carridge in *Murphy* is an ostrich, Neary an owl, Miss Dew a ludicrous duck. Celia is even compared to a goat, which is untraditional treatment for a heroine, even if the farm scenes in *Malone Dies* suggest goats are treated well. The whole cast of *Murphy* is a 'nest of vipers'.[191] Perhaps ultimately this excess of attribution confuses rather than clarifies, dissipates rather than concentrates. When Wylie is a mollusc as well as a cur, the image is in danger of seeming merely reflex, a habitual and therefore rather easy response. When asked what animal he would care to be reincarnated as, Beckett is said to have replied 'An opossum'.[192] This, we may be sure, would satisfy his Belacqua fantasy to the full.

As this analysis shows, Beckett's events and imagery are obsessively consistent. Like all solipsistic thinkers, he is obsessively concerned with himself. For *More Pricks than Kicks* Beckett plunders 'Dream of Fair to Middling Women': he is a continual self-plagiarist. It is not simply a case of all his plots resembling one another; all his heroes contain within them everything that has gone before them. It is, strictly speaking, impossible to fully understand a given work of Beckett's without knowing everything antecedent and subsequent to it; he thus at least partly satisfies T. S. Eliot's daunting dictum (in 'Tradition and the Individual Talent') that we must know all an author's work in order to know any of it. That this is an in-built limitation cannot, I think, be disputed; and some have even seen it as an indication of how very narrow Beckett's range is. But while his range of character is obviously very small in comparison with, say, Tolstoy or Dickens or Balzac, his fiction is powerfully emotional and intellectually stimulating, and in two cases at least (Arsene in *Watt*, and Madden in *Mercier and Camier*) he shows himself perfectly capable of character vignettes in the traditional mould. And the amount of special knowledge required to interpret his world is really quite small. It is helpful but not essential to know that when Molloy says 'I sometimes wonder if I ever came back from that voyage',[193] he is thinking of his previous incarnation in the *nouvelle* 'The End'. The 'faint reddish glow' of the gas-stove imagined by Moran[194] is one that Watt knew well. And in his paranoid way he observes the sheep and shepherd stare at him in much the same way as the horse watches the hero of 'The Expelled'. Malone even quotes the beginning of one of Moran's sentences,[195] then, realizing that no good will come of rehashing Moran's failure, he urges himself on to complete his own. The blow on the head that he imagines receiving in the forest may well have been dealt out by Molloy;[196] 'All that belongs to the past' at any rate. Later he asks himself 'Is it possible I got as far as London?'[197] and a subsequent passage on gull's eyes quoting Democritus's 'Nothing is more real than nothing' establishes this beyond doubt by connecting him indelibly with *Murphy*.[198] It is characteristic of Beckett's self-denigration (seen first when Walter Draffin is made author of Beckett's own 'Dream of Fair to Middling Women') to call *Murphy* an 'old shipwreck' for, as when Molloy remembers 'The End', the sea is an important agent of creativity. It is equally characteristic that objects from earlier heroes abound in Malone's little world: Watt had only one boot, and Malone can only see one; Moran had a ring he was fond of, Malone inherits it. Malone hears Watt's mixed choir and loves to suck as Molloy, unforgettably, does. He can even shout 'Up the Republic' as Beckett himself once did, when asked by Nancy Cunard to contribute to a pamphlet on the Spanish Civil War.[199]

While they are all the creatures of one man ('my people' as Beckett calls them), they are not simply spokesmen for him, as they might be if Beckett had had a political or philosophical axe to grind. 'Tears and laughter, they are so much Gaelic to me',[200] Molloy claims, a trifle too glibly, as if he himself does not believe it. Beckett certainly thinks differently – 'All that matters', he told his actors once, 'is the laugh and the tear.'[201] Beckett is, like Molloy, 'no enemy of the commonplace';[202] he believes in the integrity of his vision, he presents what evidence he has found, it is not – for him, at any rate – arcane. It is not, to be sure, something cliché-ridden like advertising; in both *Proust* and *Molloy* he explicitly rejects that vulgarity.[203] His lingua franca is colloquial, but literate. Literature in the accepted capital-letter sense of Great Art is, however, not his aim; he respects Moran's decision not to 'give way to literature',[204] follows Kafka in thinking writing 'a joke and a despair'[205] and Artaud in thinking that all literature is *merde*. The contrivance and ingenuity that 'literature' requires are not available to him because he feels that only his words are alive. But since he can only have life (however artificial) when he spins fictions with words, he is forced to endow the words themselves with some kind of personality, to compensate for his vacancy: 'All I know', says Molloy, 'is what the words know',[206] and later, 'what tenderness in these little words, what savagery.'[207] As he proceeds as a writer, his perceptions increasingly approach the status of Malone's little notes: they 'have a curious tendency ... to annihilate all they purport to record'.[208] As a result, our ultimate impression of Beckett's world is that 'all things move with the ponderous sullenness of oxen'.[209] Part of this sullenness derives from repetition ('doing the same thing over and over again', as Molloy says, 'fills you with satisfaction')[210] and part derives from the studied insouciance of the recording consciousness ('devouring my pages with the indifference of a shuttle'[211] is very much Molloy's role). Whatever Moran may say, Beckett only rarely seems to be 'writing for the public';[212] and far from satisfying the public's taste for individuals, he is usually 'content with paradigms'.[213] But things are not as clear-cut as that. The deliberate avoidance of system, of which the Unnamable speaks, is balanced by an almost mathematical 'mania for symmetry'.[214] The symmetry is of course always slightly awry, just as the details are always either too many or too few. Malone's desire 'to be clear, without being finical' is no more blessed with success than Moran's.[215] Clarity is not possible when 'the subject falls far from the verb and the object lands somewhere in the void';[216] the Unnamable recognizes that 'confusion is better avoided'[217] but finds it impossible to avoid when the hypotheses 'collapse on top of one another'.[218] The voice – and hence the form – is 'of a world collapsing endlessly', 'a crumbling frenzied collapsing'.[219] The personal vision becomes, in its way, a defence against this, a refuge, but the 'true refuge' (as *Lessness* shows) is both literally and figuratively 'issueless', a kind of death. It is only with death that Malone's desire for all things to be 'still and dark and all things at rest for ever at last'[220] will be satisfied. From the perspective of death, *sub specie aeternitatis*, even the most important subjects look puny. To speak of life and death *is*, ultimately, 'balls-aching poppycock';[221] yet equally, we cannot avoid it, it is what we are all always talking and thinking about. 'The truth that lies closest' (Kafka wrote on 21 October 1921) 'is only this, that you are beating your head against the wall of a windowless and doorless cell';[222] the only way Beckett can talk about this (to parody Arsene's familiar sentence in *Watt*) is to speak of life as if it were death, and death as if it were life. Despite the fact that there are 'no things but nameless things, no names but thingless names',[223] no bodytight mind, no mindtight body, one must have the absurd but dauntless courage to quest after such things. And the quest will take many forms. Malone is, in the end, absolutely right: 'the forms are many in which the unchanging seeks relief from its formlessness.'[224] In the process life becomes art.

4 Drama for stage, screen and radio

'What a dramatist you would make,' I said to him. 'You seem to be carrying on some experiment beyond the limits of all the sciences.'

(Paul Valéry, *Monsieur Teste*)

Two thieves are crucified with Christ. One is saved, and the other damned. Have you pondered the dramatic qualities of this theology? (Samuel Beckett)[1]

The successive mutations of a form that began in ritual and sacrifice two or three thousand years ago, and only five hundred years ago cast off its religious trappings in an attempt to involve itself in realism, have done nothing to obscure the fact that our experience of the drama is unmediated in a way our novelistic experience can never be. We are, however, in no danger of confusing this experience with the *cri de cœur* of the lyric. For it is, unlike the fundamentally private satisfactions of the lyric, something in which we all participate while remaining only spectators, something spoken aloud that, however formalized it may become, always speaks to us intimately. In holding, as its greatest practitioner said, the mirror up to nature, it presents man *en situation* in such an irresistible way that it has proved attractive to an existentialist like Sartre. It is, therefore, fundamentally a communal event and, unlike poetry, makes something 'happen', as Yeats, for one realized.[2] At the same time, as the cluster of words deriving from 'play' and 'theatre' suggest, it is a profoundly artificial medium, its effects being engineered with an eye fixed as intensely on the audience as the most thoroughgoing rhetorician could require. It is almost as if it chooses this method to compensate for being doomed, by the fact of performance, to transience and unrepeatability.

The meaning of a drama, therefore, is even less paraphrasable than the meaning of a prose work. For the drama as a totality only takes on body when spoken and accompanied by gesture, which explains why many good plays 'read' poorly in the study. It is no surprise to find a plethora of comment on Beckett's most 'literary' play, *Endgame*, and comparatively little on the plays from *Happy Days* onwards which are less and less 'readable' as the minutiæ of stage directions accumulate. Only in performance does the stunningly experimental vision of Beckett come across, so that *Eh Joe* seems something more than a *tour de force* and *Not I* something more than mere virtuosity. He is popular with theatre people, perhaps because his own virtuosity is a challenge to theirs; but nothing is sooner rejected on stage than bricks without straw, and the merely rhetorical is the simplest to achieve and the least lasting in effect.

In a sense the theatre represents for Beckett a truce with 'the mess', for impermanence dogs the spoken word even more dramatically than the written, and the presence of an audience continually destroys the illusion of reality an actor creates. This helps, perhaps, to explain Beckett's desire that *Waiting for Godot* might play to empty houses, and certainly gives one a new perspective on why he has been loath to attend the first nights of his plays.[3] He has tended, in other words, to avoid the proof of their non-reality, and concerned himself more and more (as his notebooks attest) with the points of detail that constitute their reality. It is his obsession with the theatrical fact as fact, Hamm and Clov 'as stated',[4] which leads him to look askance at certain theatrical experiments. His disaffection for the mask[5] as a dramatic property is in striking contrast to Yeats's and Pirandello's theatre. The mask in Yeats's plays is always conducive to a deeper reality, but like Wittgenstein's ladder, you eventually throw it away when you reach this reality. With Pirandello, the reverse occurs. All Pirandello's characters are wearing masks, even if they are 'naked masks', *maschere nude*; but they do not know (as Yeats's characters do) that they are wearing them, and the harder they try to be a reality, the more distant they are from it. Yeats goes to the length of allowing a prologue to cast doubts on the events that follow (in *The Death of Cuchulain*), but such daring derives from a position of strength in which his characters achieve reality, despite their appearance, without difficulty.

In Beckett's best plays, with no fuss and no paraphernalia, a similar effect is achieved by a very different method. This has sometimes surprised those more familiar with the semi-solipsistic ideas and problems encountered in the novels, since there is, obviously, a danger that the inherently dramatic conflict of being and non-being will become, when transferred from one genre to another, merely theatrical. There is no gainsaying the fact that some transference takes place: we have the author's testimony that *Godot*'s origins lie in *Murphy*,[6] and the origins of *Not I* are certainly to be found in *The Unnamable*. But it is not always a simple matter of priority for, in the same sense that *Murphy* was the well-made novel too well-made, 'Eleuthéria' is clearly a distant relative of the well-made play. It is as if Beckett's scepticism compels him to begin in each genre with something close to the conventional and accepted, unlike the fanatically optimistic surrealists, who could claim to begin with a *tabula rasa*. It may ultimately be felt that his increasing interest in theatre as much as drama – revealed by his increased involvement in production – is an inevitable consequence of a scepticism that has gone too far. Alan Schneider, who has worked closely with Beckett, has said that 'he is trying to reduce the whole theatrical spectrum to a toneless voice in a disembodied head'.[7] Most writers on the theatre contrive to agree that it is, pre-eminently, a medium that *realizes*, that makes even fantasy *real*, and the less tangible the fantastic becomes in Beckett's drama, the more one finds scepticism about the medium at the heart of the matter.

The most obvious reason why Beckett reverted to English in 1956, and has continued, with very few exceptions, to write his drama in English first, is that he found himself, in *Fin de partie*, composing a French whose richness ran counter to his real interest in the poverty of language as a medium of communication. A more prosaic, and probably more accurate, explanation is that after a radio play was 'suggested' to him by the BBC,[8] there was little else he could do but write it in English. *All That Fall* is particularly interesting as an example of how accessible Beckett can be, and its close proximity to *Endgame* confirms that the mid-1950s were a period in which Beckett was once again using the language at his disposal in the fullest possible way. In *Happy Days* and the plays of the 1960s one feels that Beckett has found a new poverty to work with, but all theatre-goers and radio-listeners must be grateful for the fact that, in taking up a language he had long ago discarded, he discovered new resources that kept his drama at a creative peak, even if nothing could be done to resuscitate prose in his native language.[9]

As a young man Beckett was understandably enthusiastic about the Abbey Theatre productions and was impressed by the achievements of the Irish Dramatic Movement.[10] Two of his early un-collected pieces ('Che Sciagura' and 'The Possessed') are dramatic in structure, and make up for what they lack in general interest by a powerful and sometimes fierce polemical tone. One of Beckett's earliest creative acts of consequence was to adapt Corneille's *Le Cid* to the manner of Charlie Chaplin. This 'Cornellian nightmare' has yet to see the light of day, but seems to have been thoroughly enjoyed by all who took part in it. It would be most misleading, however, if these early dramatic interests were to obscure the real novelty of Beckett's writing for the theatre in the late 1940s. It is easy to overdramatize this period of creativity, but Beckett himself admitted (to Israel Shenker) how important it was, and it is likely to prove a perennially fascinating area of speculation. The bare facts of the matter are that after composing *Molloy* he wrote the unpublished 'Eleuthéria', and that after composing *Malone Dies* he wrote the celebrated *Waiting for Godot*. In discussing this period, Beckett tends to adopt a dismissive tone with respect to the dramatic work, and insists that it was mainly a relaxation.[11] But it seems much more likely that he was led to experiment in drama as a challenge, at a time of great creative power certainly, but at a time in particular when, even if the poverty of conventional prose fiction had been safely left behind, he was still coming to terms with the possibly richer poverty of a new genre.

'Eleuthéria' (written in 1947), is, to be sure, something of a false start, but it is a false start which, in its absence from Beckett's published *œuvre*, introduces an element of distortion into our understanding of *Godot*, and it is, in spite of its failings, a fundamentally serious attempt to deal with the problem of freedom that had troubled Beckett so greatly in *Murphy*. It is perhaps Murphy whom the main character, Victor Krap, reminds us most of, engaged as he is in a bizarre and ultimately vain attempt to escape the claims of love, family and bourgeois life, not only in its simple and obvious outward manifestations but especially its devious, clinging emotional dishonesty. Victor's programme is disarmingly straightforward, and uttered without emotion: 'It is perhaps time someone was simply nothing.'[12] The background to this desire is left to Victor's father, Henri, to develop:

> *M. Krap* (in a doctrinal tone): The mistake is to wish to live.
> It is not possible. Living does not matter, in the life
> that is lent us. . . . But one begins nonetheless, afraid
> of doing nothing. One even imagines sometimes it will
> end, that happens. Then you see it's only bluff. So
> you begin again, with less and less. Why can't we
> accommodate ourselves to a life that's only bluff? It
> must be the origin of our sense of the divine. They
> tell you that's life, beginning and beginning again.
> But no, it's only fear of doing nothing.[13]

Despite the stage direction, the speech has the authentic ring of Vladimir's and Estragon's generalizations: the speaker abstracts himself from reality to comment on it and disables conventional intellects by exposing the crippling truisms they live by. M. Krap's death, apparently effected by the mere exertion of his will, brings an end to something his intellect has told him can have no end, because it has no beginning. But it is an event which, like so many in *Godot*, is hedged round by pointers suggesting its insignificance, as if it were merely an incentive to bring Act 1 to an end. M. Krap calls the curtain down on himself with all his usual imperturbability, and remains immobile as the full potentialities of his role are allowed to exhaust themselves.

Victor vigorously eschews even this minimal kind of heroism, and labours (if that is not too strong a word) to not exist, despite the ministrations of a Glazier and his son. The Glazier treats Victor as an object of curiosity that it is his job to bring into some definition: 'Take some kind of shape, for the love of God.'[14] He openly admits that he is a kind of surrogate artist: 'At bottom it's only words that interest me. I'm a poet who prefers to ignore himself.'[15] He is thoroughly irritated by the *idée fixe* and seems the more determined that Victor will take on unique shape in proportion as Victor achieves the shapelessness he desires. Thus he interrupts a ridiculously lengthy and predictably conventional account of Victor's psychology by Dr Piouk, in an attempt to find out why Victor wishes to shut himself up. Piouk's self-satisfied account of a man he saved from suicide does nothing to allay his suspicions that Victor is the one they should be discussing: 'Don't you see we're all circling round something that has no sense? We must find a sense for it, or lower the curtain.'[16] But the second act ends with the pathos of the first, the Glazier and his son locked in helpless mutual incomprehension.

In Act 3, after Victor has woken from a recurrent nightmare,[17] the butler Jacques attempts to explain to the Glazier what Victor's aim really is. Not surprisingly, it is like the 'difficult music' Celia heard: 'It was clear the moment he said it. It's not a thing that can be repeated. It was something like music.'[18] No sooner has the horrified Glazier launched into a harangue on the imperfections of language than a supposed Spectator materializes, complaining about the imperfection of the entertainment. Almost immediately he experiences the difficulties of a man who has moved from one closed system to another, from one category of experience to another:

> It's curious. No sooner amongst you, on the boards, and I begin to lose my faculties. (Pause.) Considerable though they were. (Pause.) Everything becomes soft and vague and I can't see so clearly. (Places his hand in front of his eyes.) I don't even know what I'm saying.[19]

With this collapse of morale, his original desire to bring the play into definition, even at the cost of ending it for good, is dissipated.

71

But the final intruder, a fervent Taoist called Tchoutchi uttering stage-Chinese and murmuring threats, proves the most effective of all; Victor at last explains himself, and the tone of his father returns to the play: 'Faced with a solution which is not death, you are filled with horror and pity. With contentment also. You are undisturbed. No need to worry your heads about it'.[20] The Spectator, afflicted with the Glazier's old malady of wanting precise solutions, is met with a calm and reasoned argument which has a certain slackness about it: 'you feel it's something else, that my life is essentially different from yours, that between you and me there's a gap like that between you and the insane, only not the same gap.'[21] It is 'a life consumed by its freedom':[22]

> I always wanted to be free. I don't know why. I don't know any more what that means, to be free . . . beyond words I know what it is . . . first I was the prisoner of others. So I left them. Then I was the prisoner of myself. That was worse. So I left myself.[23]

This formulation of what has happened, as a prelude to what is happening, proves less decisive than depressing. The Spectator can content himself with the consoling thought that periodically sustains the Unnamable: 'You have perhaps spoken the truth without knowing it. And without us knowing it.'[24] But Victor is as implacable as ever: 'I have told you a story so you will leave me alone. . . . I renounce freedom. You can't be free. . . . You can't see yourself dead. It's the theatre.'[25] The concluding sentimentalities of his fiancée, Dr Piouk and Mme Karl do nothing to prove this conclusion wrong, and we are left meditating the comfortless outlook of one who knowingly consents to return to the habitual, with not even a Godot to wait for, and the only resource available to him, to 'turn his lean back on humanity'.[26]

There are moments of great resonance in the play, as for example when M. Krap's resigned acceptance of things as they are is undermined by his awareness of how irrelevant his resignation is:

> *Mme. Piouk* I am comfortable as I am.
> *M. Krap* I know. We are all comfortable as we are. Quite, quite comfortable. Unfortunately it is not a question of our comfort.[27]

There are lively exchanges pulled up short by tragi-comic admissions, for example Dr Piouk's scheme of salvation for mankind:

> *M. Krap* And what is your solution?
> *Dr. Piouk* My solution?

M. Krap	In two words.
Mme. Krap	(severely). You have one, I trust.
Dr. Piouk	It lacks charm.
M. Krap	Inevitably. . . .
Dr. Piouk	I am a practical fellow. . . . I would forbid reproduction. . . . I would beat to death any female guilty of giving birth. I would drown the new-born. I would favour homosexuality. . . . I would encourage with all the means at my disposal recourse to euthanasia.
Mme. Krap	I was born too soon.[28]

Despite this, one feels that Beckett is too unsure of the implications and evasions of his scepticism to successfully dramatize anything more substantial than the individual perceptions it offers him. This gives the play the unfortunate appearance of a source-book for later plays. But perhaps the most damning criticism one could make of 'Eleuthéria' is that it does not encourage one to envisage its individual dramatic configurations in a way that even an unpublished *Godot* would have done.

Waiting for Godot (written 1947–8, published 1952) remains undiminished by the volume of critical comment on it. It presents us with recognizable alternatives in a way that 'Eleuthéria' never does. Vladimir is the romantic, given to nostalgia; Estragon, whom he has virtually called into existence by acknowledging his opening remark ('but for me . . . where would you be?'),[29] is pragmatically involved with easing the pain of the present. To Vladimir's conceptual intelligence ('Boots must be taken off every day')[30] which issues in useless truisms ('I remain in the dark'),[31] Estragon opposes the stricken cry of the man given to single perceptions. But it means he cannot sympathize with Vladimir's torment, and however much of a *poseur* Vladimir may seem, he takes the truth of inherited quotations ('Hope deferred . . .')[32] seriously. Only when the consultation of his hat proves inefficacious does he come round to Estragon's original position, 'nothing to be done', closing the first of many closed systems out of which the play is built.[33]

Estragon begins the next movement by parodying the last act of the previous movement: Vladimir's quest for inspiration is reduced to Estragon inspecting his boot. Vladimir's scorn for the elementary logic Estragon reveals in this enterprise does nothing to ease his own problem. His apothegms lead only to the exposure of accepted wisdom, not to the creation of new truths; the story he tells merely occupies the vacancy of time.[34] Estragon is always content to return to the point of origin; he is the architect of a closed system centring on himself ('You're merciless', Vladimir says).[35] Vladimir, by contrast, introduces a fiction that he decides to regard as true, only to find it torments him thereafter. The development of the play – if we adopt Beckett's terms from *Proust* – is that 'the observer [Vladimir] infects the observed [Estragon] with his own mobility'.[36]

To the idealist Vladimir, Estragon's pragmatism is confusing: 'Nothing is certain when you're about'.[37] As an idealist he finds that the one dream is sufficient: introduce personal freedom, as Estragon seeks to do, and it will look very much like a nightmare. Estragon's story of a brothel only torments him, and the laughter of relief is 'prohibited'.[38] Furthermore, the only moments of ordinary quotidian reality occur when Estragon decides not only to 'return the ball',[39] but to initiate the rally, and then Vladimir finds himself at the mercy of Gogo's good will. Godot, for Estragon, is simply the 'wind in the reeds'[40] from Vladimir's nostalgic 'nineties'.[41] He poisons Vladimir's intelligence by suggesting that the discriminations he seeks to make can only come to grief in identity,[42] and by asking absurd questions Vladimir cannot answer. Estragon's recourse to fatalism[43] proves so attractive to Vladimir that they become almost indistinguishable figures, and 'nothing to be done' ends another movement.

Vladimir's only recourse is to call up Pozzo and Lucky. Two worlds and two frames of reference are suddenly suspended in the same plane; hence their indecision, divided between the wish to go to his assistance and the fear of not minding their own business.[44] Such an interruption allows their fictional existence to persist at the cost of extra complications. Vladimir is careful to let Pozzo announce himself; his whole position would be in danger if the concept of Godot could not also be a percept. But like the blustering Satan of *Paradise Lost*, book 4, Pozzo is disappointed that he has been summoned and yet they do not know him.

The new arrivals increase one's sense of possibility. Lucky is like Estragon, in snatching the sleep he can get, but Pozzo introduces the notion of 'species'[45] and can laugh where Vladimir's timidity and querulousness do not allow him to. At the same time, Pozzo's epicureanism is dependent on the continued enslavement of Lucky. The human contract in even the most trifling of matters gives rise to a theatre of cruelty of alarming proportions: Beckett explodes for good and all the reassuring, almost Dickensian 'It's of no importance' of Pozzo. The pragmatic Estragon gets stuck like a broken record on the revolutionary idea of human freedom,[46] and suddenly two types of reason are seen in conflict – the sympathetic, fatalistic kind, and the inhuman one that seeks improvements which can only multiply problems, ludicrously led up to and quite bathetic when it comes. Bringing Pozzo to the point of origin has much the same effect as it did on Vladimir: it leaves his foundations in ruins: 'Perhaps I haven't got it quite right. He wants to mollify me, so that I'll give up the idea of parting with him. No, that's not exactly it either', etc.[47] Pozzo pretends Lucky is an analogue of the Kenotic Christ or Suffering Servant, but he is committed to a closed system that denies Christianity, and trying to father it on Lucky does him no good. Pozzo *acts* distraction, but he does not really want an end to the closed system of his habitual being, which is why Estragon has to ask him to sit before he can accomplish it.[48] Although Pozzo can employ his imagination without difficulty, and perform his protean repertoire of roles with considerable zest, Lucky's one role undermines his many; the convoluted torrent of Lucky's 'think', with its pathetic attempts to order material, leave his self-regarding rhetoric looking thin.

The 'think' clarifies attitudes. Estragon characteristically prefers the dance, the Noh-like prologue to Lucky's play. Pozzo's reactions to it are increasingly unpleasant. Vladimir varies between interest and anger. Lucky retains enough rhetoric for us to take Pozzo's claim that Lucky was his teacher ('Guess who taught me all these beautiful things. . . . My Lucky!')[49] fairly seriously. But the real burden of Lucky's speech gets uttered against much greater odds than Pozzo ever experiences and the ultimate conclusion, that 'man . . . waste[s] and pine[s]'[50] seems a hard-won wisdom. This is the broken-backed peripeteia towards which the speech works and away from which it dwindles, as the stream of consciousness gets caught on the rocks of intellect. The speech proves its own undoing: the facts are there, and time *has* told 'concurrently simultaneously' but the facts are already too formalized and time will tell us only what we already know. The speech catches our imagination because it is so daring, and it constitutes the nearest to heroism that Lucky can achieve. But it is really a daunting articulation of how tangential to our reality are all verbal formulations whatsoever, and how even our stream of consciousness is in a straitjacket.

Vladimir characteristically sees possibilities in this, but Lucky's hat (like his own) proves too solipsistic to tell him anything, and his plea for a repeat performance suggests he has not learnt the wisdom of the first. Lucky and Pozzo revert to their original roles with difficulty and leave the tramps to tease out the significance of their interruption. The play reveals them as men who are endeavouring (what Lucky would call 'conating') to adapt, constantly dumb-founded by the changes that take place round them. Estragon's new pain is part of the new configuration of the organism that is 'himself *post* Pozzo and Lucky', and the play takes on new colour with the appearance, at the end of the first act, of a boy. Vladimir provides him with a biography by an effort of projection not unlike Mr Hackett's at the beginning of *Watt*, and even has to propel him into uttering the message he has memorized: 'Words, words. Speak.'[51] But the boy is no surer than the Glazier's son in 'Eleuthéria' whether he is happy or not, and he is so helpless that he can only answer when spoken to. So the tramps are left at the end of the first act subject only to their own hypotheses, which conspire to keep them where they are.

Vladimir's song at the start of the second act is a symbol of creativity running up against intractability – the last line can only be repeated, as the second act can only repeat the first. Vladimir now shows himself increasingly keen on the old routines, while Estragon shows an increased desire to be off. But he is soon reduced to an obedient echo of Vladimir who, despite recognizing his isolation ('There you are again. . . . There we are again. . . . There I am again'),[52] still arrogates power to himself that Estragon recognizes ('The best thing would be to kill me, like the other').[53] The recognition does not help Estragon, who nine times in close proximity closes the dialogue in a way that suggests it may not be resumed.[54]

Stage-business is allowed to dominate, so that they may have the impression, if only momentary, that they exist, but the emotional warmth of 'Yes yes, we're magicians'[55] is dissipated by the absurdity of concerted action that reminds us of Act 1. Fictional stereotypes are revealed as a sleep and a forgetting; Estragon plays Cinderella to Vladimir's Prince Charming, Vladimir plays Westerns, Estragon appropriates a nightmare from the Victor of 'Eleuthéria'.[56] The culmination is a hat routine out of Laurel and Hardy which ends with Vladimir wearing Lucky's hat, and admitting the possibility of voluntary role-playing. But the whole sequence is rendered absurd by the failure of Pozzo and Lucky to arrive. It is briefly suggested[57] that this is because the uncreative object Estragon has had a vision of his own, which explains Vladimir's irritation and Estragon's ultimate insult of 'Critic!' If the vision has taken place independent of him, a critic is precisely all Vladimir can be, and it is disarming to find the word used as an insult at precisely the moment formal criticism would want to step in and start rewriting the play.

It is an indication of how much deterioration there has been that even a blind Pozzo is something to be glad of; we feel the confrontation is now not so much two realities in one plane as two aspects of one reality. Vladimir's delight expresses itself in a sentimental mystical trance, in which he forgets the cries of Pozzo altogether in musing on what they might mean. The rhapsodic philosophizing of Vladimir so infects Estragon that he utters a glib and gnomic utterance he would have found almost unthinkable in Act I: 'We all are born mad. Some remain so.'[58] Nevertheless, his creative power remains on the increase (he sees Pozzo and Lucky as Cain and Abel)[59] and Vladimir again begins to feel protective about his own. It is he, after all, who 'wear[ies] of this motif'.

As the play nears its end, we realize that the deadly, mechanical point of origin, 'We're waiting for Godot' involves a deliberate destruction of significance; it gets progressively emptier of content as the play continues, and all the analogies they have constructed for themselves fail to clothe their nakedness. Vladimir is desperate to prove that he is experiencing a repetition but Lucky's 'concurrently simultaneously' has been replaced by the random 'one day'[60] that expands to fill the life that has been invented for it. He is no more interested in Estragon's dream than he was earlier in his nightmare, but Estragon manages at last to bring him to an understanding of something outside himself, and however self-indulgent Vladimir's philosophizing may seem, he is at the heart of the matter. He is right to see habit as 'a great deadener',[61] though it has taken him a long time to see it, and involved him in habitual deadness on the way. Unfortunately his response to the perception of an image of God (Godot with a white beard) is habitual and *ex hypothesi* without real content. It does not lead to a greater content, only to the stale reiteration of the one perception: 'Tell him . . . tell him you saw me and that . . . that you saw me.'[62] The impossibility of systematizing the unprecedented (Watt's problem) leaves Vladimir unsure of Godot's salvation and, for the first time, seeking the way out Estragon has long been looking for. The end of the play is suddenly on us in a rush, with the studied elegance of Act 2's repeat of the end of Act I no comfort at all in a world where everything seems to happen for the first time.

Endgame (1956) has the 'power to claw'[63] because it is clearer in definition, but many have felt that the situation is in some way less dramatic than that of *Godot*. It is much more obviously a 'mind-drama' than the earlier play, and Beckett clearly sought a chamber environment, as Yeats and Strindberg had done before him, with something similar in mind. If there is something Greek about *Godot*, where the only things that matter (even the significance of Godot) are on stage, it is even more obvious here. If there was 'no outside'[64] in *Waiting for Godot*, where it was Beckett's aim to encompass all reality, to see eternity in a country road at evening, *Endgame* reveals how absurd that aspiration was: in a contracting universe, there is even more reason to realize that there is 'no outside', and therefore less reason to move.

Clov's laugh at the outside is as brief as Vladimir's or Krapp's laugh, but he laughs at memory with more of the alacrity of Krapp than the reticence of Vladimir, the first indication, perhaps, of the 'power to claw'. Only the thought of Hamm stays his laughter, because he is still slightly in awe of him (though eventually he laughs at Hamm as well). He is absurd from the start, mixing the roles of amateur philosopher and harassed housewife (in the original drafts Clov dressed up as a woman)[65] indiscriminately. The fact that he speaks first adumbrates his eventual liberation from Hamm, and Hamm reminds us of this with his first words. Hamm allows himself to be sidetracked by an object that leads him back into the past, and a mangled quotation from George Herbert that is immediately undermined. But the self-questioning is unhurried as yet, and he finds time to exemplify Bruno's law of maxima and minima: 'the bigger a man is the fuller he is. . . . And the emptier.' At last the crucial decision is taken: 'it's time it ended.'[66] This elaborate formality completed, the opening game is perfected, and the middle game begins.

The rest of the play is devoted to examining the preconditions that will allow 'ending' to take place. It can only be articulated outside of words, but within the play countless stress-fractures are introduced with the stage-direction 'Pause' which proleptically embodies and points forward to the final end. In this dialogue between self and image (more inquisitive of the *origin* of perceptions than Yeats's self and soul),[67] the creative mind reveals itself as exhausted, seeking an honourable way out from dependence on its fictions. The brief tableaux at beginning and end may seem to put the blame for the recurrence of the problem squarely on the fictional identity of Clov, but the central part of the play makes questions of praise and blame seem irrelevant.

There is a cauterizing simplicity about the exchanges that comes from the avoidance of rhapsodic and lengthy speeches (in which respect *Godot* already represents a considerable advance on 'Eleuthéria') and also from the feeling that the two central figures feel things to be absolutely clear from the start. The artifact bears a grudge against the artificer, as microcosm always must, according to the *Proust* volume.[68] But 'Outside of here it's death' for Clov.[69]

Gazing at the wall, Clov sees no writing, though he has been weighed in the balance and found wanting; what he does see, with commendable serenity and equanimity, is his ultimate destruction, he sees his 'light dying'.[70] The visionary quality of these perceptions is as rudely stamped on by Hamm as Estragon's by Vladimir, in order that nothing should go astray in this expulsion of the primary offender.

Hamm preens himself on his success ('We're getting on') but his parents clearly represent an obstacle. The suggestion is that what is troubling him comes from an unpleasant conflation of sympathy and intellect: 'There's something dripping in my head. . . . A heart, a heart in my head.'[71] This admission does nothing to exorcize the ghostly memories of his parents (whose second interlude proves longer in duration and once again nostalgic in orientation), but introduces a complicating factor when we see that Nell leaving Nagg parallels Clov leaving Hamm. It is almost as if Hamm is trying out the implications of the image that leaves its reality. What prevents the play at this point seeming a tissue of receding mirrors is the openness of the technique; nothing else could convey the unifying consciousness of the creative organ. Nagg's sudden need to tell a story[72] may be seen as almost a psychological defence mechanism on the part of Hamm, unable to face a separation which will bring him face to face with his real self, a necessary comic relaxation of the imagination that clears the way for the harsh business to come.

Endgame is a play more conscious of its ends than *Godot*, more teleological. Whereas in *Godot*, the repeated elements tend to get robbed of meaning through never being embodied (the classic example being the non-arrival of Godot), in *Endgame*, in accord with its greater sombreness, each reiteration of 'Something is taking its course' is accompanied by a new understanding of things on the part of Hamm. Hamm seeks a solution to his problem by suggesting that a meaningless relationship, in simply occupying a space verbally and gesturally, must in the course of time begin 'to mean something'.[73] But to situate this satisfactorily in his bundle of perceptions he is forced (like Vladimir and like Winnie later on) to postulate an outside observer who can only be the audience, and Hamm remains unamused at the thought of a 'multitude . . . in transports . . . of joy'.[74] The problem for Hamm is that his speculations have a disturbing habit of taking on body. Clov's discovery of a crab-louse crawling on him follows so closely on Hamm's speculations about what is left alive that it is difficult not to find Hamm's hatred for generation part of the vicious circle he has created around him, and is seeking to get free of. He momentarily considers, romantic-fashion, the geographical escape of the Drunken Boat, but his main energies are devoted to a 'prophetic' set-piece Pozzo would have been proud of. It is instructive to see how close this vision of the unconstricted image, 'a speck in the void ... a little bit of grit in the middle of the steppe'[75] is to Arsene's experience in *Watt* that takes him 'off the ladder', or Murphy's third zone that is so difficult to achieve. It is, perhaps, even more instructive to see Hamm's prophecy founder on a footling point of detail only a constricted image like Clov could take any pleasure in; in moments like this,[76] the irremediable isolation of Beckett's characters seems to sanction the extremest forms of sado-masochism.

Hamm faces the implications of Clov's dependency by claiming to be his father, but it is part of the reverse logic of this play that this idea is immediately qualified by Clov treating Hamm as a child over the issue of the toy dog. Hamm's 'I'm taking my course', reminiscent of Estragon's strident personalism ('I'm waiting for Godot')[77] is more complex because it embodies Hamm's realization that to liberate himself from Clov, he must be again what he has been. His sense of timelessness ('What does that mean? Yesterday?') is a result of his ability to follow such a course; Clov, as a conditioned object, is doomed to the perception of unrelieved, tedious successiveness. Clov's riposte reveals, however, that no truth content is to be attached to such perception:

> *Clov* (violently) That means that bloody awful day, long ago, before this bloody awful day. I use the words you taught me. If they don't mean anything any more, teach me others. Or let me be silent.[78]

He is as utterly conditioned as the Unnamable, 'made of other's words', or (in this important preparation for the conclusion) the Caliban of Shakespeare's *Tempest*. Clov tries to confuse the issue by suggesting a new course of action loosely based on the old; he continues to feel every moment as a crisis. However, Hamm's horrifying story of the painter who is the only survivor of a holocaust suggests how equivocal apocalypses can be. Like Vladimir, he believes that 'habit is a great deadener', which is why Clov's determined attempts to turn their situation into some profound metaphysical statement outrage him so utterly. He spikes Clov's guns on 'the life to come'[79] with rare panache, and shouting 'To hell with the universe', reveals the fundamentally educative basis of his role.[80] He realizes that Clov will, in a sense, never be free of him and so he attaches, like some fallen Prospero, great weight to educating him to the same intellectual eminence, perhaps hoping that this is the way to liberate him also.

Hamm's sense of timing is, therefore, especially acute. He knows instinctively that the telling of his story (his second) will be the crucial predisposing factor, and he wakes his father because Clov is not yet ready for its wisdom. It is, admittedly, a difficult wisdom to learn. The story is littered with pauses, but serenely resigned, and smooth. The careful repetition-with-variation of key elements is part of a deliberately withdrawn stance that allows him to think of himself, momentarily, as an employer of servants (like Mr Knott), with a Sherlock Holmes meerschaum, and holly to put up. The effect this has on the play is not unlike that of the sudden barrel-organ music in Bartók's Sixth String Quartet; only concentrated attention can appreciate the hidden pattern behind the mere daring. The lull at the termination of the narrative, when other characters seem to be required for its completion,[81] reminds us of Hamm's dependence on Clov, at precisely the point when he has been hoping to express his effective freedom from all human claims. Nagg seizes this opportunity to make a veiled plea for sympathy by explaining his role: 'I hope the day will come when you'll really need to have me listen to you, and need to hear my voice, any voice.'[82] Hamm cruelly, but necessarily, cuts this idea down to size, by revealing his Prospero role: Nagg's account is subject to his jurisdiction and if Hamm does not want that day to come, it never will. Clov's self-satisfied speech in praise of order[83] consequently irritates Hamm even more than Estragon's claims to self-determinacy irritated Vladimir. Hamm therefore punishes Clov by requiring him to ask questions about a story that Clov has been irrelevant to, and confusing him about the origin of creativity: it is the sea (as for Henry in *Embers*, whose every pause it drags into speech) not the earth that is Hamm's concern now.[84]

In what is perhaps the most difficult part of the play, the origin of creativity proves difficult to articulate. Hamm is faced with his own apocalypse, an apocalypse he himself has engineered. He begins to perfect his own will-lessness, to reveal the power of absence: 'there are no more navigators' (Clov's more practical mind echoes, 'there are no more tugs')[85] and the great winding-down of the endgame has begun. For the one and only time in the play Hamm exhibits a mercy coextensive with his justice:

Clov   Then I'll leave you.
Hamm   (head bowed, absently). That's right.
         (Clov goes to door, turns.)
Clov   If I don't kill that rat he'll die.
Hamm   (as before). That's right.[86]

In a new and calmer mood, Hamm attempts a second prophecy, self-orientated this time. It centres on the 'old refuge'[87] of fiction, which names its victims: 'I'll have called my father and I'll have called my . . . my son.' The world of fiction is revealed as a world of order that Clov can never experience (as Clov's beautiful final speeches about departure make quite clear). But the construction of such a world is followed, for Hamm, by a period of undifferentiated flux in which one becomes 'a speck in the void' and 'all life long you wait for [the millet grains of time] to mount up to a life'.[88] In such a condition, or approaching such a condition, Hamm cannot prevent Clov from singing, for the conditioned image is on the point of escaping from his jurisdiction. To Clov's limited perception, the apocalypse has occurred outside, in some recognizably traditional deluge; Hamm asserts his absence from such events ('It all happened without me')[89] as part of his programme of will-lessness.

The separation proves more difficult than for Pozzo and Lucky leaving Vladimir and Estragon, because we are at the climax of the creative mystery: the liberation of the image. Hamm pictures it to himself as self-murder, which in a sense it is. In liberating Clov, he liberates himself from the fiction of being. The anguished cry 'let it end . . . with a bang'[90] shows how intimately Hamm is involved in his own apocalypse, and he is *compos mentis* enough to see the possibility of reading the small boy as an 'underplot' or fictionally redemptive agent. Clov signally fails to understand this. Whereas Hamm knows that Clov signifies the end of one relationship and the seeping in of another image, Clov thinks, too literally, that the boy is merely a 'potential procreator'.[91] Hamm still requires, for his own (and our) sense of order, a farewell from Clov, delivered 'tonelessly' despite the plangent cadences. Clov's description is far from clear, but Hamm is clearly resigned to the triumph of losing this endgame with very considerable verve. The 'they' Clov speaks of are presumably cognate with the 'they' Molloy and the Unnamable speak of: the inexplicable inquisitioners sent out by the creative mind as it seeks to compel an image to come into consciousness. 'They' can only be silenced by an image that attains full identity: 'you must be there better than that if you want them to let you go.' It is entirely characteristic of the image's intolerable plight – desperate to be free but forced by the creative mind to become free at the moment it decides – that Clov should not comprehend what is happening to him: 'Then one day, suddenly, it ends, it changes, I don't understand, it dies, or it's me, I don't understand that either. I ask the words that remain. . . . They have nothing to say.'[92] They have nothing to say, partly because they have still to tread the same path, and partly because they have taken on identity and have no commerce with those still striving to attain it.

Hamm's delight in finding himself at the end at last issues in the throwing away of gaff and dog and whistle and the need to utter ('reckoning closed and story ended'; 'let's play it that way . . . and speak no more').[93] All that remains is the St Veronica handkerchief[94] miraculously bearing the impression of his own features. The liberation of the image leaves him face to face with himself in a perfect closed system; replacing the handkerchief on his face allows the real and the image to coincide and the need to create lapses. Only wordless gestures remain, and the only threat to Hamm's bliss consists in the submerged recognition that it will all have to be gone through again.

It is very doubtful if any performance of *Endgame* could bring to light more than half of what the play is saying. This does not, of course, mean that it is undramatic. It is, however, difficult to imagine how even a poor performance of *Krapp's Last Tape* (1958) could be undramatic. It is one of Beckett's most accessible plays, and represents a further clarification of his investigation into the sources of creativity and the characteristics of the artifact. It is, as all monodramas seem to be, a virtuosic play, continuing the solipsistic trend established by the last few words of *Endgame*. It begins, like *Endgame*, with a 'brief tableau', but it ends with something new – the endless movement of the tape and the silence of the creative mind. The colour of *Endgame* has rotted down to the black and white of *Krapp*; it is brief, elemental, and more classical in structure than any previous work. The concentration on one figure is made even more severe by the strong white light that lights up his table and the immediately adjacent area, leaving the rest of the stage in utter darkness. He is not circumscribed like Hamm, but he never leaves the stage area as Estragon does, and he has the 'laborious walk' that hampers other Beckett figures.

What is perhaps most striking about the play is that the extreme concentration does nothing to make the problems simpler. Dualisms of self and world only give way to dualisms of self against self. There are certain compensations. The demands of the body are expressed in unrecordable gesture, and as audience we never forget his walk and his voice – his *presence*, over and above what he signifies. His monomania is as attractive as any other genuine expertise, because it is carried out with such relish. He has, unlike Hamm and Clov, no weather eye, or telescope, upon the audience; he is an audience in himself. He does not, even with the banana skins, participate in the humour he gives rise to; he defines himself solely in reaction to the absurdity of past selves enshrined on tape, his most bellowing laugh (after three brief laughs that bring the tramps and Clov to mind) reserved for a Providence that has the 'false ring' he had always suspected.[95] The tension is still generated by the conflict of disparate selves, but the selves are now inhabiting the same location.

Krapp-on-tape equates the self with grain, the same grain, no doubt, that stood for time in *Endgame*.[96] Krapp-as-auditor knows to his cost where this organicism leads. In spite of the infinite regress (for Krapp-on-tape has been listening to himself on tape) time has wormed its way forwards, and the 'husks' can no longer be separated out with ease. The conditions of creativity in the past, with 'eyes closed against the glare' as one possible solace, and eyes open the other, now involve pain: it is no accident that Krapp should switch off the tape when he hears the words 'When I *look*',[97] and fortify himself with drink and a song celebrating the delights of darkness.

The voice on the tape is that of an accomplished *littérateur*, in his element with vocabulary like 'viduity', and not above stealing 'chrysolite' (to describe the eyes of his girl-friend) from Shakespeare's *Othello*.[98] There is a perfect consonance between the perceiving eye and the object perceived: 'Whenever I looked in her direction she had her eyes on me' is much less paranoid than the experience the hero of 'The Expelled' has with the horse.[99] The same kind of consonance between self and world is articulated in the scene in the punt: 'We lay there without moving. But under us all moved, and moved us, gently, up and down, and from side to side.'[100] Its inability to endure, briefly revealed in the separateness of 'Her moments, my moments. The dog's moments'[101] could not be more clearly shown than in the separation of recorded voice from actual life. And much of the tranquillity of the on-tape experience disappears when we remember it takes place in landscapes racked by wind, whereas the recording is accompanied by 'extraordinary silence'. Furthermore, since the 'light of the understanding' is coextensive with the 'fire' of imagination and the darkness of destruction,[102] the scene in the punt, for all its beauty and serenity, begins to seem more a wish-fulfilment than a reality. As the girl opens her eyes, we have a repeat of the Murphy–Endon situation, achieved by a bending movement not unlike that which brought Proust's Marcel one of his *moments privilégiés*. But it is more than Mr Kelly's doll-like movement reorchestrated for two; it effectively collapses sexual penetration and the artistic conflation of subject and object as in the French poems of 1937–9.

The Krapp we actually see before us has only one speech, whose bluntness and irritation thrust an acerbic thorn into the more rosy lyricism of young Krapp. This Krapp has realized his creative inadequacy, and is reading Fontane.[103] Terrified at the prospect of all escape-routes being closed, he tries to recapture the past and contrive the kind of act of consonance that was once so easy to achieve, even if only in mind. However, as the tape is allowed to complete its message this time, an absolute and more complex congruence is established. The wish-fulfilment of the Krapp before us is of a piece with the rationalizations of the Krapp on tape. The 'fire' of imagination that makes the loss of happiness no matter for remorse seems to constitute a less 'real' reality than the one we have had the privilege of witnessing. And the consonance achieved with the girl in the punt seems suddenly a possible reality that was wilfully destroyed, in the misguided belief that artistic creativity would suffer if it continued. It is part of the magic of this dazzling play that the new material, following something we have already heard, alters our understanding of what has gone before, in a simple, but quite decisive way. We are left with a much more equivocal Krapp at the end than we had any right to suspect at the beginning.

The dramatic experience in *Happy Days* (1961) has been further refined. But the refinement does not involve an increase in sophistication; it issues in what the stage directions call 'Maximum of simplicity and symmetry', and a backcloth described as 'very pompier trompe-l'oeil' which makes no pretension to realism. The increasing sense of drama as a ritual to be gone through is exacerbated by the realization that Winnie is entirely subservient to the bell that wakes her up, where Krapp could control his tape (if not his drinking) and Hamm was at least a Prospero of sorts. Willie is a blot on the symmetrical pattern visually, but verbally his contributions are less and less distracting after his first, and most amusing, gratuity. We have seen the flowing style of the young Krapp exposed to the withering brutality of the old; Winnie performs a similar act – her telegrammatic style is so bare that even the briefest lyricism is extinguished. In *Happy Days* the trivial and clichaic has taken over the foreground, as in *Play* and again in *Come and Go*, where the important is reduced to a guarded whisper, and utterance assumes a formulaic status. In *Happy Days* language and gesture are on the way to becoming discrete: the important question of pain is accompanied by a quest for a toothbrush: 'no better, no worse – (lays down mirror) – no change – (wipes fingers on grass) – no pain – (looks for toothbrush) – hardly any.'[104] Accordingly, what had seemed like a musical form in *Endgame* and *Krapp* undergoes considerable alteration: rather than suggesting that all melodies are analogous because they all use the same notes, Beckett is now content to concentrate on playing as few notes as possible. Thus, although the extension of particularity into generality still involves an important change of focus, the focus does not widen greatly – 'slight headache sometimes' is virtually equivalent to 'occasional mild migraine', and the 'old things' are perceived by the 'old eyes'.[105]

The past, called up by the dead hand of newspaper obituaries, is revealed as the only source of happiness; the 'old style' is a question of time rather than literature.[106] Any other solace will have to be located in an unrealizable future, 'the happy day to come when flesh melts at so many degrees and the night of the moon has so many hundred hours'.[107] The immediate future, constantly translating itself into the present, causes nothing but difficulty; but experience wearily absorbs the unexpected and accommodates it to its preconceptions. Willie's 'invisible hand' returning her fallen parasol is unexpected, and his gesture seems almost to lack foundation. But he performs the very important function of restoring the *status quo*, and our realization of this robs even his suddenly bloodied head of some of its shock. Their relationship is subject to numerous minor shocks requiring continual psychological adjustment, but they only impinge on each other at moments of unavoidable contiguity. Winnie's overstatements save her from disappointment; Willie's ability to lead a life of self-satisfaction effectively removed from all significant contact is such that he takes on almost the qualities of an object. Personality becomes a collection of atoms free to appear and disappear at will. Winnie disturbs Willie (as Vladimir disturbs Estragon) merely for her own gratification, to give her what Estragon would call the 'impression' that she exists.[108] She does, however, realize that Willie is the precondition for her speaking, and it is increasingly obvious that *she* only has an existence for herself in so far as she continues speaking. 'That is what I always say' may be reassuring to Winnie, but 'even words fail, at times'[109] and her continual talk adds to, rather than diminishes, her problems. She relies on hypotheses: 'just to know that in theory you can hear me even though in fact you don't is all I need.'[110] This is because there has been a rupture of subject and object, so that for Winnie, unlike the young Krapp, a glance is not necessarily reciprocated: 'I know it does not follow . . . that because one sees the other the other sees the one.'[111] This means that Winnie can make no comment of general relevance, not even on such weighty matters as 'peace' or 'the other'. Despite her excited interest in an emmet, its actions remain unendowed with any of the metaphysical resonance of *Endgame*'s rat. Throughout the more reflective central section of the first act, we are not allowed the distraction of gesture. Everything is reduced to a single level. The monosyllabic exchange linking the proliferation of insects with the continuous creation of God provokes none of the bellowing uproar of Krapp; they both laugh quietly, in severely symmetrical form.[112] The discriminations here are required to be finer; Winnie's concluding comment on this section reveals a more complex irony than we have met before: 'How can one better magnify the Almighty than by sniggering with him at his little jokes, especially the poorer ones?' The multiplicity submerged in comments like this sustains what is basically a monologue; but such compensations for the loss of a genuine dialogue are brief and low-key. We are fortunately spared Winnie's exhaustive inventory (the experience of Malone suggests her instincts about it are correct: she never would complete it); but the dramatic aim is to offer us no escape whatever from the unvarnished fact of Winnie's continuing prattle.

Because of this, Winnie's sensation of being held ('if I were not held . . . I would simply float up into the blue'),[113] which gets stronger as time passes – ultimately giving rise to the absurd and anguished inquisition she hypothesizes for Carter – seems a kind of analogue to the creative act of author and audience. Perhaps it helps to account for why, as the play gets under way, the dramatist's control over his material becomes more and more confident. In most dramas, the fact that certain steps are taken at the outset means that (to remain meaningful) less possibilities remain open; this play is by contrast, rather like a game of chess, in which, up to and including the beginning of the endgame, possible moves increase dramatically, but good moves decrease alarmingly. In this play, almost anything seems possible; hence Winnie's 'fear so great, certain days of finding oneself',[114] just prior to the Earth extinguishing her parasol. This ridiculous and seemingly superhuman act is preceded by a 'maximum pause' in which it seems the creative mind, disturbed by ramifying possibilities, has ceased to record facts at all. It is almost as if the creative mind says to itself, as Winnie says, 'Something must happen, *in the world* . . . if I am to move again.'[115] The gloomiest moment of all is when she realizes she has been dependent on 'empty words'.[116]

It is, perhaps, a play that, unlike *Endgame*, seems to lack a sense of its own logic. This is perhaps a result of its rootlessness in time. Winnie mentions a set time for her song, but the song is separated from this reference to it by the curtain between acts. Winnie's

D

feeling that time does not pass is, however, in conflict with her hypothesis: 'And should one day the earth cover my breasts, then I shall never have seen my breasts, no one ever seen my breasts.'[117] She is, like Watt, experiencing a nothing, that has occurred and is still occurring. But her situation is worse, because it lacks all the formal elegance of Watt's 'nothing'. The perception of uniformity strangles even the veneer she tries to put on it: it is crucial that she cannot complete her statement of wonder. She is enslaved by something outside herself. The someone looking at her, for whom she is 'clear, then dim'[118] begins to seem like the predatory creative mind, but this in itself begins to seem nothing less than the communal mind of the audience, called upon to confront their responses *in medias res*. Like the Unnamable, Winnie finds that 'all is strange' and we are suddenly faced with our own almost unrecognizable features, Winnie gazing at us and saying 'And you, she says, what's the idea of you, she says, what are you meant to mean?'[119] This is not the gaze of Murphy at Endon, or Krapp at the girl; *we* are inescapably involved, and much more dramatically than when one of our number supposedly leaps on the stage, as in 'Eleuthéria'. At the same time Winnie remains consummately self-orientated; as far as she knows, there is no gallery to play to. There is only the recognition of how limited and repetitive Willie's life is, giving her a sense, however paradoxical it may seem, of liberation. The delight she registers at learning what a hog is presents us with a new image of morganatic fate, up to her neck.

Winnie's speculations in the second act are more cosmic than before, partly because of her more rigorous, less conversational manner, and partly because she is concerned to record all she can see and be certain of, in an attempt to placate the light. Echoing the morning hymn of our first parents proves useless. Neither the outside world ('What reeds?') nor the past ('What day?') nor the present world of her body ('What arms? What breasts?') is now acceptable.[120] She is left with only the mind (still prone to 'deep trouble',[121] however much she may think she has cured herself of that), and the eye (no longer troubled by the face that was looking at her, since the eyes belonging to that 'float up [and] seem to close in peace . . . to see . . . in peace').[122] It is her eye and her mind that are the consolations of her present predicament ('I call to the eye of the mind . . . Mr. Shower – or Cooker'):[123] 'What would I do without them, when words fail?'[124] She is, however, forced to admit that her perceptions are as much outside as inside her, that the world-stuff is alive (despite an earlier, dissenting opinion) and that 'things have their life', a life no human construct, such as logic or reason, could possibly explain. Winnie has not yet lost her reason; it is her reason that enables her to discriminate one sensation from another. Winnie is much less fussy, much more precise in Act 2; she has comprehended her problems; her affiliation is with Aristotle (whose name she can remember) rather than with Browning (whose name, and lines, she cannot).[125] But the phrase 'That is what I find so wonderful' begins to seem an utterly mechanical application of a ridiculous optimism; like 'Godot', it reappears in different contexts without filling out in meaning. She has not realized that if 'things have their life', the doll cannot be moved about at will; her own perceptions are irrevocably controlled by something outside her. The need for movement outside ('something must move, in the world'),[126] the need for the God of Rilke's *Sonnets to Orpheus*, is made much more specific than in Act 1. Consequently the notion of changelessness acceded to there is qualified here; God becomes 'just chance, I take it, happy chance'.[127] Their distance from Him is articulated in Winnie's obsession with the 'black night without end' (compare Pim's 'black night of boundless futurity'),[128] and Willie's obsession with the past. Willie's entire part consists of eighteen sentences, five of which repeat what he has said before. His only significant action is to reawaken her memory of the courtship, and Winnie stands aside from what his appeal might mean. But the final bell mocks her song, and she is left at the end as she always feared she might be, beyond words.

In *Happy Days* the perspectives are so shifting (despite the fact that it is all seen, as it were, in one plane) and the words show such a strong tendency towards contradiction ('To have been what I am, and so changed from what I was')[129] that any subsequent drama had to move into another area. It is a transitional play which, for all its painstaking detail, sometimes lacks definition. The set may be simple and symmetrical, but the play remains determinedly asymmetric and uncompromisingly oblique.

Play (1963) restores a certain amount of symmetry, and starts Beckett on the road towards the unvarnished theatrical facts of *Come and Go* and *Not I*. *Happy Days* throws up the question of changelessness but is not always able to make subject-matter and dramatic experience coincide; this happens without difficulty in *Play* by the simple expedient of repeating the play, and even suggesting a third performance. The faces of *Play* face 'undeviatingly front', and have no commerce with their bodies. It is a world of spirits as meretricious and tormented as the earthly existence where such commerce existed. The voices are 'toneless', the faces 'impassive'. The light is inquisitorial; the voices are 'largely un-intelligible' and utterly passive. Although Beckett seems to have remained in some doubt as to what the light *exactly* represents,[130] he is quite clear that the inquisitor is 'unique' and 'human'. It may be one of the Master's minions, but it has become a Master of sorts. There is no longer a 'they' to be blamed; there is in fact no praise or blame of any kind to be made. The light cannot be shaken off. The faces remain abjectly passive in parallel urns; there is, in consequence, a total absence of communication, our dramatic apprehension of which is ensured by separating out three narrative threads for individual exploration. At the beginning of the play, the three faces seem like three atoms of a single creative cell which refuses to come into focus. The light requires them to separate out into separate constituent parts and take on flesh for brief snatches of time. They begin to seem like the faint flashes of light in the unrelieved darkness of the creative imagination that Beckett has often spoken of. They are so constituted that they form recognizable stereotypes: nagging wife, wayward husband, blowzy mistress. At the same time each atom is endowed with its own idiosyncrasy, which is why their concerted efforts to utter, much like their tawdry earthly existence, cause them to come into conflict. Each utterance requires to be understood as a particular, and then carefully joined to the preceding utterance by the same voice, and then related to the total experience. The problem is, first, that the utterances of the other two characters do not, at first hearing, concentrate the original character's statements, but rather dissipate their effect; and second, that the dramatic experience cannot rely on a verbal memory alert and capacious enough to add, subtract and multiply in the way a novel-reader's can. The repetition of the play is therefore a very necessary mechanism, as well as a dramatization of part of the play's meaning. The light, refusing to entertain the idea that its initial movements in the first run-through might have been mistakes, requires them to repeat their 'chorus', their semi-metaphysical considerations, their vulgar love affair, their deeper meditations. The repetition is tormenting because one feels that the light should have been able to unscramble the essentials more successfully the second time around. But the unscrambling is to be done by us; we are as much passive sufferers of the light as the heads are.

The situation is infernal, but to locate it in hell would be a comforting sentimentality quite alien to this play. It takes place in a disturbingly median location, a kind of limbo. All previous Beckett locations yield to this in respect of tawdriness and uncertainty. The darkness and silence so often longed for are now found to be unsatisfactory; they are clearly not continuous either. It is because the light still flashes that M and W2 are led to the vanity of asking if they are perceived; and the three figures can actually see very little external to themselves because the light dazzles them. Clov, even if he never saw the earth lit, at least had the chance to observe his 'light dying'; these three can remember the earth only fitfully, and repeatedly experience the death of the dark. The 'face to face' promised those who have shuffled off this mortal coil by I Corinthians, 13, turns out later to be the eyes of *Words and Music* which 'widen to a stare and begin to feast again'[131] (what *Imagination Dead Imagine* calls the 'eye of prey').[132] *Words and Music* suggests that one glimpse of the 'wellhead' will take us to a place where all eccentricities are consumed;[133] but *Play* suggests there is only an inquisitor and his victims at the end of an ordinary life. It confirms, in other words, Winnie's suspicion in *Happy Days* that the source of all things is outside her, without any suggestion that it is the 'zephyr' Winnie imagined. W2 is, however, optimistic:

> To say I am not disappointed, no, I am. I had anticipated something better. More restful [. . .] less confused. Less confusing. At the same time I prefer this to . . . the other thing. Definitely. There are endurable moments.[134]

And even M, meditating on fantasies involving a dinghy reminiscent of Krapp's punt, faces the logical conclusion to his meditations with a certain equanimity:

> *M* Such fantasies. Then. And now – [. . .] And now, that you are . . . mere eye. Just looking. At my face. On and off. [. . .] Looking for something. In my face. Some truth. In my eyes. Not even. [. . .] Mere eye. No mind. Opening and shutting on me. Am I as much – [. . .] Am I as much as . . . being seen?[135]

W1 is less fortunate, afflicted still by a residual desire to understand: 'If only I could think. There is no sense in this . . . [. . .] I can't. The mind won't have it. It would have to go.'[136] She concludes by leading the assault on the light itself, claiming there is 'Nothing to be asked at all. No one asking me for anything at all',[137] because the 'whole thing', all the events, hypothetical or otherwise, that made them what they were, are 'there, all there, staring you in the face. You'll see it. Get off me. Or weary. [. . .] Weary of playing with me.'[138] But even this request is tempered when we think of her bewilderment ('no, that does not seem to be the point either') and humility ('Perhaps it is more wickedness to pray for more').[139]

The importance of *Play* is that it establishes beyond doubt that 'all that' [i.e. existence on earth, real or fictional] 'was just . . . play'[140] and that beyond the 'change', as the Unnamable discovered, it is still all play. It enables Beckett to suggest that the metaphysical strain and the melodramatic strain, into which the play neatly divides, are effectively coextensive, and it helps to explain why he is intent in this work on destroying the banality of the domesticated theatre with precisely the material that made it what it was.

Come and Go (1965) and *Breath* (1969) continue the formalization of the theatrical experience, without adding anything significant to the situations and ideas Beckett has already explored. *Come and Go* is so bereft of significance that it must have been intended to situate dramatically precisely this inability to go further. The play points briefly to a world of suffering we are all presumed to be familiar with, but refuses to allow us more than the barest facts on which to exercise our imaginations. The 'colourless' voices are 'as low as compatible with audibility'. Solutions and problems are out of the question here. Even to speak of a location seems irrelevant. Unlike the three witches of *Macbeth* to whom the first words of the play briefly refer, they are dedicated not to a future in which they may hope for success, but rather to the restitution of the past at the expense of a present that can only be enshrined in whispers. Vi, like the characters in *Play* or *Happy Days*, thinks of 'the old days' as separate from 'what came after'.[141] But the perfectly executed ballet of exits and entrances confirms rather Molloy's *aperçu* on 'the unchanging': 'The forms are many in which the unchanging seeks relief from its formlessness.'[142] In this particular form, the characters suffer the deprivation of a future without demur, but it is the forward-directed work of *Godot*, *Endgame* and *Krapp's Last Tape* (in which, for the first time, the future begins to seem nothing more than the past) which makes the stage a place of power and significance.

Breath, offered to Kenneth Tynan in response to his request for a piece on the 'man–woman' situation (and illegitimately used by him as prologue to *Oh! Calcutta!*), compresses birth, copulation and death into thirty-five seconds without at any point justifying its extreme brevity. Presumably, at a moment of desperation, Beckett saw less and less reason for the kind of fine discriminations he made earlier in his career, which seemed to have only multiplied his difficulties. But of course the dramatic experience is more limited, and even *Not I* represents only a partial return to the challenging brilliance of his earlier work.

Not I (1973) allows us no distraction from the gaping mouth at the centre of the stage. The hooded figure to the left is 'faintly lit', and the four movements 'of helpless compassion' he makes become increasingly indistinguishable from the darkness. The mouth has taken over the inquisitional role of the light in *Play*, apparently without rancour, as if there were simply nothing else it could do. The auditor is the pitiful residue of a dialogue Beckett has for several years been trying to preserve. But the monologue is all that ultimately matters, with its fivefold 'refusal to relinquish third person'. It is almost as if the voice has finally, as it has always threatened to do, got out of control of whoever its master is (there is no Opener, as there is in *Cascando*) and has arrogated power to itself above and beyond its hesitancy and querulousness. We do not, however, feel the power generated by irresistible emotional force coming into conflict with immovable intellectual object; the voice circumvents all its difficulties with a 'try something else' philosophy. The compensation is that certain things are clearer than ever before: the experiencing consciousness is beyond life, a Persephone snatched from the fields of Enna at the age of seventy; from the moment of birth to the moment of death it has had no identity; the moment of death which seems a guarantee of real being involves the return of feeling and the buzzing in the head, not to mention the cold moonish light which, from *Malone Dies* to *Play*, exhibits disquieting variations in intensity.

Beckett's notebooks contain a synopsis of the work which reveals its organization around five basic clusters of biographical experience, rather than, as one might have expected, around thematic abstractions. Beckett was keen to amplify the details of biography, and also to make clear the connections between such things as the mechanism of thinking and the perception of the moon. But the work was written relatively quickly,[143] and the extreme concentration of a play like *Endgame*[144] is clearly a thing of the past. The voice is remorseless and yet moves jaggedly back and forth in time, encapsulating the event and reflections upon the event, but in too much of a hurry to do more than drop hints. The voice is interested in what it says, but not desperately so; and the repeated cry ('What? ... who? ... no! ... 'she!') is not so much agonized as 'vehement',[145] as Beckett's stage notes suggest. At the most noisy moment of all, the two screams superseded by a silence into which the echo drains away, the voice even seems to recognize its own experimentalism as a conditioning factor in the desire to do away with all echoes. At the same time, the voice contributes to a continuous project without ever being precisely aware that there is any project to contribute to. The attempt to get to the heart of the creative problem involves, as previous explorations had suggested it would, a separation of the expressive organ from the conceptual mechanism, followed by an attempt to suggest that there is no conceptual origin anyway. This last move seems to have been dictated by the voice of *Eh Joe* saying: 'You stop in the end. . . . Imagine if you couldn't.'[146] It means in effect that the drama has to exist literally in the pauses between the utterances, as Beckett has always felt it should, rather than in the collision of one utterance against another, which has always multiplied his problems. *Not I* is perhaps the closest Beckett has come to dramatizing the totality of what he hears in his head, but its arrangement of material is less dramatic than the work it most reminds us of, *Cascando*.

The radio plays suggest Beckett had realized that live theatre could not encompass successfully his developing themes of the relationship between creativity and identity. The irresistible *presence* and tangibility of the actor constantly tend to make speculations about identity seem absurd. In Pirandello, where this is central to the play, the developing action seems often to be only a wrangle as to what names we will agree to pin on things. Beckett moves his speculations into another mode because the things, under scrutiny, have a disturbing habit of multiplying and changing, whatever we agree to call them. In addition, the adoption of a new mode means new technical problems to solve; and some of the diffuseness of a play like *Embers*, for example, seems partly due to inexperience rather than muddled thinking. It is obviously best to consider the radio plays as a separate genre, provided it is remembered that they contain the solutions to certain problems which the later theatre takes for granted.

The comparative realism of *All That Fall* (1957), much stressed by all writers on the play, is a matter of some complexity. The radiophonic instructions are as lapidary as Beckett's stage directions, but it is clear that the earliest sounds of all are devoted to creating a sense of environment against which the subsequent events may be imagined. They are, however, deliberately exaggerated to remind us of the fictional status of those events, and it is no surprise therefore that the central characters should also be periodically afflicted with the feeling that they, too, are mere fictional constructs. The human voice and the sound induced by radiophonic devices thus interact to create a world constantly aware of its artifice, powerfully engaging because of our habitual suspension of disbelief, but disturbingly transient and insubstantial when we try to examine it, constantly tending to fragment itself into individual, disconnected sounds. The characters exacerbate this unavoidable property of radio drama. Mrs Rooney is so much given to reflecting on her mode of behaviour that it amounts to an undermining of her carefully particularized reality; Mr Rooney's quietly eccentric attitudes are put under less stress (except at the end when the 'thing' he carries about with him is exposed to public curiosity), but his mastery of two distinct tones – one to recount his narrative of past events, one to record his experience of the present – does much to diminish his reality as a character. And yet, in spite of this, one feels that Beckett was, in the writing of *All That Fall*, as much attracted by the prospect of having to confine his vision within conventional forms as by the prospect of doing something in an entirely new medium. He exploits, with more relish than perhaps anywhere else in his work, his mastery of local colour and character vignettes, already revealed in *Watt* and *Mercier and Camier*, and used again, most effectively, in his Irish version of Robert Pinget's *La Manivelle*, *The Old Tune* (1960).

The actual environment inhabited by such personalities is subject to the familiar Beckettian rule of decay, all the characters suffering forms of more or less irremediable bodily malaise. The very prevalence of this decay prevents one dwelling on it, and what other dramatists might have used as significant background information, or material for explaining motivations, is here absurdly squandered on characters who do not reappear, telling stories of others who never appear, in a manner that perfectly undermines the 'plausible concatenation' Beckett has always despised. We are left to concentrate only on the individual moment of utterance. And yet the presence of such elements as suspense ('Surely to goodness that cannot be the up mail I hear already'),[147] which Beckett normally eschews fairly severely, gives the work an end-directed quality which is uncharacteristic. Beckett seems to have recognized that this kind of approach requires what he calls 'mitigation of contour',[148] and it is entirely characteristic of him to leave the central issue of Mr Rooney's involvement in the death of a child totally unexplained, in an extension of the technique, found even in Henry James, that concentrates attention on what turns out ultimately to be enigmatic.[149] The suspense reveals, on the level of psychology, the crippling tedium of the lives uncomplainingly lived by the Boghill locals; the arrival of the up mail becomes a matter of importance when it provides material for an argument with the station-master. From the point of view of the audience, the creation of what we take to be ends in themselves involves us, endowed with a perspective that is happiest with objects at a distance, in ignoring what lies under our noses. It is precisely this world that Beckett seeks to dramatize. Mrs Rooney almost calls her environment into existence around her as a pledge of her reality, with the philosophical melancholy of the solitary Vladimir:

> All is still. No living soul in sight. There is no one to ask. The world is feeding. The wind – (brief wind) – scarcely stirs the leaves and the birds – (brief chirp) – are tired singing.
> The cows – (brief moo) – and sheep – (brief baa) – ruminate in silence. The dogs – (brief bark) – are hushed and the hens – (brief cackle) – sprawl torpid in the dust. We are alone. There is no one to ask.[150]

Beckett is repeatedly aware, with the vigilance of a phenomenologist, that the projection of another reality ultimately proves detrimental to our ability to endure the present. Consequently the banter and triviality of ordinary conversation involves no aspirations in the manner of Chekhov. There is at the same time none of the documentary exactitude that seems to cling to popular minor drama throughout the ages. There is a certain mannerism about Beckett's approach, deriving from his desire to give pattern to the most meaningless item as well as to the most significant, because human utterance predisposes one to take its products seriously, however unsatisfactory they are ultimately seen to be. So he implacably records our repetitions: 'Nice day for the races', 'Divine day for the meeting', 'Lovely day for the fixture'.[151] And continues to suggest that phenomena require to be maintained by a will rather more powerfully active than one might expect from such acquiescent creatures: Mrs Rooney's doubt as to the ability of the day to 'hold up'[152] proves so prophetic that it is almost as if she has precipitated it – in this sense, it *is* 'suicide to be abroad'.[153]

In a similar way, Mr Rooney's attempt to maintain his own equilibrium appears to have required the brutal cessation of someone else's; he has seemingly perfected his desire to 'Nip some young doom in the bud'.[154] His abilities are very severely compartmentalized ('Once and for all, do not ask me to speak and move at the same time'),[155] the rigid habits of a man who finds counting 'One of the few satisfactions in life'.[156] He is consequently no enemy of the symmetrical, whatever associations it may call up: 'you forwards and I backwards. The perfect pair. Like Dante's damned . . .'.[157] And we may not doubt his histrionic ability to deliver a narrative of the interior life, the 'moments of lucidity'[158] in the enclosed space of the unoccupied compartment, where computation prospers very much better than on the steps of Boghill station, not to mention the railway-line itself, where a train can get fifteen minutes late on a thirty-minute journey. The confined stasis of the compartment is not as pleasant as Murphy's third zone, because it is only a qualified freedom: it is, in fact, if Mr Rooney is to be believed, preferable to move because the train moves rather than to have to actively introduce movement into the stasis of one's own real existence (for example, by walking).[159]

Mr Rooney finds the artificial stasis induced by an accident unsatisfactory; Mrs Rooney, by contrast, is delighted that there may have been a collision, but outraged at Mr Barrell's domestication of such a contingency under the umbrella of a cliché: 'Retarded! A hitch! Ah these celibates!'[160] The power Mr Barrell arrogates to himself is shown to be as derisory as that arrogated to Himself by the Lord of Psalm 131: 'We all know your station is the best kept of the entire network, but there are times when that is not enough.' Of course the Rooneys' laughter at the latter strikes home with more vehemence than Maddy's anger at the former, but the play does not allow us a simple decision as to which is the more important. The impotence of the deity involves catastrophe and death along the line, but 'fully certified death' retains its attractiveness for Mr Rooney,[161] who harbours the romantic desire to be buried alive. The impotence of Mr Barrell involves us in a short-circuiting of our aspirations and desires; when things fail to fall out pat, it forces us into conversation we do not want with people we do not like. It forces us into the unpleasant recognition of the existence of others at moments when our own most precious sensation of identity is seriously undermined ('Don't take any notice of me. I do not exist. The fact is well known')[162] and involves us in arch jokes about impotence and sterility when our most intimate satisfactions can no longer be achieved by normal physical union (hence the difficulty of completing the act of seating the bloated Mrs Rooney in the car). Mrs Rooney's haste is rendered meaningless by the delay of the train; her desire for comfort has broken the perilous balance of the closed system we must learn to endure.

It is a landscape full of catastrophes that do not materialize, of warnings that are ignored and explanations that are merely self-justifying. Mr Tyler almost runs into Mrs Rooney, only to experience a 'narrow squeak' at the wheels of Connolly's van. Mr Slocum's car will not start, but when it does, it kills a hen. Genuine sexual experience is not remotely possible: Mr Rooney prefers auto-erotic acts, and Mrs Rooney's energy is dissipated in absurd innuendoes, and frenzied offers of satisfaction. She withholds sympathy from those who come up with a catalogue of ailments, the climax being the hysterectomy which has threatened the end of the Tyler line, as the death of Minnie has the Rooney line before it. Whereas Joyce's Bloom is seeking a symbolic replacement for Rudi, Mrs Rooney sees no prospect of replacement – there is only helpless silence and wondering at the fact that anyone can be kept out of pain. Mrs Rooney's desire to be atomized (inherited from the hero of 'From an Abandoned Work')[163] represents a logical extension of the conditions that the play dramatizes. There is only the void Mr Slocum gazes at through his windscreen, in which objects (especially human objects) refuse to take on shape: 'I suppose the truth is I am not there, Mrs Rooney, just not really there at all.'[164] 'Piercing' sight reveals only a 'big pale blur'[165] and is literally piercing, as when the hinny (like the horse in 'The Expelled') gazes steadfastly at her until she cries 'pull her eyes away from me'.[166] In such a cosmos, the eyes become a dubious privilege; they do not consolidate reality, they only consolidate one's sufferings: 'I see it all, I stand here and see it all with eyes . . . (the voice breaks) . . . through eyes . . . oh if you had my eyes . . . you would understand . . . the things they have seen . . . and not looked away.'[167]

The suffering cannot be exorcized; the 'dead language'[168] cannot encompass the vision, so 'the voice breaks'. A tempest of wind and rain is the climax to meteorological conditions worsening throughout the play, and the characters are all left 'like Dante's damned', 'on the rim' as Mr Tyler weightily expresses it, 'crucifying gearboxes'[169] in an attempt to provide themselves with some kind of existence from moment to moment.

Embers (1959), Beckett's second radio play, was the first dramatic product of Beckett's increased experimentation at the end of the 1950s that gave rise to such uncompromising assaults on convention as *How it is* and *Happy Days*. It is the first of Beckett's dramatic works that seems to lack a real centre: it relies very considerably on repeating a cluster of phrases ('bitter cold', 'great trouble', 'white world', 'not a sound'), and it has a structural slackness deriving from the two main topics failing to blend. It is, despite this, a very moving work, full of vivid fragments of biography and poignant fictional scenes. The problem is that Henry sees no connection between his life and his art. Krapp, like Malone before him, has faced the fact that he is an artist of sorts; Henry, by contrast, seems largely unmoved by his ability to summon up realities at will, and he is the first of Beckett's artist figures to leave us, as audience, quite free to make whatever connections we will among his disparate material. This does not prevent the play being one of Beckett's most interesting confrontations of the configurating mind of the artist with the atoms of aesthetic material that he tries to make sense of. But it does place a very considerable onus on the audience and is part of the attempt, still not completed by the time of *Not I*, to bring the audience into the centre of the dramatic experience as a compensation for the increasing interiorization of the drama.

The play begins with a vacant space, the sea 'scarcely audible' and the sound of an arrival; it ends with what Mrs Rooney would call a 'lingering dissolution'[170] and the reinstatement of the sound of the sea. In between, Henry utters two long speeches which frame two central incidents, in which the voices he has summoned up threaten to multiply. The puzzling thing is that Henry's control over voices does not extend to the most crucial figure of all, his father; what reality the figure has for us is made up of allusions, attributions and images that we respond to visually. The failure to incorporate into the physical existence of the play its most important figure is not so much a failure of conception – though it might have served to link Henry's life to his story of Bolton – as of tact. There seems, in fact, no good reason for the omission, since some kind of synaesthetic construction (which could have been used to portray his father) is openly entertained from the beginning: 'I mention it because the sound is so strange, so unlike the sound of the sea, that if you didn't see what it was you wouldn't know what it was.'[171] A similar conflation unites the idea of a horse stamping in a courtyard and the daily swim of his father that hastened his death: 'Listen to it! (Pause.) Listen to the light now, you always loved light.'[172] The juxtaposition is extreme, as if there has been a collapse of space between two previously distant realities. But the movement from one subject to another is never more than brisk; it never becomes a matter of haste. One topic inevitably drags another in its train. It is clear that fiction became Henry's medium out of 'need', the same need that Hamm implicitly spoke of, when discussing the 'solitary child'.[173] But it is also clear that fiction could not provide any lasting ordering of experience (such as Clov, and even Krapp, dreamed of): 'I never finished anything, everything always went on for ever.'[174] This realization is perhaps an indispensable prolegomenon to Winnie's difficulties in a time continuum without beginning or end.

The specimen fiction narrated, poignantly elaborated in the last speech of all, is a strangely anaesthetized affair of an old doctor (Holloway) visiting a patient (Bolton) who, through long years of suffering, has become a friend and who is asking to have an end put to his misery. Bolton seems dedicated to reproducing the exterior circumstances of a snowy evening ('white world, not a sound') in the interior world he inhabits ('only the fire, no flames now, embers').[175] He is unable, however, to separate out the two strands that he wishes to bring together, and can only stand at the window (a familiar threshold in Beckett, in 'Dream', in *Murphy*, in *Poèmes 37–39*, iv), helplessly trying to enact an impossible union: 'Bolton at the window ... back against the hangings, hand stretched out widening the chink.'[176] Bolton's gestures become clearer and more irritating. Holloway cannot minister to the diseased mind that is oscillating between two mutually exclusive states:

> Bolton starts playing with the curtain, no, hanging, difficult to describe, draws it back, no, kind of gathers it towards him and the moon comes flooding in, then lets it fall back, heavy velvet affair, and pitch black in the room, then towards him again, white, black, white, black, Holloway: 'Stop that for the love of God, Bolton, do you want to finish me?'[177]

Awareness of the moon, which Molloy watched with such concentration, which Belacqua speculated on, awakens in Bolton the same desire for a companion as Henry has already registered in meditating on his father ('to be with me, in this strange place').[178] But gazing in Holloway's face, eye to eye like so many other Beckett pairs, leads only to Holloway covering his face, withdrawing from the offer. It is meditating on this symbolic moment that enables Henry to make the liberating admission that it is simply an image constructed by his imagination ('that's it, that was always it')[179] which he cannot get beyond and hence cannot regard as a solution to his problems ('no good. (Pause.) No good'). He recognizes that no imaginative power on earth can satisfactorily relate the actually lived to the constructions we make of it, as he stands at the edge of the sea into which he is about to lapse. His 'real' life is revealed as a study in vacancy, the soundlessness of the story a reflection of, or converted into, the emptiness of solitude.

Ada is called up partly to demonstrate how all-embracing the sea can be, partly to criticize Henry's uncertainty in the face of it ('it's a lovely peaceful gentle soothing sound, why do you hate it?'),[180] and partly (and most importantly) to act in the manner of other Beckett females, as an agent that allows (or prevents) the creative act to take place. Thus her trivial goading can create (or enable to be created) the two noisy scenes with the Music Master and the Riding Master, and her emotional range runs the full gamut of stereotypical female roles. She is insensitively logical, as if it truly were the mere matter of black and white Bolton wishes it was: 'if you hate it why don't you keep away from it?'[181] She is not simply 'a little cruder than usual';[182] she is cruel, in the manner of the 'they' who span the works from *The Unnamable* to *Cascando*: 'It's silly to say it keeps you from hearing it . . . even if it does you shouldn't be hearing it, there must be something wrong with your brain.'[183] She is, however, un-cannily prophetic and by the end of the play her forecast has come true: 'The time will come when no one will speak to you at all. . . . You will be quite alone with your voice, there will be no other voice in the world but yours.'[184] The time has come, and, as with the 'precipitates' of *Echo's Bones* twenty-five years before, the 'embers' are cold, and the plumber calling for the waste the following day will find only the ash of 'so much toil and play'.[185]

The short, sharp bursts of noise that punctuate the work are greatly outnumbered by the pauses, which are so effectively used in *Happy Days*. But they are entirely suited to the organization of the play around sudden violent climaxes and the daring juxtapositions of one area of experience against another. The least tolerable experience of all is the one that seems to have the least to do with the experiences recorded elsewhere: Addie's persistent failure to strike the F of the Chopin Waltz she is learning. But the discord reverberates forwards, to make more complex the sexual struggle on the beach (itself an extension of Henry's father violently slamming shut the door on life), and backwards, to explain Henry's violent distaste for the triviality of normal family life. The hooves Arsene heard pounding the road in *Watt*, which expressed for him the changeless tedium of ceaseless repetition,[186] have here become more distinctly apocalyptic. Even the apparently irrelevant interest in training a horse to mark time,[187] to become changeless like an aesthetic artifact, takes its place in the remarkably complex, almost molecular, structure of *Embers*.

Yeats's words were 'for music perhaps';[188] Beckett's *Words and Music* (1962) leaves one in no doubt that the two are essential components of the radiophonic vision. Croak is a portrait of the artificer on his last legs trying, with more or less desperation, to bring the two halves of his vision together. Words bears immediate, eloquent testimony to the cramped conditions pertaining in the creative cell and launches himself at once, apparently in rehearsal, into an almost catechistic disquisition on the Deadly Sin that has always interested Beckett most, Sloth. Croak's late arrival is not, however, due to sloth. It has been caused by the face of a girl seen on the stairs, bringing his past so dramatically alive that it seems like a Proustian *moment privilégié*. Croak is unwise enough to abuse this privilege by attempting to import this experience into the narrow confines and uncertain rewards of creativity, and is disappointed by Words's inability to rid himself of 'orotundity' when the topic is changed at short notice. The belief that the creator is not in control of what he creates, dating from the *Proust* book, could not be more clearly articulated.

Croak's only recourse is to summon Music, who drowns all Words's complaints. But, in a spirit of misguided tolerance, and in an almost indulgent moment of wistful intellectual reflection, Croak allows Words to continue the analysis he has begun. Words is no more successful than before, and Croak realizes that his kind of formulaic utterance is only a partial solution to the problem, and that the two modes must ultimately be brought together. Words is the more truculent, and yet on the subject of age, after tremendous difficulty with the simplest repeated elements, he finally bursts into a kind of blasted song, softly uttered and with the deliberate coarseness of scansion one associates with late Yeats. (Words actually quotes Yeats's early poem 'The Lake Isle of Innisfree' at one point.)[189] The song brings together Love and Age in a manner reminiscent of Malone, but altogether more sentimental. The conflation of microcosm and macrocosm is managed better by the poet of *Poèmes 37–39*: 'that old light / The face in the ashes / That old starlight / On the earth again'[190] seems more clumsy than clever. Where *Happy Days* and *Play* are works of fragmentation, exploration and ultimate dislocation, *Words and Music* is ultimately a work of clarification and unification. But, unfortunately, any treatment of the creative problems of an artist that tends to suggest that on the one hand there are discrete and distinct elements and that, on the other, a 'poetic tone' and mere cleverness can actually bring the elements together through the agency of one of them, runs the risk of seeming either simplistic or confused.

Words seems to be so cheered by his neo-Yeatsian, semi-mystical intuition that, when asked for a description of the girl's face, he can provide a passably smooth and professionally dispassionate account. However, the solidity and resonance of his utterance are fractured by his uncertainty and his inability to encapsulate that 'clarity of silver' which helps to make up the 'radiance' of the woman's face.[191] Croak is greatly disturbed by this, and reveals his disturbance in the 'groans' which ultimately silence Words for good. The analytical power that Words has shown in discussing abstractions proves to be no use at all in dealing with particularities, any more than the song that had to be composed on the spot proved helpful. But Words begins to warm to his educative role of catharsis and exorcism (a clear anticipation of his ultimate dominance over the creative act, with all its disappointments, as his sighs close the piece), and his attempt to make clearer the remoteness lurking in the 'starlight' image is so successful, despite Croak's anguish, that he is once again prepared to try a song. Words stresses the lifelessness of the construct he pictures: 'the whole so blanched and still . . . that it seems no more of the earth than Mira in the Whale . . . shining coldly down – as we say, looking up.'[192] At the same time he gives as much scrutiny to the evidence of life – breathing – as Lear with Cordelia dead in his arms, or as Beckett himself in *Imagination Dead Imagine* and *Breath*. His anatomization of Lily comes to rest in the recognition that her 'natural . . . aperture' is a place where, as the song says, it is 'All dark no begging / No giving no words / No sense no need'.[193] The conclusion is not new, and confirms how important an accurate reading of the sexuality in the pre-war poems in French is. For the creative act of the artist is seen to be as much a fulfilment of private desires as the act of love, and Croak's shuffling departure suggests he has brought his two principals to the point he always sought. This aids the symmetry of the experience and sows a doubt in the listener's mind as to who controls who, compounded when Words's initial shock at the vision of the 'wellhead' is softened, at the end, into an acceptance of Music's superior description of ultimate bliss.

The last few moments suggest that there are only two possibilities: either the 'wellhead', or the repetition of elements already used. Beckett announces here how important repetition will be in his later works. It is doubtful, in fact, if *Ping* and *Lessness* are fully comprehensible without a recognition of the strategies involved in a neglected work like *Words and Music*. But this does nothing to mitigate the feeling that it is one of Beckett's least effective works, perhaps a result of over-careful planning, or more probably due to the fact that it is a discursive, and not a dramatic, examination of creative problems.

Cascando (1963) has always seemed to me one of Beckett's masterpieces, and the excitement of the breathless Voice set against the austerity of Opener derives from an unerring sense of the possibilities of rhythm that can hardly be subjected to critical explanation. Despite its simple structure and its familiar subject-matter (quest, boat-journey, acceptance of absence equalling loss of conventional identity leading to true selfhood), it sets up more resonances more economically than any other radio play of Beckett's.

The 'cold' voice of Opener ('dry as dust' in the magazine version)[194] is muscular without being strident, and clear without being definite. Voice maintains a similar consistency in his more frenzied mode, reminding us of the Unnamable and pointing forward to *Not I*. Opener's four major speeches of explanation remove any traces of equanimity that may seem guaranteed by his disinterested resignation. He is a more isolated figure than any we have yet met, partly because his own skeletal utterances strike home directly as irresistible facts; no concession at all is made to lyricism, and the lightest possible rhetoric is employed. But, even more importantly, his resignation seems to have been won against much more intransigent odds than those faced by any preceding artist-figure. He is under no illusions that the impressively earnest flow of words from Voice can do anything to ameliorate his isolation (there is 'No resemblance'[195] between them); he has solved Winnie's problem of what is inside and what is outside not only for himself, but for all subsequent creators – which is, perhaps, why the subject, and the use of radio as a medium, dies out. He has faced the inescapable fact that all utterances are only a representation or metaphor of human experience ('An image, like any other'),[196] but has decided that there is no way the distance between the two may be collapsed, without alteration of the medium. He is no longer troubled by voices outside him that he can pin on to a mysterious 'they', though the experience of the listener invests his repeated 'Good' with rather more uncertainty than he himself experiences. He remains as stunned as was Croak at the ability of music to express the numinous ('Good God');[197] this effectively liberates him for the final burst at the end, as the two forces join hands (like the shadowy couple in *Enough*) to perfect their own absence. His cyclic sense is as understated as it possibly could be ('You know, the re-awakening')[198] and presumably assuaged by the silence that closes the text. But the conclusion is necessarily equivocal, partly because the pressure of Voice's wish-fulfilment is so insistent that it undermines its own apotheosis, and partly because Opener's resignation ('I have lived on it . . . till I'm old. Old enough')[199] cannot entirely cloak his parasitism: 'It's my life, I live on that.'[200] Despite the final ambiguity, the unadorned definition of a position that has been carefully deliberated ('There is nothing in my head')[201] rings in the mind of an auditor long after the piece has lapsed into silence.

Voice embodies what Beckett elsewhere calls 'babble'.[202] His babble consists of short, primarily monosyllabic bursts; when accompanied by music, the voice is primarily a commentator, and the story of Woburn simply marks time. As the story proceeds, however, certain attitudes harden: motivation ceases to matter in the face of the unvarnished fact ('he goes down . . . falls . . . on purpose or not . . . can't see . . . he's down . . . that's what counts'),[203] and in the face of the need to exorcize the compulsion towards fiction ('saying to myself finish this one . . . and finished it . . . and not the right one').[204] The character Woburn is endowed with a psychology almost as an afterthought ('in his head . . . what's in his head') and the contents of this consciousness slowly and painfully emerge from vacancy ('a hole . . . a shelter . . . a hollow . . . in the dunes . . . a cave . . . vague memory . . . in his head . . . of a cave').[205] The impulse towards abolishing the reality accessible to the senses (especially sight), pointing forward to the final paragraph of *Enough*, is here made momentarily equivocal by implying that this is the only material fiction can employ: 'no more trees . . . no more bank . . . no more cover' is followed by 'no more stories . . . no more words'. Voice is aware that his own identity is bound up with his fiction ('I'm there . . . somewhere') and that it is his own quest to find himself: 'to see him . . . to say him . . . for whom . . . that's it . . . no matter . . . never him.'[206] As Opener says immediately afterwards, speaking of Voice and Music, 'From one world to another, it's as though they grew together'. Prior to this, the sympathy of the constituent parts, quite unlike the conflict of Words and Music, has been indicated by their 'weakening' successively. The movement from interior to exterior, from land to sea, implies a consummation; the boat is equally subject to dissolution ('no tiller . . . no thwarts . . . no oars')[207] and the island that proved a fake Hesperides in *Malone Dies* is here avoided. The open sea of undifferentiated flux is what attracts Woburn; he leaves the island astern of him, to the great delight of Opener, who takes over the rousing cries Voice has up to now sustained himself with. The sea represents a place where there is 'no more coming . . . no more going'.[208] It is a new version of *Words and Music*'s 'wellhead' and remains one of Beckett's most attractive conceptions. The last words of Voice articulate the difficulty of distinction; Woburn is clinging on (to the boat, to the narrating voice) and it is because he is clinging on that he cannot become spiritually dispersed through space ('he need only turn over . . . he'd see [the lights] . . . shine on him').[209] The 'drawing together' that is a precondition of a theory of correspondence (criticized as inadequate in *Proust*) is in this work revealed as once more a possible solution. It seems, indeed, inevitable, rather than a matter of chance. Perhaps this explains some of the ambiguity that remains in the work, since for Beckett the inevitable always smacks of a constriction that is profoundly unattractive.

It is no exaggeration to say that, despite winning several prizes, Beckett's *Film* (1964) is one of his least successful works, marred by technical ineptitude as much as deliberate technical limitation, and needlessly obscure for those spectators who have not had the benefit of consulting the shooting-script beforehand. The story of the film's making (1964) is marvellously entertaining, but beneath Alan Schneider's engaging honesty one feels the 'home movie' approach was a salutary warning that everyone connected with the enterprise sensibly heeded afterwards. It is clear that financial difficulties prevented the completion of the Evergreen Film Project, but the experience with *Film* must have alerted the principals to the fact that books were easier (as well as cheaper) to produce, and much more profitable.

Beckett's gifts are, indeed, singularly unsuited to celluloid. His dramatic sense, consolidated by his sharp eye for the right kind of actor, is much more obvious in the theatre or on the radio. *Film*, as it stands, even without the section at the beginning which 'opened up another world'[210] is both too strictly located in time and space and not enough imbued with the spirit of place Beckett usually catches unerringly. The country road of *Godot* and the den of *Krapp* are 'givens' that we never wish to question; the grim streets of lower Manhattan, the staircase like something out of Dostoevsky, the almost vacant room at the top – these never, somehow, convince. Part of the problem is that the theme – *esse est percipi* (to be is to be perceived) obtrudes too insistently (which is not at all the same thing as saying that it is articulated clearly). Another difficulty (solved in *Eh Joe* by confining Joe to one location only) is that we are exposed to the kind of distraction Beckett never allows (and cannot afford) in his best theatre. The temptation to include one or two grotesques, germane to the story only in so far as they confirm the truth of the theory of perception, was mercifully resisted; but Beckett himself, in his notes, admits that the early section is 'undefendable except as a dramatic convenience'[211] which turns out to mean 'to suggest as soon as possible unbearable quality of E's scrutiny'. Leaving aside for a moment this question of the relationship between E and O – except to point out that Beckett is well aware that the convention on which a work is based cannot be established by personal fiat – it is obvious that this kind of thing is a luxury the Beckett of *Endgame* would have done without. Which is not, of course, to commit oneself glibly (as many reviewers did) to the point of view that *Film* is the thoroughly meretricious product of an enterprise that should never have got off the ground. It is simply to suggest that the real centre of the film (as the time-schedules suggest) is the scene in the room, and that this terrifying dénouement might have made as much sense without the preliminaries.

Many of the elements that make up this scene are things Beckett has been obsessed with over the years. The photographs provide the same link with the past as Krapp's tape-recorder does for him, and the rocking-chair is an irresistible reminder of Murphy – the gruesome headrest that distinguishes this chair being a fortuitous addition that got written into the text.[212] The fascination with eyes that open and shut like a doll's and, more importantly, with two sets of eyes that gaze at each other, is nothing new. (One of the early titles was, appropriately enough, *The Eye*.)[213] The portrait with its face to the wall in *Endgame* has now been turned round to reveal the face of God the Father. What is disappointing is that nothing new has been added. The configuration has changed in emphasis, but not gained in meaning. It was surely for precisely this final scene that Beckett was moved to try the cinema. Perhaps no other mode could embody so dramatically this scene which haunts him. The final frames are powerful and shocking, and they provide an emotional focus that is very much lacking at the end of *Eh Joe*, the play he later wrote for television. But there is something brash and simplistic about this conclusion which derives directly from the separation of E and O around which the film is based. *Eh Joe* solves the problem of *percipi/percipere* much more economically, by presuming, rather than exploring, the fact that the two elements are in reciprocal relation one to another. This obsessive situation in Beckett has yet, perhaps, to be successfully embodied in any of his dramatic work; which may possibly be because its first articulation in prose (in *Murphy*) was so precise and complete that he has nothing much to add to it, only variant configurations to record. Certainly the clarity of the conclusion places the comparative irrelevance of the beginning in high relief.

The silent film is disappointing not because it is an anachronism, but because (as with the mimes) the area that most torments Beckett, language, has been mysteriously and arbitrarily lulled to sleep. No tension is possible; there is merely the balletic vacancy of the gesture to engage our attention.

The reinstatement of the voice in *Eh Joe* (1965) is a tacit acknowledgment of the limitations of *Film*. Like all the voices of Beckett's most recent drama, it has 'little colour', but it is more 'remote' and 'slightly slower' and steadier than some. The phrases it utters end more often than not in a question. The 'penny-farthing hell'[214] of Joe's mind he inherits from *Play*; the eyes of 'the green one' that opened after love-making appear as far back as 'Dream'; his desire to destroy the past, and his intentness, he gets from *Film*'s E/O. The camera moves relentlessly forward, but the play fails to suggest *why* camera eye and object should be reciprocally interactive. Beckett recognizes the documentary realism of *Film* was false; in *Eh Joe* there is 'No need to record room as a whole'.[215] But it never becomes clear why Beckett has adopted the medium of television as a whole, and in recent years he has not felt the need to revisit the studios.

The move into film and television may come to seem of considerable historical interest; Genet and the practitioners of the *nouveau roman* have shown a similar interest. But Beckett's interest in the applied visual arts dates back at least as far as 1934, when he showed an interest in Eisenstein before it became fashionable to do so,[216] and probably earlier, to the Chaplin and Buster Keaton films that impressed him so deeply.

The mimes bear witness to Beckett's need to make substantial the fears and hopes that torment him, in the hope of exorcizing them. But, as one would expect from someone who is constantly aware of the problems of the god-like creative artist, he remains largely unmoved by such practitioners as Marcel Marceau, who are very often improvisational and not bound to follow an author's text. His comment on Marceau – 'With Marceau, I always feel the absence of words'[217] – can, in fact, be applied with much more justice to his own written mimes, *Act Without Words I and II* (1957, 1963, written earlier), which are strident and unsatisfying. In the last analysis, as *Not I* was not the first play to reveal, he is much more interested in words without acts.

Writing on Bram van Velde and the surrealists, Jacques Putnam says, 'the very wish to enter is enough to ensure that one never does'.[218] This serves to remind us that Didi and Gogo, like Kafka's Joseph K, should never have come (or been allowed to come) at all, that they should never have engaged on the quest in the first place. This is particularly true in view of the fact that all the signs are that it is not a quest at all, in the normal sense. It shows no signs of coming to an end. The signposts (when there are any, and they are fewer and farther between in Beckett than in Kafka) point in the wrong direction, as they always seem to have done since Browning's 'Childe Roland to the Dark Tower Came'. Unlike his predecessor in the Greek drama, the messenger has no story to tell; the stranger who in the traditional quest reveals to us the inner nature of our pilgrimage turns out to be more agitated than we are. *Waiting for*

Godot, however, maintaining presence on the stage, may be seen to have advantages over waiting on God and his mercy offstage. Violence is done to Estragon off stage, and the eruption of Pozzo and Lucky into their lives in a way degrades our exemplars into mere clowns, mere grovellers, mere sadists. They only regain their feet with difficulty because what little dignity they had has been taken away. The effort to restore the equilibrium of the immensely complex field of forces that we call our situation is bound to be exhausting. *Endgame* confirms this. The decisive act of Clov's leaving (if indeed he does) will liberate Hamm only for a moment; the boy will come through the door, and it is himself Hamm will meet, as surely as Stephen Dedalus met himself in the National Library. It is as if Beckett's own creativity has come under scrutiny: the necessary liberation to compose one's narrative (*compose* in every sense – order, make secure, restore) is ousted by the remorseless repetition of event – what the *Proust* book calls 'habit' – to which passing time commits us all. As the plays become more and more elemental there is less and less time for the narratives we tell ourselves; but our fictions have their revenge by taking on independent life, and compelling us to go on telling them. This explains the inquisitional light of *Play*, where the narratives overlap like a snapshot out of focus, insistently offering us (at least for the first half of the play) their meretricious content for our outraged consumption. Confronting the particles of the dramatic experience, and trying to assign a role to each (in *Words and Music* with a certain levity, in *Cascando* in deadly earnest) leads, for a while, to the abandonment of narrative in *Come and Go* and *Breath*. But its persistence in *Not I*, where the dramatic experience has swelled to become *all* narrative and the means has diminished to a mouth, shows that the stories continue wherever we 'open and close'. The silence at the end of *Cascando* suggests momentary fulfilment (however much the last word 'nearly' echoes in the air-waves); *Not I* reveals this to be illusory – the voice comes mysteriously out of the dark and just as mysteriously returns into it. It is even more 'a text written to come out of the dark'[219] than *All That Fall*.

5   The intellectual and cultural background to Beckett

> I once took an interest in astronomy, I don't deny it.
> Then it was geology that killed a few years for me.
> The next pain in the balls was anthropology and the
> other disciplines, such as psychiatry, that are
> connected with it. . . . In the end it was magic that
> had the honour of my ruins. . . .   (*Molloy*)
>
> I always loved arithmetic it has paid me back in full
>   (*How it is*)[1]

Some of the most sensible words on the critical approach to a writer
through his 'influences' were uttered, in passing, by Norman
Douglas:

> If you hide your plot, how shall the critic be expected to see
> it? . . . you must hit the nail on the head and ask him to be
> so good as to superintend the operation. . . . He can then
> compare you to someone else who has also hit the nail on the
> head and with those writings he happens to be familiar. You
> have a flavour of Dostoievsky *minus* the Dickens taint;
> you remind him of Flaubert or Walter Scott or somebody
> equally obscure; in short, you are in a condition to be
> labelled – a word, and a thing, that comes perilously near to
> libelling.[2]

Beckett has, perhaps, suffered more from labels and libels than most
other modern writers. He is inevitably an attractive figure for historians of ideas, partly, one suspects, because his work seems to
sanction influences from the unlikeliest places; partly because as a
close friend of Joyce (and one of the few, indeed, to survive his
influence) he is a man who has met most of the key figures in
modernism, from Stravinsky to Ezra Pound, at one time or another.[3]
Beckett can seem, at first reading, to be a writer almost without
forebears, but it is obvious that no creative man works in a complete
vacuum, and it is unthinkable that he should. Beckett's work need
not (indeed should not) seem less original when we have traced back
through literature and philosophy and discovered which elements
of other people's work have been added to his own individual tem-

perament to make his vision what it is. It is, in fact, perfectly natural that a sensitive and intelligent man will be affected (profoundly, in some cases) by the authors he reads. Some authors, such as Hardy, are obliging enough to quote and name the writer at the back of their minds. Beckett does not usually go as far as this, but much of his reading is reflected directly in his work, and an intelligent guess will usually unearth what is not. The lumber of erudition which occasionally (though, perhaps, with less and less frequency) surfaces in Beckett's work is doubtless mainly a result of his critical and scholarly activities during the early years of his creative life. He has been free of such labour for years, but he has been known to search, with an earnestness above and beyond a writer's natural concern, an earnestness only a scholar could fully understand, for the umlaut inadvertently omitted from a German quotation in the reprint of *Proust*.

Obviously, the main difficulties in outlining the importance of background material in reading Beckett resides not in discussing accepted influences like Descartes, but rather in attempting to discuss influences which are more superficial, or so entrenched that the writer himself is unconscious of them. In this respect Beckett's own criticism provides us with much useful information. Clearly it is important to maintain a sense of perspective: we must distinguish from the start those authors (such as Dante and Proust) who affected the details of his outlook; between, as it might be said, those who provide the rooms and those who provide the furniture. At the same time, we can usefully preserve an often artificial, but convenient, distinction between philosophical and literary influence, and it is with the first of these that one should begin.

Philosophical problems have, over the centuries, tended to congregate around certain key terms and key concepts upon which, in the very nature of things, the final word can never be spoken. Beckett, who has received no formal philosophic training (unlike, say, Sartre), is not unnaturally sceptical about philosophy's claims to answer the questions it raises. He finds the articulation of his own personal distress, and, more importantly, the ultimate reasons for that distress, are not significantly clarified by formal philosophy – once again, unlike Sartre. Nothing would be easier than to dismiss the philosophical dimension of Beckett from our discussions, except for the one crucial fact which is insistently forced on us: that he has read, and been attracted by, most of the major philosophers from Pythagoras onwards. It is perfectly characteristic of Beckett that he should send one scurrying to a philosophical dictionary to discover why Murphy should react so strongly to the 'extreme theophanism of William of Champeaux',[4] and yet curtly dismiss Plato as a 'Borstal Boehme',[5] only to send one back to remind oneself who Boehme was. He admirably exemplifies, in fact, the first part of Goethe's dictum that a writer must know all philosophy, the second part of which (that he must keep it out of his work) no writer has ever totally satisfied. And yet he is an amateur, a dilettante, an aesthete where philosophy is concerned, impressed by the dispassionate and clinical manner of Spinoza's *Ethics* and immensely attracted to the ideas of order that Spinoza's mathematical form conjures up, but at no time so committed to the premises that he could meaningfully be called a Spinozist.[6] We need, therefore, in discussing his philosophical affiliations, a framework flexible enough to allow several philosophers ostensibly very different (at any rate to the academic philosopher) to figure together under certain basic headings, keeping constantly aware that at no time does one idea commit Beckett necessarily to all that follows from it, and, most importantly of all, that only those philosophers who can be shown to have changed the direction of his thought (dramatically or over a long period) are relevant to our present concerns.

It is clear (from Beckett's first separately published work, the poem *Whoroscope*) that his first exposure to the philosophy of Descartes gave him a concrete model from which to seek satisfaction on the fundamental questions, metaphysical, epistemological and linguistic, that philosophy asks. It is a philosophy which, as is now generally recognized, marks the beginning of modern thought, moving away from abstract metaphysical system-building, and beginning with one's epistemological relationship with the outside world, under the (for Descartes) beneficent aegis of the First Cause we call God. It is above all, a philosophy that involves, for the first time, the systematic employment of the element basic to all previous scepticisms, whether Grecian or Renaissance: namely, doubt. While agreeing with Montaigne that our judgments are fundamentally relative, Beckett was doubtless aware that this relativity could only exist against a fundamentally metaphysical belief in an ultimate reality of absolute truths.[7] Descartes goes at least one step further in so far as he does not assume what he sets out to prove; he in fact seeks to guarantee the accuracy of his truth by adopting what at first sight seems the least profitable method. It is difficult to imagine anything more likely to appeal to Beckett's imagination: the truth will be arrived at after the toughest possible journey thither, honour will be satisfied, and the sceptical spirit will be lulled to sleep. There is just the right balance between activity, leading to apparently unforeseen conclusions, and passivity, each subsequent question being ceaselessly conditioned in a rigorously determined way, by the answers to previous ones. Unfortunately it is not nearly such plain sailing as it seems.

Broadly speaking, Descartes's philosophy states the following: the evidence of the senses and of tradition can be dismissed; it is such things that engender doubt in the first place. The only clear and true ideas, Descartes claims, are the ideas of mathematics, which aim to establish relations between items, and an order determined by relations. The celebrated Cartesian method obeys certain rules that are directly evolved from this: Descartes decides that we must divide every problem into as many parts as is feasible and requisite for its better solution, and that we should conduct our argument in an orderly way, beginning with the simplest objects and ascending to knowledge of the most complex. He aims, furthermore, to be exhaustive: we must make throughout 'such enumerations that we can be sure of leaving nothing out'[8] (what Beckett's people constantly try to do, and constantly fail to achieve). Descartes is aware of limit, for the decision to doubt inevitably admits it; nevertheless, he postulates the unity of human knowledge and bases his examination of human knowledge on the one thing he cannot doubt – the fact that he thinks, *cogito ergo sum* (I think therefore I am). In much the same way, however much his body may disintegrate, no Beckett character doubts that, at least for the duration of the fictional work which calls him into existence, he is engaged in the act of thinking. This is a *reductio ad absurdum* of one of Descartes's most controversial ideas, an idea that necessarily follows from the formulation of his *cogito*, namely that mind is more certain than matter, and that one's own mind is more amenable to examination than the mind of any other person. Descartes's problem at this point is that, in answering the sceptical arguments that doubted the existence of the external world, he has erected a method that seems to perpetually recede from it, and he has come up with a fundamental dictum that locates the ultimate reality in the mind. Descartes suggests, in fact, that the external world of matter can only be inferred from what is known of this internal world of mind. His answer to this is to prove the existence of God, at which point Beckett (like many others) cannot follow him. One of Descartes's proofs is this: no finite being has the capacity to conceive the idea of the infinite, as has already been established; therefore the idea must be given to us by the infinite being. There is no such thing as free thought. The problem here is that Christian philosophy conceives of a God who has endowed man with free will, whereas Descartes's theory of the material world (and, by inference, the parallel world of mental events) is rigidly deterministic. Man in fact becomes, in this view, an automaton, and the seeds of eighteenth-century materialism are sown.

There is much here that interested Beckett centrally. First, the method which made Descartes the founder of modern philosophy, defiantly individual and inventive. Second, the fundamentally subjective orientation of the method, well described by Paul Valéry:

> If . . . feeling for the Me takes on such an awareness and such a
> central mastery of our powers, if it deliberately makes itself a
> system of reference for the world, makes itself the very hearth
> for the creative reforms which it institutes against the
> incoherence, the multiplicity, and the complexity of this world,
> as well as against the insufficiency of the explanation given,
> it then feels nourished within itself by an unutterable sensation,
> before which the devices of language are empty, similitudes
> are of no worth.[9]

Descartes claims that if one follows the method, no deceiving demon can get in to spoil it. But one only needs to equate God and the deceiving demon (as Beckett is constantly tempted to do), and one is only left with the *cogito* (which states that the thinking I must exist even if nothing else does), and a language that cannot signify. Beckett is the more desperate because he cannot help himself; Descartes at least *chooses* to doubt. Hence Descartes's serenity, expressed in a French that has become the model of lucidity, the style of a man who habitually spent the morning in bed. Beckett (as Peggy Guggenheim's scurrilous memoirs reveal) did the same, but found neither the serenity nor the style, however much Descartes's *Méditations* seem to echo behind every page he writes.

The whole of Beckett's subsequent philosophical thinking is determined by his acceptance of Descartes's methods and rejection of Descartes's consolations. His interest in Cartesianism led him to study the often neglected followers of Descartes, Geulincx and Malebranche. As Nietzsche later pointed out, 'Descartes could only demonstrate the reality of the empirical world by appealing to God's veracity';[10] it was the business of the followers of Descartes, the so-called 'occasionalists', to make the second more convincing, but they pursued this in such a way that it had bizarre consequences for the first.

Although there is a spirit of mystification and fascination with arcana in Beckett that an unsympathetic reader might be constrained to dismiss as mere Irish whimsicality, there can be no doubt that the experience of reading the 'beautiful Belgo-Latin of Arnold Geulincx'[11] in the Trinity College library was a great intellectual excitement for the young Beckett. This difficult thinker's works (still not translated into English) made a very deep impression on Beckett, but must have contributed to his increasing dissatisfaction with Descartes's solutions. Beckett only quotes Geulincx once, or rather he quotes one of Geulincx's dicta repeatedly: *Ubi nihil vales, ibi nihil velis*. As later with Schopenhauer, it is the form of the statement as much as the content ('Where you are worth nothing, there you should wish for nothing') that attracts Beckett. But it is clear that Beckett was very impressed with Geulincx as a whole. The Cartesian problems have been shifted into the very difficult area of ethics,[12] and the Geulincxian solutions involve deterministic answers much more rigid than Descartes had ever envisaged. Geulincx is quite unimpressed (as Montaigne had been) with the arrogant claim of a Sophist like Protagoras that 'Man is the measure of all things'; Beckett, in a post-war essay of art criticism, exposes Protagoras' presumption with a withering scorn.[13] Geulincx is quite unimpressed also (as Schopenhauer, for different reasons, was to be) with the stoic attitude to suicide; none of Beckett's characters (not even Murphy) regard this as a happy issue out of all their afflictions. What Geulincx does require of man, by contrast, is that he should transcend himself in a genuine activity that he has striven for without it being imposed from without; endeavour (what Lucky in *Godot* calls 'conation')[14] is as much the keynote of this philosophy as it is of the gallery of incompetents that throng Beckett's works. Endeavour is not, however, something man can take pride in; *inspectio sui* (inspection of the self) leads to *despecto sui* (contempt of the self) which in its turn leads to an abrogation of the power of the will: there is no point (any more than there is for Molloy, or Malone) in willing change in the world outside ourselves for we have no power over such matters and are acting quite irrationally. Diligence, humility and obedience are as strongly recommended as in a medieval book of religious rules; the passions (especially concupiscence, as Murphy would, in his best moments, wholeheartedly endorse) are outside human control and therefore morally irrelevant. Geulincx encourages his reader to take up a stance in relation to them which is of the utmost importance when we think of Beckett's characters: indifference. At the same time he reminds his reader that he must act, and that the only consolation he can derive from doing so, is that he cannot do what he does not know how to do.[15] It is a grim wisdom, and all the niggling, carping little phrases that undermine and ultimately erode a Beckett narrative ('No, I can't. . . .') stem directly from Beckett accepting this.[16]

Malebranche (whom Beckett refers to in *How it is*) offered no way out. Doubtless Beckett's attraction to this thinker was, as with Descartes and Geulincx, in part stylistic; Leibniz, Diderot, Fontenelle and Voltaire all praised Malebranche's grace and lucidity, a lucidity achieved despite his contempt for what Beckett would call the 'literature of notation'.[17] On purely philosophical grounds, Beckett admired Malebranche's hesitancy, his feeling that there is no real reason for the world to exist at all, and his understanding of the difficulties involved in trying to observe oneself. Malebranche revises Descartes's dualism by objecting that Descartes allows interaction between the substances of mind and matter while claiming that they are disparate. (Descartes was honest enough to admit this.) The finite mind cannot, Malebranche claims, have the power that Descartes assumes it has; he follows St Augustine in saying that man cannot be a light unto himself, and suggests that being is only possible because God intervenes every second. Berkeley (*Principles of Human Knowledge*, section LIII) commented on the strangeness of this belief that existence was arbitrary, but the strangeness of a belief has never prevented Beckett from taking an interest in it, and it must have seemed a possible answer to his prevailing sense of non-being: a cruel God had failed, in his case, to intervene. Malebranche's other major claim, that to think of God is sufficient to prove his existence, was clearly less relevant to Beckett. In this case, Hume's argument (partly anticipated by Fontenelle) that agency is as unintelligible in divine beings as in finite beings is much closer to Beckett's thinking. Whereas in Malebranche the world remains outside God (and the world is culpable), in Hume, God remains outside the world (and it is God who is at fault). In sum, Malebranche is altogether too close to Leibniz's 'pre-established harmony' (which Beckett attacks in *Murphy* and *Molloy*) to be entirely satisfactory to Beckett. As so often, he receives confirmation from Malebranche that there is an irreconcilable gulf between man and God and between mind and matter, and feels perfectly free to reject the melioristic parts of his theology. What *How it is* calls 'Malebranche less the rosy hue'.[18]

'The rosy hue' is something that also clings to the philosophy of Bishop Berkeley, the definitive edition of whose works was edited by Beckett's tutor at Trinity, A. A. Luce. Beckett pays Berkeley the compliment of basing his *Film* on Berkeley's best-known dictum, *esse est percipi* (to be is to be perceived). The idea that bodies possess no other reality than that of being perceived has obvious attractions to a man like Beckett, obsessed as he is with the passivity and potential non-existence of human beings. But the consolation Berkeley provides – that the perceiver is God – Beckett finds quite untenable, and so once again he takes only what he himself has found to be true, and leaves out the transcendent being. He remains mildly amused by the eccentricity of Berkeley's philosophy, as the reference to 'idealist tar' in *Murphy*[19] (Berkeley's late work, *Siris*, is about tar) shows. But in the same work the narrator is a little embarrassed at having to abuse the 'nice distinction[s]' of this philosopher.[20]

Of Beckett's opinion of the other famous British philosopher, Hume, only a splendid tale of Joyce and Beckett together survives. 'How could the idealist Hume write a history?' asked Joyce, to which Beckett replied, 'A history of representations.'[21] What Beckett means is that Hume is not describing a course of events, rather he is simply describing one representation after another. He is not, in other words, contradicting himself (Beckett is a better philosopher than Joyce); but if he were heart and soul an idealist, he would not see any point in writing a history. Of Hume's important sundering of cause and effect – which might be expected to appeal to the Beckett of *Proust*, irritated by the 'vulgarity of a plausible concatenation' – we hear nothing. Of the natural history of religion, more predictably, Beckett has nothing at all to say.

At this point it is extremely important to be clear about why Beckett rejects the deity these thinkers are concerned to promote, and this involves a brief sojourn in areas somewhat more familiar and less ethereal than those explored in the last few paragraphs. As befits a man brought up 'almost a Quaker',[22] Beckett's religious position is essentially a severe one. We have no way of telling exactly when his religious faith lapsed, but it is clear that from his earliest years he found death and suffering difficult to accommodate to the traditional idea of a benevolent God, and the seed of his later severity in this area was obviously sown early. His response to what seemed a meaninglessly arbitrary, or worse, a derisory fiction, has taken many forms, but never, despite the newspaper who billed him as 'the Atheist from Paris', a simple atheism.[23] Just as he has been impressed by the faculty certain philosophers have for pursuing truth and facing the ultimate problems even after they have apparently been solved by system-building, so he has continued to be obsessed, personally, by the fundamentally religious questions concerning the existence of God, His justice and mercy, and the afterlife. The excessive literalism of traditional theology, especially certain thinkers still revered in the Catholic Ireland he has exiled himself from, he is quick to scorn; although his familiarity with it at all suggests he was momentarily attracted by it. In fact, the brilliant mixture of seriousness and hilarity found in Moran's theological questionnaire in part two of *Molloy* suggest a mind at once closer to, and more distanced from, the religious life than, say, the Stephen Dedalus who composes a similar questionnaire in *Portrait of the Artist*.[24] What unbeliever would one expect to be familiar with Cangiamila's *Sacred Embryology* and Pope Benedict XIV's *Diocesan Synod*?[25] At the same time what believer would allow his path to be (even momentarily) halted by the occasional absurdities of Comestor and Adobard?[26] No more poignant example of the divorce between Reason and Revelation, Knowledge and Belief, could be imagined, and Moran's amusement gives way to rancour as he recites the 'pretty', 'quietist' Pater, inescapably attracted to the forms he seeks to subvert.[27]

Beckett clearly regards the trifling disagreements on points of dogma and detail with a withering scorn; at the same time, however, he sees them as perfectly natural strategies engaged in by the human mind faced with an insoluble problem. He recognizes that the truly fundamental religious questions have only been satisfactorily faced – if they cannot be said to have been answered – by the greatest and most sensitive minds. St Augustine is clearly one of these, a thinker who remains perpetually attractive partly because he was once far from saintly and never allowed his acuity of mind to degenerate into sanctimoniousness. Beckett's interest in Augustine went at least as far as him reading some of his work in the original Latin, and his first published essay shows his familiarity with Augustinian terminology.[28] He was, however, reading Schopenhauer at much the same time and he must have been impressed by the force of Schopenhauer's attack on Augustine's theodicy in *De Civitate Dei*:

> If anyone studies the Augustinian theology . . . (especially in the fourteenth book) he experiences something analogous to the feeling of one who tries to make a body stand whose centre of gravity falls outside it; however he may turn it and place it, it always falls over again . . . the contradiction between the goodness of God and the misery of the world. . . . The only dogma which was regarded as fixed by all parties was the existence and attributes of God, and they all unceasingly move in a circle, because they seek to bring those things into harmony, i.e. to solve a sum that will not come right, but always show a remainder at some new place whenever we have concealed it elsewhere. But it does not occur to anyone to seek for the source of the difficulty in the assumption itself, although it palpably obtrudes itself.[29]

It occurs to Beckett to seek for the source of the difficulty in the assumption itself. God, if he exists, must clearly be omnipotent and omniscient. In the world of *How it is* he is the one who (hypothetically) provides the sacks. But *How it is* is a savage parody of the Leibnizian idea that this is the best of all possible worlds, a panorama of aggressor and victim perpetually encircling a world based on cruelty. It is more like the worst of all possible worlds; and Voltaire's *Candide* was one of the earliest important texts in Beckett's thinking. Beckett stresses that only one half of the divine contract is fulfilled: He is just ('that's our justice', says the voice of *How it is* with outraged regularity), but not merciful. It is in fact, the world of the Old Testament Jehovah rather than the world of the New Testament Jesus. God, in conceiving the world, brought forth suffering, and it would be better for us all not to have been born. Beckett's attitude, is gnostic or manichean. The God who created the world was Satan.

Once this has been grasped, it is not difficult to see why he mocks Duns Scotus 'haecceity of puffect love' in *More Pricks than Kicks*[30] and can find in Scholasticism (to which Joyce was always attracted) only immense energies of mind wasted on a problem the gnostics had already satisfactorily answered. The God of the scholastics has no need of the world, but Mr Knott in *Watt*, who has set himself up as a kind of God, needs to be constantly witnessed, and even shows his face to Watt in a parody of God showing his face to Moses. It is the gnostic/manichean context which explains Beckett's characters' emphasis on abstention from intercourse, and his obsession with the battle of darkness and light. For the manichean aim is to extract all that is good from the world, and sexual relationships only retard the liberation of the light into the realm of the spirit. Every conception and every birth are a repetition and parody of the first conception and birth, which was the double birth of Cain and Abel from the coupling of Satan and Eve.[31]

This explains why Beckett's characters face their parents with hatred and fear. The father (like the artist, as we see with Krapp and Malone) usurps God's role,[32] and must consequently be punished; but it is the mother who actually gives birth, and so it is her that the protagonist particularly reviles. In this respect, God's power appears to have been displaced from man to woman; as Beckett puts it in 'Dream of Fair to Middling Women' (using the Talmudic expression for 'majestic presence or manifestation of God which has descended to dwell among men'), 'The true Shekinah is woman'.[33] Woman, however, is at the same time prostitute; the madonna–prostitute figure is of course common in late nineteenth-century literature that Beckett is known to admire. In *First Love* it is the death of the father that leads directly to marriage and confrontation with the prostitute; at the end of the story the protagonist is haunted by the cries of a child he may have conceived upon the girl, Lulu, whose name is changed to Anna, almost as if the narrator fears our easy identification of her with the notorious heroine of Wedekind's tragedies. The women in Beckett's work are strangely protean; Lulu becomes Anna, and Molloy's women – his mother his mistress Ruth–Edith, his hostess Lousse – all merge imperceptibly into one stereotype. Beckett concentrates on woman because she is the medium for incarnation. And he concentrates on the moment of incarnation because this is the point where eternity enters time, and being enters existence. It is, in fact, the point where the most pressing theological difficulties begin, since it is the point of intersection between human and divine.[34]

At times, however, it seems to be Christ's death rather than his birth that causes Beckett most difficulty. It is clearly the acid test of the redemptive qualities Christ has claimed as his *raison d'être*. Belacqua, his first hero, finds Christ's death 'slick' compared to that of the philosopher Empedocles,[35] and the story of the two thieves crucified with Christ has troubled Beckett's thinking for many years. References to this story abound in Beckett's work, and he returned to it in a 1956 interview: 'Two thieves are crucified with Christ: one is saved and the other damned. How can we comprehend this division?' Beckett is attracted by the neatness of Augustine's explanation: 'Do not despair, one of the thieves was saved. Do not presume, one of the thieves was damned.'[36] But the neatness of a solution does not guarantee its truth; in fact, for Beckett, it makes its truth suspicious. The arbitrary separation of good and bad endemic in Christianity is inevitably unpalatable to a man believing in a precarious and sensitively articulated balance of forces in art and life. 'If there were only darkness', Beckett is quoted as saying, 'all would be clear.'[37] It is because we have both darkness and light that our difficulties multiply. It is no wonder Murphy finds the raising of Lazarus 'the one occasion on which the Messiah had overstepped the mark'.[38] Not only does Jesus bring him from darkness to light and from peace to pain, but he breaks up the necessary partnership, what he calls (in the 'Denis Devlin' review) the 'Dives–Lazarus symbiosis'.[39] Beckett is doubtless aware that this story became the *locus classicus* for disquisitions on the nature of purgatory (an idea that has fascinated him since first reading Dante), and can only see the story in terms of Jesus forgetting to temper his justice with mercy where Dives is concerned.

Christ is, in fact, a singularly unattractive figure in many ways.

Moran points out that he was never known to laugh.[40] Christianity's great emphasis on the Crucifixion (pointed out with considerable force by D. H. Lawrence)[41] establishes it, for the agnostic, as a religion of death. A manichean would be tempted to stress the escapist aspects of the Crucifixion rather than its aspect of utter commitment. Jehovah in fact becomes preferable to Christ, not simply because of the quality of his jokes (although *Murphy* bears witness to the fact that 'In the beginning was the Pun'), but because he is a more comprehensive figure, cruel and worldly as well as mystically remote. Beckett's interest in Jehovah[42] (the Yahweh who becomes Youdi in *Molloy*, the figure with the white beard in *Godot*) may account for a quality in Beckett's work that might almost be called Talmudic – its witty, legalistic, labyrinthine, balanced quality. Certainly, from Beckett's point of view, it seems true to say that Christ's Love is resistible almost because of its greater flexibility, whereas Jehovah's Law must be either accepted or rejected wholesale.

Acceptance of the Law and the Divine Lawyer has much to recommend it. As Kant says in the *Preface to the Metaphysical Elements of Ethics*: 'that he who is accused by his conscience should be conceived as one and the same person is an absurd conception of a judicial court; for then the complainant would always lose his case.'[43] It may indeed be absurd, but it is an image which has dominated twentieth-century 'absurd' writing, from Joseph K to the *Texts for Nothing*. It is only a short step from accepting this absurd state of affairs to postulating that the literal (as distinct from the figurative) court no longer has any relevance. Thus we find Beckett, in *Proust*, borrowing (without acknowledgment) from Joyce the notion that Dostoevsky's famous novel *Crime and Punishment* contains neither crime nor punishment in the accepted sense.[44] The crime is to have been born, as Calderón realized; the punishment takes the form of remaining alive. And suicide provides no way out because it involves making a God of oneself in a situation in which God has already been seen to be useless. All one can do is search for the self.

Beckett does not dismiss the traditional roads to truth; all he rejects is the palace of wisdom at the end of the road. He in fact uses a number of theologically sanctioned methods to find out not the truth about God, but the truth (if it exists) about the self. Murphy's self-laceration is, for example, strangely reminiscent, even down to details, of the career of the thirteenth-century mystic Henry Suso;[45] but his end-in-view is very far removed from that of Suso, consisting in the discovery and perfection of the self as a hermetically closed sphere. The experience of Romanticism may make this aim seem Faustian but it is an end approached by totally un-Faustian means, by means, in fact, that any mystic worth his salt would immediately applaud: the discomfiture of the body to liberate the mind, and the incantatory repetition of certain items of speech or movements to bring the desired end nearer – not to mention an almost inhuman patience and endurance. Beckett's ultimate desiderata – silence, darkness, will-lessness – may seem at first sight to link him to a thinker like Eckhart, but he is, as he says in 'Dream', a 'dud mystic' and his early description of Giambattista Vico indicates where his real sympathies lie. Vico is a 'mystic that rejects the transcendental in every shape and form . . . whose Providence is not divine enough to do without the co-operation of Humanity.'[46] 'Negative mysticism', in other words, contains certain attractions, but these are almost all on the side of man rather than God. Its deeply introspective hesitancy, its basis in contradiction, testify (as Jung said the Book of Job testified)[47] to a more finely developed discriminatory and spiritual sense in man than in God. It is partly the contradictions that explain why, though far from being a Buddhist, he can quote Gautama's 'mad wisdom' with such relish in his essay 'Henri Hayden; homme peintre': 'Gautama . . . said that one is fooling oneself if one says that the "I" exists, but that in saying it does not exist, one is fooling oneself no less.'[48] In fact, the religious problem is squarely bound up with the aesthetic expression of it (as we found with Augustine on the two thieves). And it is astonishing to find this realized by Beckett as early as 1929, in his first published short story 'Assumption'.[49]

In this story Beckett meditates on the plight of a man, an artist, who can 'whisper the turmoil down' in others, but who remains in turmoil himself, since he finds utterance extremely difficult. His utterance, when it comes, will be an ejaculatory scream ('Perhaps the most perfect form of being', said Beckett in 1962, 'would be an ejaculation'),[50] but when it does come it will be, like the song of a swan, the sign of death. A vague omnipotent power seeks deliberately (it seems) to prevent him achieving his end, and his only recourse (since he both wants to utter, and cannot utter, is afraid to utter) is to hope that he may ultimately fuse with the 'cosmic discord'. Just as every wish of Balzac's Raphael in *La Peau de Chagrin* brings nearer his demise, so every word spoken by this figure seems to bring the deluge nearer. This particularly troubles him because, as an artist, he would ideally like to keep everything in perfect balanced suspension. In this respect, a love affair (as later in *First Love*) proves critical, since as a result of it he loses the desire for, and the possibility of, balance. Sexual ecstasy leads him to a religious ecstasy in which he becomes the Power that previously sought to thwart him; in this way he is liberated from the three-dimensional world, the 'Satanic dimensional Trinity'. The sexual death of orgasm leads on to 'the blue flower, Vega, GOD'.[51] The woman has acted as a catalyst for utterance, but his scream, when it comes, sweeps her out of the way, as he fuses 'into the breath of the forest and the throbbing cry of the sea'. He clearly becomes what Murphy's third zone describes as 'a mote in the mind of absolute freedom'. And yet the final focus of the story is on the dead body he leaves behind, and Beckett's characteristically dualist stance is reasserted.[52] It is not only the woman who is a vulture; it is the artist also, as Beckett's early poem (based on Goethe's 'Harzreise im Winter') makes clear. The artist is creator and procreator; in liberating his mind, he can reach the light of eternity only through the death of the body. The imagery, indeed the aspiration, may seem uncharacteristically romantic for Beckett, but it has, of course, strong affiliations with the Decadents. The *belle dame*, like God, is *sans merci*, and it is a rough justice she metes out. The end and the means to the end are very much two-edged.

'Assumption' is arguably Beckett's worst piece of writing and clearest articulation of theme. The religious problem is seen from the start not as an isolated matter, but as a question involving the predicament of the artist and the difficulties of the lover as well. This explains the emphasis on eros and anteros in his early poems (well described by Lawrence E. Harvey), an emphasis resulting from the decay of agapé. It is in the end no use quibbling that Beckett is really a believer because Godot contains God, because all his life Vladimir has compared himself to Christ, because Hamm has his St Veronica handkerchief. As Beckett has carefully explained, 'I use religious symbols because I am perfectly familiar with them.'[53] But the French diminutive cuts down to size a God that for all our waiting does not come; and Vladimir's and Hamm's comparisons do nothing to suggest they can save or be saved. Any suggestion that Beckett's inner voice is a near relation of the 'still small voice' of which Christianity speaks can only remind us of the calm he has never been able to find.

It seems perfectly logical that anyone disappointed of Christian consolation in the way Beckett has been seen to be, is bound to turn (if not for religious satisfaction, at least in the spirit of returning to the origins of thought) to the writings of the pre-Socratic philosophers. These very fragmentary writings only became the common property of twentieth-century intellectuals because of Eliot's recommendation, in the epigraph to *Four Quartets*, of Diels's edition of *Die*

Fragmente der Vorsokratiker; John Burnet's account in *Early Greek Philosophy* was, until recently, the best treatment of the subject in English, and was doubtless consulted by Beckett. Beckett was impressed by the 'terse dicta' of Heraclitus[54] and the famous suicide of Empedocles, but he seems to have been most attracted to the figure of the 'laughing' philosopher Democritus,[55] whose proposition 'Nothing is more real than nothing' has always been one of Beckett's favourite phrases. This eccentric formulation, at first sight totally alien to the predominantly materialist Atomists among whom Democritus is usually grouped, is used by Beckett in a way not entirely fair to Democritus. Democritus' theory states that random atoms move strictly in accordance with certain laws in an infinite void; Beckett is attracted by this and by the equable temperament of the man who puts this rather terrifying news forward. But he regards the proposition 'Nothing is more real than nothing' as only the second real truth he can rely on (the first being Geulincx's statement of human value); as a result, he slightly distorts it, and the phrase occasionally seems a wish-fulfilment regarding an unattainable state of consciousness that Beckett can never record successfully in his creative work. The importance Beckett attaches to it is nowhere more dramatically demonstrated than in his reply to an inquiry on the sources of his writing: he told Lawrence Harvey in 1962 that if he were a critic setting out to write on the works of Beckett he would begin with the quotations from Geulincx and Democritus.[56]

Of the other early philosophers Beckett doubtless found Pythagoreanism superficially attractive; he shares with the Pythagoreans an interest in music, mathematics, mysticism, the coincidence of opposites, the problem of an intellected world not revealed to the senses, and even their interest in animals. His early long prose work 'Dream of Fair to Middling Women' (1932) shows him aware that their scheme is wrong, but regretful that it is so:

> If all our characters were alike . . . we could write a little book
> that would be purely melodic, think how nice that would be,
> linear, a lovely Pythagorean chain-chart of cause and effect. . . .
> But what can you do with a person . . . who is not a note at
> all but the most regrettable simultaneity of notes.[57]

Just as Voltaire (in *Le Philosophe ignorant*) portrays a Pythagoras at the mercy of irrational forces he cannot control, so Beckett, in *Murphy* (written in 1935) aligns himself clearly with Hippasos, who first revealed how inefficacious music and astrology could be.[58] By 1949 in the Duthuit dialogues, Beckett's tone in discussing

Pythagoras has become harsher and more mocking as, with the passing of time, his evidence of the irrational has increased.[59] The singular figure of the philosopher Zeno is important here, since Zeno's dialectic was mainly directed against the Pythagoreans, and sought to deduce two contradictory conclusions. He did this so successfully that even Aristotle had difficulty in refuting him, but his triumph is pre-eminently on the level of logic, since his conclusions are contrary to common sense. Beckett likes Zeno because he is a destructive philosopher, recommending nothing; basically monist in aim, but content to show the shortcomings of accepted systems. He has also been particularly impressed by Zeno's power of image; we find Zeno's heap of sand referred to in *Endgame* and *The Lost Ones* and actually on stage in *Happy Days*. At no time is Zeno's name actually used; he is simply 'that old Greek'.[60]

Equally, at no time does Beckett actually refer to Gorgias the sophist, but it would be clear – even without the testimony of his close friend A. J. Leventhal[61] – that this philosopher's beliefs are strikingly coincident with Beckett's. Gorgias' thought resolves itself into three propositions: Nothing is, it cannot be comprehended, and even if it can be, it cannot be communicated to anyone. Gorgias has been interpreted as a serious sceptical denier of all existence and as a joker parodying philosophers; Beckett would warm to him on both counts.

Aristotle he has rather more time for than Plato, although in his first poem *Whoroscope* he refers affectionately to the anti-Aristotelian brothers Boot of Dublin, and he nowhere wholeheartedly commends him. His most interesting reference to Aristotle lurks behind the Latin in one of the fragmentary notes at the end of *Watt*. They are the apocryphal last words of Aristotle.[62] It is not simply that Beckett is attracted by the summation of wisdom in death-bed remarks (though he is certainly the kind of man to read such collections, and a notebook for *Krapp* shows him collecting together the most gruesome 'in memoriams' imaginable); it is more important to realize that here Beckett underlines (as if any underlining were necessary) the major theme of *Watt* – the defeat and death of reason – by referring to the pessimistic last words of the man who, as 'master of those who know', first offered a systematic and comprehensive account of the world from rational principles. It is further interesting to note that among his notes for *Watt* Beckett visualizes and develops a situation by means of Aristotle's ten categories. It is almost as if he set out believing Watt's quest, based on rational principles, would eventually succeed if pursued uncompromisingly enough, only to find, as he came to write it, that it would not. But the reduction of escape-routes consequent upon reading the pre-Socratics is so comprehensive that Aristotle could hardly have made a great deal of difference.

Our discussion so far has shown how Beckett – no doubt much less systematically than I have suggested – was forced to drop or select from, philosophies that had offered superficial attractions that proved ultimately to be of no help. At this point, it is important to remind ourselves that post-Cartesian philosophy has tended to develop the epistemological consequences of Descartes's thought at the expense of the metaphysical concerns that were central to him. As Beckett is very familiar with this later philosophy, it would be impossible to deal with every influence in detail.

Beckett read Kant in 1930, the year of his return to Ireland, to teach at his old university. At only one point in his writing does he refer to Kant[63] – in the second of the 'Three Dialogues with Georges Duthuit' – and it is by way of Freud that he comes to do so. The conclusion of Kant's *Critique of Practical Reason* (1788), finds the philosopher who gave his name to the 'critical' philosophy in an uncharacteristically transcendental frame of mind, unable to doubt the existence of God because the stars are so profoundly beautiful. Beckett (unlike Freud, who only registers his puzzlement that God has not dealt equally with all of us) is amused at this not because the idea is laughable (although there are very few instances of such an idea in his own writing),[64] but because it involves the great philosopher in something like an inconsistency. One of the most celebrated sections of Kant's earlier work, the *Critique of Pure Reason*, is an attack on 'cosmological' proofs of the existence of God that can have no validity. This is presumably why Beckett allows the technical inaccuracy of calling Kant's later discussion a 'cosmological proof' to enter into his discussion with Duthuit. It tells us that we need not expect any major Kantian influence to be at work in his own writing. The closest he can get to Kant, in fact, is signalled by his character Molloy, who instead of wholeheartedly embracing the 'categorical imperative' which is the basis of Kant's moral law, finds himself unable to even obey the 'hypothetical imperative', which Kant associated with those who were still benighted in a world of will and relativism.[65]

The Beckettian world is very much a world of this kind, in which the exploitation of the will can do nothing to extricate one from an irremediably relative situation. At this point in his thinking Beckett finds himself anticipated by the influential 'pessimist' philosopher Schopenhauer, whom he read in the same year. Beckett's debt to Schopenhauer is very considerable; much of the discussion in *Proust* is based on Schopenhauer's very original aesthetics, and Beckett has never concealed how much he delights in Schopenhauer's presentation of his philosophy as a whole. It is not simply a question of being impressed by his manner, however; Beckett is in profound agreement with many of his ideas. Unable (like many others) to accept Kant's 'thing-in-itself' because the rest of Kant's critique, showing the limits of what we can and cannot think about, is unanswerable, Beckett takes refuge in Schopenhauer's 'thing-in-itself' the will, because it is something all mankind is familiar with, and it does not need thinking about. Schopenhauer's arguments, usually described as 'irrationalist' so as to leave an unpleasant taste in the mouth, resolve themselves into one basic conclusion: the less we exercise the will, the less suffering we endure. And if we are fortunate enough to actually silence the will for good, we will be restored to the ineffably peaceful condition of effective non-existence. The conclusion to *The World as Will and Idea* is only the most resonant of many similar passages, and it is a passage Beckett and his characters would unhesitatingly endorse:

> to those in whom the will has turned and has denied itself,
> this our world, which is so real, with all its suns and milling
> ways – is nothing . . . time and space . . . subject and object;
> all are abolished. No will: no idea, no world. Before us there is
> certainly only nothingness.[66]

In as thoroughgoing a pessimism as this, philosophy itself comes under scrutiny. It has already been attacked, by Schopenhauer removing metaphysics from the inquiry: the contemplation of things before, or beyond the world, and consequently beyond the will, he declared, is open to no investigation. But it is clear that we are close to a situation in which, as a Schopenhauer specialist, Patrick Gardiner, describes it, 'the end of philosophy is silence'.[67]

With the removal of God, therefore, goes the removal of metaphysics. If epistemology is not also to be removed, its linguistic foundations (the elements that have kept it from silence) have to be analysed. This, broadly speaking, is what modern philosophy, and a writer like Beckett, has tried to do. And following Descartes and Schopenhauer as key figures in Beckett's thinking is Fritz Mauthner, an Austrian logical positivist from whose work Beckett read aloud to the blind Joyce in the late 1930s.[68] Beckett told me recently that he had been particularly impressed by Mauthner's *Beiträge zu einer Kritik der Sprache*, but stressed that it was Joyce who had first drawn it to his attention.

Schopenhauer only approaches silence; Mauthner encounters it head-on. According to Mauthner, ordinary language, which we cannot go beyond, is of no use to us in our quest for truth. 'Only in language do these two words "mind" and "body" exist, in reality they cannot be separated', says Mauthner;[69] as a result, 'the so-called self-observation has no organ'.[70] Since for Mauthner there is 'no thinking without speaking',[71] and since, when we speak, there is no distinguishing between the report and that which it is supposed to be a report of – a problem we meet in part two of *Molloy* – we are continually uttering meaningless statements. Only by transcending the limits of language (which Mauthner considers impossible) will we get to know things as they really are. And this can only be achieved by a critique of language, which Mauthner describes as 'the heavenly stillness and gaiety of resignation and renunciation',[72] a phrase reminiscent of Schopenhauer, but even more prophetic of Beckett.

The problem for Mauthner (and for Beckett) is that this desideratum can only be articulated through language. As Gershon Weiler says, 'it will either increase the confusion implicit in language by using it, or else it will eliminate language and then there will remain nothing to criticize and the critique itself will become impossible'.[73] The critique's success coincides with its own destruction; as Mauthner describes it (in terms that remind one irresistibly of Beckett's 'Denis Devlin' article), the critique of language is not the solution of the 'riddle of the Sphinx' but 'it is at least the redeeming act which forces the Sphinx into silence'.[74] The critique tries, as Beckett tries, to say the unsayable. And in the same way as Beckett makes capital out of his failure (by writing when writing is impossible), so does Mauthner. As Weiler says,

> The explanation is this. Although the critique rejects the idea
> that terms have a clear and distinct meaning, it must,
> *qua* critical practice in a particular field at a certain time,
> assume that at least some terms have clear and constant
> meanings; otherwise the critical enterprise could not even get
> going.[75]

It would be difficult to overstate the relevance of this for students of Beckett. The premises are the same, the conclusions are the same; only the realm of discourse – drama and fiction rather than philosophy – is different. Mallarmé's aim of purifying the language of the tribe has been replaced by the even more challenging one of purifying the language of the clerks, with the unavoidable prospect of failure.[76] Mauthner in fact provided Beckett with the necessary ammunition to destroy all systems of thought whatever, even 'irrationalism'. If there are 'as many logics as there are languages with different structures', the 'suicide of thought'[77] becomes not only necessary but inevitable. It is a good deal less consoling than Bergson's intuitionism – on which Beckett lectured at Trinity – but it is worked out with a philosophical rigour that commands respect, and it is as important in its own way as Einstein's relativity was to be for physics.

In twentieth-century thought positivism and phenomenology have been largely dominant, the former promoting an increased interest in linguistics, the latter preparing the way for existentialism. Linguistic approaches to Beckett are obviously important in determining questions of tone and style. Existentialism is a much abused term covering a multitude of sins, and is frequently used by Beckett critics as a handy label for something really rather more complex. Beckett has explicitly differentiated his own manner of exploration from theirs: 'When Heidegger and Sartre speak of a contrast between being and existence, they may be right, I don't know, but their language is too philosophical for me.'[78] His *area* of exploration, however, is much the same as theirs, especially his obsession (found as early as the 1938 review of Denis Devlin) with the inaccessibility of 'the other'. This idea is clearly not far removed from the existentialist's basic premise that to make others the object of my perceptions is to view them as other than they are. However, the existentialist emphasis on choice hardly bulks large in Beckett's work and only occasionally (as, for example, in 'The Expelled') does a distinctively existentialist 'dread' manifest itself, and in this case the impulse is more likely to be the fairly common psychological condition of semi-paranoia. It is true that the existentialist philosopher Karl Jaspers has stressed the importance of 'boundary situations' and that many of Beckett's most important scenes are of this kind (Molloy by the sea, for example), but it is clear that Beckett regards existentialism as primarily important for continuing the erosion of the rationalist position already begun by empiricism. Sartre's dramatic art in *Huis Clos* was doubtless a useful example of what could be done with such ideas, but any closer connection between the two remains to be proven. Sartre was at the École Normale at the same time as Beckett, and they still occasionally meet, 'without design but without embarrassment'.[79]

Philosophy's failure to come up with satisfactory explanations of the world did not deter Beckett from taking an interest in psychology. He appears to have been impressed by the new discoveries made by experimental psychology as it shook off nineteenth-century behaviourism. In an early review he describes MacGreevey as 'the

Titchener of the modern existentialist lyric',[80] and *Murphy* is full of references to psychologists and psychological ideas. One of the gestalt psychologists Külpe, had an assistant named Watt whose discoveries suggested that our behaviour is so conditioned by our original intentions that any secondary elements that are part of our consciousness are effectively without content. This sheds new light on the problems of Beckett's Watt some forty years later.

When we come to psychoanalysis, Beckett's anagrammatic playfulness in *Molloy* (Freud's libido becomes the 'character' Obidil), reinforced by a wry remark about the 'fatal pleasure principle', suggest that he is not prepared to swallow Freud wholesale.[81] However, the fact that Beckett quotes from the difficult (and misnamed) *Introductory Lectures in Psychoanalysis* in his dialogues with Duthuit, when seeking a stick with which to beat Kant, reveals that he is far from being dismissive in the manner of Nabokov. Freud's discussion of repetition (in *Beyond the Pleasure Principle*) and parricide (in *Totem and Taboo*, etc.) doubtless helped to confirm what Beckett himself had already found to be true: that sexuality was at the root of our difficulties, that masturbation, solipsism and the imaginative faculty were closely connected, that obsessive images revealed themselves in dream-states, and that bifurcation of personality stems from loneliness (in *Endgame* Beckett speaks of the solitary child who 'turns himself into children').[82] Equally, Freud's description of the general guilt of mankind in the late metapsychological work *Civilization and its Discontents* is an especially acute analysis of the spiritual condition which Beckett (following Schopenhauer) had found in Calderón's 'Crime of having been born':

> Whether one has killed one's father or abstained from doing so is not the really decisive thing. One is bound to feel guilty in either case, for the sense of guilt is an expression of the conflict due to ambivalence, of the eternal struggle between Eros and the instinct of destruction or death.[83]

Beckett is certainly the kind of writer whose work encourages Freudian interpretations. His obsessive repetition may be seen in Freudian terms as an attempt to achieve the impossible, to experience in his work the fact of death (like Hermann Broch's Virgil) since, as Wollheim has shown, 'the compulsion . . . to repeat can be seen as the effort to restore a state that is both historically primitive and also marked by the total draining of energy, i.e. death'.[84] Beckett's very acute memories of life in his mother's womb (an area Otto Rank explored in the 1920s) will in any case continue to be of interest to psychoanalytically orientated critics. The psychoanalytic approach to literature is still not as intellectually water-tight as it might be, but when Freud speaks of eros and thanatos as controlling principles, it is clear that such terms provide an interesting way of thinking about the troubadours and Dante. What is certain is that neither psychology nor psychoanalysis constitute, for Beckett, a total answer to the condition of man, any more than does the physicist Schrödinger's account *What is Life?*, a work he is known to admire. But equally, as one of his characters says, 'I'd like to be sure I left no stone unturned before reporting me missing and giving up'.[85]

The literary background
to Beckett

The heart of the cauliflower or the ideal core of the
onion would represent a more appropriate tribute to
the labours of poetical excavation than the crown of
bay. *(Proust)*[1]

In considering the literary influences on Beckett, we first of all find
that the experience of reading Dante early on in his university career
was as overwhelming as his reading of Descartes at the end of it. It is
not difficult to see why. *The Divine Comedy* is one of the great masterpieces of the world because it enlivens the aridities of scholastic
theology and the bickerings of thirteenth-century Florence in poetry
that is celebrative, without being sentimental, and weighed down
with misery, without being defeatist. At the same time as satisfying
medieval canons of decorum in being a multi-structured allegory of
almost geometric precision, its relevance remains undiminished
because of the range of its total vision. It dramatizes the characteristically medieval sense of the gap between man and God, which
is insurmountable and brings irremediable sadness, while at the
same time dramatizing the dauntless spirit of quest and aspiration
upwards to the godhead.

Since the rediscovery of Dante in modern times,[2] the *Inferno* has
perhaps been the most frequently admired section of the work and
Solzhenitsyn (in *The First Circle*) is the latest in a long line of writers
to be impressed by the brilliance of Dante's imagination there.
Beckett himself refers most frequently to the *Inferno*, which has a
harrowing clarity similar to his own work. He is, however, profoundly aware of the magnificent last words of the *Inferno*, which
stress the beauty of the sky and stars,[3] and even if Dante's breadth
of vision and stylistic elegance can no longer be emulated, there
can be no doubt that emphasizing the relevance of the *Inferno* at the
expense of the *Purgatorio* and *Paradiso* would smack of sentimentality.
At the same time the twentieth century, while not necessarily wallow-
ing in its own despair, has not often found cause for hope in the way

Dante could. It is true that hope is in short supply in Beckett's work; Moran sees even the very presence of hope as infernal: 'That would keep hope alive, would it not, hellish hope.'[4] Yet it is nothing more tangible than a kind of blasted hope that keeps Vladimir and Estragon waiting for Godot, and although it is the dialogue that keeps Clov where he is,[5] he clearly expects something from it. While Beckett's vision is nothing like as comprehensive as Dante's, we may be sure that Beckett was sensitive to the whole of Dante's great work, even if certain parts left a particularly strong impression on his mind.

What is important about Dante for students of Beckett (above and beyond the numerous verbal reminiscences of Dante in Beckett's work)[6] is that Beckett was at one time tempted to conceive of reality in similar terms. His reinterpretation of Dante's tripartite cosmology for the essay on Joyce's 'Work in Progress' establishes beyond doubt that he found reality (as we might expect) purgatorial. Hell and paradise are both static and lifeless; there are 'no eruptions', everything is exactly as it has always been, as it always will be.[7] The middle state of purgatory (from which section of Dante's work Beckett chose Belacqua as representative hero for his early work) he equates with earthly existence, as Schopenhauer (in the essay 'On Religion')[8] had done before him. Earthly existence is a perpetual eruption of movement of immense complexity, in which we can find no footholds at all, only the 'absolute absence of the Absolute'. Living in a world without absolutes, the Unnamable has no idea of what world he is in: 'strange hell that has no heating, no denizens, perhaps it's paradise, perhaps it's the light of paradise. It isn't the earth, that's all that counts, it can't be the earth.'[9] We see here disbelief mingled with hope: can things be as bad as they seem? or: is it really the earth at last? The earth may seem like a refuge from the 'hell of stories', but it is remorselessly purgatorial, a world of perpetual 'eruptions', as the Unnamable's narrative abundantly testifies.

Dante has been justly called 'the greatest realist in all literature',[10] and whatever meaning we give to the slippery word 'realistic' it is a quality that we find beautifully exemplified in one of Beckett's favourite lines from the poem. His hero Belacqua (a student of Italian as Beckett was) is particularly attracted (in the story 'Dante and the Lobster') by one of Dante's quibbles: *Qui vive la pietà quando è ben morta.*[11] It is a phrase that sums up Dante's tension between doctrine and sympathy, ethos and pathos: 'There pity must be dead for piety to live', as Thomas MacGreevy (one of Beckett's friends in the early years) rendered it.[12] It is interesting to find

J. C. Powys celebrating in Dante the quality that comes directly from such 'realism', which all Beckett's people possess: 'whatever his *doctrines* may say . . . the far truer emanation that proceeds from his *style* indicates endurance as the supreme human virtue.'[13]

Needless to say, biographical speculation of the kind Beckett found in Giovanni Papini's *Dante Vivo* (which he reviewed)[14] interested him no more than 'the legendary life and death of Marcel Proust' had done. But he read much more of Dante than simply the *Commedia*. He singled out Dante's prose work *De Vulgari Eloquentia* for special praise in his early article on Joyce's 'Work in Progress'.[15] Seeking a parallel for Joyce's practice, he was led to stress the hybrid quality of Dante's language, rather than (as Dante had done) emphasizing the question of eloquence. He was not, however, unaware of the historical importance of Dante's emphasis, for his own taste in literature at this time included the early Italian poets, and the troubadour and Minnesinger poets of France and Germany which constituted (as Ezra Pound had claimed in *The Spirit of Romance*) the first European literature of the vernacular. Among the early Italian poets it is not difficult to see why he preferred Cavalcanti, who is now best known to the English reader as the presence behind the first lines of T. S. Eliot's *Ash Wednesday*. Cavalcanti is arguably the greatest of the 'new-style' poets that Dante labelled 'dolce',[16] sometimes difficult and intellectual (as are many of Beckett's favourite writers) but in his most engaging poems profoundly aware of how sensuality distorts our reason, and pessimistically sensitive to every suffering we are heir to. Bruno's frenzies may be heroic but there is nothing heroic in Cavalcanti; he is fearful, dissatisfied, morose. He is a poet who concentrates on the eyes, since 'it is the eyes which enjoy most and are most enjoyed in love',[17] and his greatest heroism, in fact, is to keep his eyes open, in every sense. Beckett, whose fascination with eyes facing each other, eyes opening and closing, and even the mechanics of the eyeball, began early, must have been profoundly impressed by this poet. He was certainly very interested in Pound's essay on him: 'Cavalcanti . . . is a most terrific organon. . . . Guido emerges *gran maestro* not of *amor*, as the chinamaniac Petrarch would insist, but of the entire medieval *scribile* which Mr Pound may possibly consider to be the same thing.'[18] The allusion to Petrarch's *Trionfi* is no doubt the result of being forced to study the poet for examinations,[19] but he certainly did not feel attracted to the smoothness and sweetness of the poet whom Coleridge thought represented 'the final blossom and perfection of the troubadours',[20] whose influence was so extensive in the centuries that followed.

We find him, in fact, in the same review, relieved to come upon the *Tagelied* of the German Minnesinger Heinrich von Morungen. The Minnesinger poets were lyric poets writing in the courtly love tradition, who ultimately adopted a more colloquially direct and unaffected style, to express insights about the male–female relationship which might have raised the eyebrows of the originators of that tradition. Of this group it was the most inventive and individual, Walther van der Vogelweide, who made the greatest impression on him, and Beckett's early poetry is dominated by 'albas', 'enuegs' and 'serenas' in the Vogelweide manner. It is not difficult to see why this fine poet interested Beckett. Walther is racked, in a distinctively medieval way, by the conflicting claims of eros and agapé, piety and pity, matter and spirit. He is constantly aware of a vast gulf separating man from God, and so depressed by the condition of the former that his prayers to the latter seem bred of a hysterical and almost heretical despair. Love, especially sexual love, is seen to be subject to the rigours of decay from the moment day dawns, and its eternal aspect seems constantly threatened by the random and meaningless intrusion of death. Two centuries later Villon, continuing the vernacular tradition, decides at the beginning of *Le Lais* (in a passage echoed by Beckett in one of his early poems)[21] to renounce eros altogether, and to live alone. But this aim, for both Villon and Beckett, proves difficult to achieve, and it is no surprise to find Ronsard summing up (with Beckett's whole-hearted approval) 'L'Amour et La Mort n'est qu'une seule chose' ('Love and Death are but the same').[22]

Huizinga's *Waning of the Middle Ages* has accustomed us to thinking of the dominance of love and death in the medieval world,[23] and this was certainly the configuration that most interested nineteenth-century romantic artists. But it is classical too. Unfortunately the situation cannot be eased by factitious appeals to old ideals. While Joyce recommended 'the classical temper'[24] and Proust was seen as 'the founder of impressionist classicism',[25] Beckett cannot accept its claims to 'omniscience and omnipotence'.[26] Ionesco's remark 'I aspire to classicism'[27] shows a similar sensitivity to the fact that despite one's admiration for the restraint and clarity of classicism, it is something one may never achieve. One of Beckett's favourite authors, for example, is Racine. But he admires Racine because he is a man who seems to 'write without style'[28] and because his style, especially 'the preterites and past subjunctives',[29] allows him to be as exact and penetrating as any dramatic artist could wish to be. And the stylization of passion is so great in both that such luxuries as tenderness and pity are as irrelevant to *Andromaque* as to *Godot*.

135

Concomitant with this is Racine's ability to suggest how claustrophobic the human condition is, and how terrifying the infinite spaces can be. In *Endgame* the shrinking of possibilities is charted as unsparingly and as terrifyingly as in Racine. But it is no longer possible for the hard, clear lines of classical tragedy to express the total human condition that Beckett sees. 'For those of us who are not Jansenists nor Greeks', says Beckett, 'no such certainty exists.'[30]

This means, of course, that not even the dubious alternative tradition of Romanticism – dubious because it can seem all too much like 'spilt religion'[31] – can be entirely resisted. 'Anti-Romanticism', as Northrop Frye has written, 'had no resources for beginning anything other than a post-romantic movement.'[32] Beckett commends Huysmans for speaking of 'the ineluctable gangrene of Romanticism',[33] but finds himself supporting the irrationalism of Schopenhauer and the post-romantic dogma that 'he who does not have the power to destroy reality does not have the power to create it'.[34] The self-indulgence of Ossianic antiquarianism and the 'Elysium of the roofless'[35] that was so much a part of the late eighteenth-century taste for ruins have no attraction for him. The retreat into the mountains which Hölderlin's Hyperion finds so efficacious[36] (and which later, in Ibsen, becomes the source of spiritual vision) brings no joy to Beckett's people: 'In a cowpad a heart had been traced, pierced by an arrow. And yet there was nothing to attract tourists. I noticed the remains of abandoned nosegays. . . . The scene was the familiar one of grandeur and desolation.'[37]

Although Beckett's studies involved him in Wordsworth, Byron, Keats, Shelley and Tennyson, only Wordsworth's fondness for tramps and Shelley's intuitions of a pre-natal life[38] could have had a particular poignancy for him. Since it is the fact that we come from a body at birth that means we ourselves have a body, and since the body is the seat of all that is sensual and base, and pre-eminently the prey of disease, it is our habitation of this mortal coil that involves us in suffering. Beckett would have found this powerfully, if a little melodramatically, put in Rousseau:

> Being forced to speak in spite of myself, I am also obliged to conceal myself. . . . The ceiling under which I live has eyes, the walls that enclose me have eyes. Uneasy and distracted, surrounded by spies and by vigilant and malevolent watchers, I hurriedly put on paper a few disjointed sentences.[39]

The later Rousseau (in *Reveries of a Solitary*, which was on Beckett's undergraduate syllabus) is more decisive: 'My body is nothing to me but an embarrassment, but an obstacle, and I shall in advance disengage myself from it as much as I can.'[40] It was in Leopardi, whose sincerity made his rhetoric acceptable even to Ezra Pound,[41] that Beckett found his feelings most profoundly mirrored.

Where Dante wavers between pity and piety, Leopardi is unsure whether to feel pity or scorn when faced with the 'unhappy children of Mortality'.[42] His position is an unrelievedly pessimistic one because it does not, any more than Beckett's, allow a value to hope. 'Where is no hope is no place for inquietude',[43] wrote Leopardi, careful above all to avoid the traditional sentimental pieties: and, with a vehemence Beckett could echo, 'it is absurd to attribute to my writings a religious tendency'.[44] While Leopardi is not jealous of his own individuality like his countryman Vico,[45] his philosophy of despair is unflinching and intransigent; what Beckett added to this was a temperament that could not help laughing (whereas Leopardi never smiled) and, more particularly, laughing at itself. There was consequently less danger that his sincerity might be suffocated by a fulsome rhetoric, although the towering presence of poets as great as Dante and Leopardi may also have been the force driving him to seek genres less obviously rhetorical than poetry.

When he came to write 'The End', for example, he was clearly trying to eradicate the romantic strain which he recognized as an element in his early writing. The self-imposed drowning in a boat of the unnamed hero takes its place in the series of romantic and post-romantic quests for oblivion which Beckett had encountered in Shelley, Rimbaud (whose 'Drunken Boat' he once translated), Baudelaire and Eliot.[46] But this hero goes one step further: he actually does drown himself, without fuss or bother, and 'lives' to record his own demise in fiction. This possibility is something Romanticism, even at its high-water mark, did not choose to face; much of its strength, indeed, resides in its ultimately life-giving faith in the new values it discovers. The hero of 'The End' is closer in his attitude to writers of the later nineteenth-century, or such writers as Hölderlin, for whom the romantic reintegration of self and world was impossible to achieve. Hölderlin shows the Faustian gestures of an Empedocles or a Hyperion to be ultimately meaningless in the face of the disinterested remoteness of the gods. The full text of the fragmentary poem quoted in the addenda to *Watt* reads:

> But to us it is given
> Nowhere to rest,
> Suffering men
> Falter and fall

> Blindly from one
> Hour to the next,
> Like water flung down
> From cliff to cliff,
> Yearlong into uncertainty.[47]

In a situation like this, there is only one obvious answer, and most of Beckett's heroes after Watt carry on their person the means whereby they can perfect their absence from the world. But none of them after 'The End' actually use their phials of morphine as they might, for they become embroiled in the possibility that a solution may be achieved by moving into another plane altogether.

The romantic aim to restore such lost paradises as the womb involves them in correspondingly severe terrestrial hells. A more feasible aim is retirement into the mind, as Rousseau indicated. This has, for Beckett, the advantage of simplifying Descartes's dualism, but it leads, if engaged in responsibly, as Beckett's narrator–creators find out, to new problems. First, is the mind passive? Second, what happens to an utterly passive, helpless mind that has no interest in its contents? 'Have men', Balzac wrote, 'the power of bringing the universe into their skulls, or is the skull a talisman with which they abolish the laws of time and space?'[48] Beckett does not answer the first question, because he cannot answer the second. All he knows is that if knowledge is sorrow for Byron, it is at least logical that ignorance should be bliss for Gray. Whereas, if 'knowledge increases unreality' (as it does for him as much as it does for Yeats),[49] and if ignorance does as well, he is bound to suffer more than the romantic writer. His yearning is just as intense, but it is undercut by a much more profound scepticism.

At this point some modern heroes immediately spring to mind: Rilke's Malte, Gide's Lafcadio, Svevo's Zeno. But Beckett explicitly repudiates them because they have failed to 'kill the marionette' in themselves that is always enabling them to return to the normal world.[50] Much more successful, from Beckett's point of view, is Paul Valéry's Monsieur Teste, 'the mystic without a god',[51] and if we examine the origins of this figure in Valéry's *Introduction to the Method of Leonardo da Vinci*[52] it is very easy to see why.

The mystic without God is left with only negatives. Instead of the quest leading to God, 'Every road', says Valéry with the kind of unflinching courage Beckett's heroes try to achieve, 'leads back to oneself.'[53] Instead of seeking vainly for personality, on a quest that must be circular, the man of intellect, 'must at last bring himself to an unqualified refusal to be anything whatsoever'.[54] Pure consciousness 'differs as little as could be wished from nothingness'. Beckett's nothingness is much less perfect than this, and much less volitional, but he is, in spirit, very close to the darker side of Valéry: 'There is no temptation that stirs one so deeply, none more intimate, and also, perhaps, none more fruitful, than that of self-repudiation.'[55] It is a similar self-repudiation that explains Beckett's unwillingness to talk about his work. But self-repudiation also means that Beckett, in each successive work, aims at a more quintessential statement of his vision. Every new utterance is a repudiation of what has gone before; 'All these Murphys, Molloys and Malones do not fool me', the Unnamable says.[56] As a result of this, both the external form of his work (its physical dimensions, its linguistic virtuosity) and the internal content (the bodily condition of his 'people', the focus of vision) become more and more reduced. The man of the greatest mind, said Valéry, speaking of Leonardo, will avoid all forms of action and 'by dint of rigorous thought, will end by reducing himself to a state of practical hebetude'.[57]

'There is', Beckett says, 'at least this much to be said for mind: that it can dispel mind.'[58] The ultimate end of such self-repudiation is usually retirement: Rimbaud's celebrated repudiation of literature is one kind of retirement, Proust's immurement in the cork-lined apartment in the Boulevard Haussmann (to write in bed, as Malone will do) another, Mallarmé's, behind a smoke-screen, a third. Beckett lacks the strength of purpose to go off, like Rimbaud, to Africa as a trader; Proust's solution is to make creation reciprocal with destruction.[59] Mallarmé claimed to have created his work by mere elimination ('Destruction was my Beatrice')[60] but outlines his problems so cogently that one suspects the extremity of the condition.[61] Beckett, at least, has wrung the neck of rhetoric in a way that cannot be labelled self-deception. Rimbaud describes himself in the poem 'Enfance' as 'maître du silence' ('master of silence') but, as he says elsewhere 'J'ai tous les talents' ('I've got all the talents'),[62] and having used them to the full, there was nothing left to do but embrace silence. What he aimed to do he could do: 'I wrote of silences and of nights,' he goes on, 'I expressed the inexpressible.'[63] It was the path Joyce followed. Mallarmé's aim, like Beckett's, was impossible. We have seen Mauthner, in 1906, reaching a similar conclusion where philosophy is concerned. And we find Kafka writing to Max Brod in 1921 of 'the impossibility of writing',[64] three years before his own self-repudiation in the face of death. Erich Heller has said of the poetry of Baudelaire, Hölderlin and Rimbaud: 'in their poetry, speechlessness itself seemed to burst into speech without breaking the silence.'[65] Maurice Blanchot's description of

The Unnamable shows that things have changed, and changed utterly: 'when the talking stops, there is still talking; when the language pauses, it perseveres; there is no silence, for within that voice the silence eternally speaks.'[66] Suicide may be 'an eminently philosophic act',[67] 'the consequence for the existence of pure thought.'[68] But pure thought for Beckett is impossible, and philosophy has been exposed for what it is. The surrealist ranks were spectacularly depleted by suicides, but Beckett finds Schopenhauer's reasoning – that it only increases the amount of will in the world – preferable. And yet the idea inevitably haunts him. He speaks in *The Unnamable*, of 'those whose sang-froid is such that they throw themselves out of the window'[69] and, in doing so, bizarrely forecast the fate of the painter Nicolas de Staël in 1954. The event was still fresh in his mind when he was interviewed in 1956 for the *New York Times*. 'There are others, like Nicolas de Staël', he told Israel Shenker, 'who throw themselves out of a window – after years of struggling.' We would do well to remember this story whenever we are tempted to sentimentalize his own struggle.

Once these general influences have been assimilated, it is obviously important to see Beckett in relation to more particular themes and techniques. The question of influences on his poetry can safely be shelved until we come to consider his work in that medium; the novels and drama have already been discussed, and require a more precise placing in terms of tradition.

Beckett's comments on his novelistic forebears are not much more voluminous than any of his other remarks about his work, but they are especially helpful in defining the area that we need to look at. 'I read romances', says the narrator of *First Love*, 'under the guidance of my tutor, in six or seven languages, both dead and living.'[70] The word 'romance' is perhaps an even more slippery literary term than most of the others in constant use, but, however we choose to define it, we end up with something that is in a particularly problematic, and almost perilous, relationship with 'reality'. Historically, the word expresses something more developed than 'ritual' but less developed than 'realism'. It is in fact a much more hybrid form than these, less a genre than a mode, a way of looking at reality rather than a codified convention. To a writer continually aware of his own non-existence, and therefore singularly ill-qualified to develop a large gallery of individual characters, painstakingly provided with particular psychologies, it is an especially adaptable medium to use. Without being strained beyond bearing, it can accommodate the satirical and outward-looking as well as the intimate and introverted, and is flexible in a way the nineteenth- and twentieth-century novel demonstrably is not. It need not, therefore, occasion surprise that Beckett's real forebears are those writers of prose that critics have felt least comfortable with, and have been unable to pigeonhole, 'romancists' rather than straightforward novelists.

When Beckett was asked if he minded being placed in the company of Rabelais, Swift, Fielding and Sterne, he replied, in his characteristically lapidary manner, 'No'.[71] Other influences, such as Marivaux, Cervantes and Voltaire have been suggested. Obviously, with such a wide range of reference, we need to precisely locate where Beckett may be in debt to these writers. Marivaux (and Furetière) have already been discussed elsewhere;[72] Voltaire provided the title of one of Beckett's earliest works;[73] Fielding is fairly easily discernible behind some of the phrases in *More Pricks than Kicks*;[74] the painter in *Don Quixote* proves an essential part of Beckett's argument in one of Beckett's pieces of art criticism.[75] Any really Rabelaisian influence remains to be proven; at present the case seems to rest on the disputed fifth part of *Gargantua and Pantagruel*[76] and a writer who 'participates in the immediate effects of his humour'[77] in a way most people have found attractive but which tells us little about Samuel Beckett's own particular way of laughing. Cervantes provides a useful point of reference, as we shall see, but the most important figures for our purposes are Swift, Sterne, Diderot and Joyce.

Swift is, in some ways, the most important of all, a fellow-countryman of Sterne and Beckett whose prose style is a model of clarity and economy. His subject-matter has not always been accepted as healthy, which response would, no doubt, have satisfied to the full his desire to get under complacent skins. As far as Swift was concerned, as man developed, there was increasingly little commerce between the body that defecates and the mind that proposes, and he was so resolute in his refusal to be comforted (least of all by his own imaginings) that they finally parted company for good, the body helpless in the face of a mind that could only find its image in God: 'I am that I am.' Although in his most popular works Swift remains outside his characters, using them as the stalking-horse from behind which he can send forth his satiric shafts, his greatest ironic performances (such as *A Modest Proposal*) offer so many façades that we cannot take up any fixed position when faced with them. We are jostled out of our conventional complacencies, and dramatically involved in the conditions under examination. The ironic narrator in a work like *Modest Proposal* is crucially implicated in what he thinks himself free of; and we, and the author, are implicated with him, as human beings who have failed each other.

We are made to feel, as dramatically as Ivan Karamazov, that we *are* our brother's keeper. So the blunt instrument of satire is made even more devastating by being refined to the point of sympathy. It is the same kind of thing that happens at the end of *Watt*, where the absurd figure of the eponymous hero is at the mercy of Messrs Gorman, Case and Nolan gaping ahead of themselves at 'nothing in particular' and reiterating stale truisms ridiculously inappropriate to his dilemma:

> All the same, said Mr. Gorman, life isn't such a bad old bugger. . . . When all is said and done, he said.
> Riley's puckaun again, said Mr. Nolan, I can smell him from here.
> And they say there is no God, said Mr. Case.
> All three laughed heartily at this extravagance.[78]

As in Swift, all real communication has long ago ceased, leaving each of them helpless before the contents of their own consciousness, the very process of thinking an alienation and the only dialogue of any account an internal one. Swift, who counted 'finie la rigolade' ('let the farce be done with') among his mottoes, would surely have been very impressed with this.

There is nothing of an ironic nature in Sterne and Diderot that Beckett could not have learnt from Swift, but each has a façade of whimsical playfulness that requires to be penetrated (like *Murphy* or *Watt*) before we can see what they are up to, and why they should adopt tactics of concealment. Both Sterne and Diderot admirably exemplify the theory that 'the business of the novelist is not to relate great events, but to make small ones interesting'[79] and make us feel that our life is little more than an 'immense agglomeration of trifles'.[80] Beckett is particularly attracted to this approach because it provides him with a bulwark of substance to set against his continuing sense of transience, and because it satisfies the materialist side of his nature, which is precisely what makes him so sensitive to the world of random contingency Sterne creates in *Tristram Shandy*. Faced with such a world, Beckett tends to adopt the approach of Diderot's fatalist Jacques: '[I tried] to make fun of everything . . . [so as to be] master of myself.'[81] It is the only defence we have when we are 'equally foolish in our wishes, in our joy, and in our affliction'.[82] The tradition of the 'wise fool' is still operating here (as it still is in Dostoievsky) but the quality of his wisdom, and the quality of his foolishness, have dramatically changed and they are in a new and unsettling relationship one to another. The narrator who in Swift was revealed to be part of the scene he was abstracting himself from (for purposes of criticism) is now even more to the front of the stage. Or rather, he is making a lot of very dishonest gestures, to explain why he can no longer be master of ceremonies: 'What I know on the subject of Mr. Knott, and of all that touched Mr. Knott, and on the subject of Watt, and of all that touched Watt, came from Watt, and Watt alone.'[83] Sam has obviously been reading *Jacques le fataliste*: 'All I tell you here, reader, I have from Jacques.'[84] The jester is at last revealed to be running the show; no wonder the element of distortion has increased. But what happens when it reaches its apogee?

'I have spent two unforgettable days of which nothing will ever be known', says Malone,[85] who claims to have lost his pencil; 'there is at this point a truly lamentable lacuna', says Diderot,[86] posing as the editor of the papers in front of him. There are lacunae in Swift, expressive of the emptiness of minds that go beyond their proper station. But there is something more terrifying about the lacunae of Malone and Diderot, or the blank page in *Tristram Shandy*, commemorating Yorick's death and yet like a black hole sucking us all into the domain of death. Faced with an abyss of this kind, the jester tries desperately to distract us, making us laugh at Moran's painful knee (inherited from Jacques), at the smutty joke (Moran's description of Turdy and Bally; Diderot's Bogger country and the cabinetmaker Balls), and at the absurdity of language (Sam's maddening repetitions in *Watt*; Jacques beginning a whole series of sentences with 'The fact is. . . .'). Most seductive of all, perhaps, is the distraction of philosophizing. There is an unembarrassed willingness to philosophize in Beckett's people, the kind of thing one finds in Bruno's play *Il Candelaio*, or in the dialogues of *Jacques le fataliste*:

Jacques	When I cry, I often find I am stupid.
The Master	And when you laugh?
Jacques	I find I am still stupid.[87]

The pained recognition that life has all been a game, that we will without doing and do without willing, that stories never end and are difficult to start, and that those who listen never understand those who speak, is why in the modern picaresque[88] – Beckett's *Mercier and Camier*, Flaubert's *Bouvard et Pécuchet* – the traditional reversal of roles (wise servant, foolish master) has ceased to matter. Lucky, though granted the wise fool's inalienable privilege of philosophizing, is no luckier than Pozzo.

We are faced then, here, with a scepticism which affects the physiognomy of the work of art, by fragmenting the external form, by constantly adverting to the novel's fictional status, and by treating as process what is more often considered product. These three effects are all manifestations of the same spirit, and difficult to separate. The frequent appearance of the author as puppet-master (as in Thackeray's *Vanity Fair*, or Beckett's *Murphy*), in bringing about the second of these aims, necessarily also brings about the first and contrives to suggest the third. And once we have been reminded of the semi-parasitic nature of all fictions, by an author whose puppets are a compound of previous stereotypes that have succeeded and failed, we find that the work constantly draws our attention away to something outside itself, thereby perpetuating the disjunction between fictional realism and lived reality, and 'opening up' the 'closed' form of the book that is being read. The greatest works compensate for this by offering us glorious paradoxes, encompassing a larger number of possible meanings than quotidian reality could ever do. *Don Quixote* is the great chivalric romance at the same time as being a critique of all romances ever;[89] *Candide* is a great philosophical tale at the same time as being a (very unphilosophical) critique of philosophy; Swift's *Tale of a Tub* and Rabelais's great work are monuments of learning even when the most sparkling attacks against learning are being mounted; Sterne's *Tristram Shandy* is at one and the same time a critical meditation on the nature of fiction, a sentimental story of rare excellence, and a brilliant send-up of all activities whatsoever.

All these works openly acknowledge that they are artifacts; they are, in the fullest possible sense, literary. The apotheosis of the whole tradition is, of course, Joyce's *Ulysses*, which provides the key by which to read it, as well as the locked door and enormous room which the first-time reader encounters. In *Ulysses* the ultimate factitiousness masquerades as the ultimate realism – and not, as in Sterne and Cervantes, the other way round. In other words, where Sterne and Cervantes are in the end orientated towards the real (like Rabelais and Voltaire), Joyce, with the whole weight of symbolist thinking behind him and the curious aesthetic of Aquinas in front of him, is in the end orientated towards the art-work as in some way a primary fact of reality, prior to reality (because it is self-contained) and strictly controllable (because it can be arbitrarily stopped at any point in time), which reality is not. Swift and Sterne, with their elaborate paraphernalia of footnotes, lacunae and citations, recognize this fact but, for different reasons, turn their backs on it. Swift's *Tale* is a dramatization of the failed book, the book that requires reality to complete it; *Ulysses* is a dramatization of the successful book. Beckett is closer to Swift, as we see from his celebrated account of Joyce: 'The more Joyce knew, the more he could. . . . I'm working with ignorance, impotence.'[90] For this reason Joyce, who seemed able to make the artifact contain the whole of reality, though a masterly writer in Beckett's eyes, could only be a negative influence, something to admire, without attempting to emulate. In this respect, 'Dream of Fair to Middling Women', for all its occasional sourness and frequent ineptitudes, was a liberating factor. And the practice of Swift and Sterne, who knew that you could not help leaving something out, sanctioned a new fictional approach that could, in Beckett's terms, 'accommodate the mess, without pretending that it is other than it is'.

One of the key issues in making sense of 'the mess' is judging whether things recur; but since it is the very basis of our understanding of the world, it is not surprising that two very different attitudes towards recurrence have been developed. The notion that history repeats itself brought serenity to Plato and Buddha, and a quivering and anxious optimism to Nietzsche; it was the guarantee of spiritual existence for Kierkegaard; it provided Vico with the structure of his argument, and has been explained by such contemporary thinkers as Mircea Eliade as part of a fundamentally regenerative attitude to life. However, Ecclesiastes – one of the earliest, and certainly the most celebrated proponent of the darker side – found nothing new under the sun, and the first sentence of *Murphy* (for all its humour) indicates that Beckett shares his troubled *ennui* rather than the melioristic accounts of the alternative tradition. When it comes to the question of successive incarnations (which, given Beckett's compulsions, it must), Beckett is close to the position of Matthew Arnold in 'Empedocles on Etna' – that 'each succeeding age in which we are born . . . will make ourselves harder to be discerned'.[91] With a conclusion like this only a kind of ultimate death (what Beckett calls 'fully certified death'),[92] the end of time, offers any hope of solace, not a death from which one may awake to haunt reality again (like the ghosts of Hardy) but a permanent death which is real rest at last. And the voice that survives beyond death in *The Unnamable*, *Play* and *Not I* renders even this rest illusory.

The composer of fictional histories, in coming to terms with such ideas, can choose broadly speaking, one of two extreme solutions:[93] the articulation of undifferentiated flux in which items randomly recur, or the construction of a static world by means of a circularity of structure. Joyce, in *Ulysses* (very much concerned with problems of time and history), straddles the two: the stream of consciousness provides the flux, while the dominance of detail, and the recurrence of phrase and incident provide the stasis. Beckett also tries both. A circular structure frequently hovers behind his work as a possibility; but in *Watt*, *Molloy* and *How it is*, and even in *Play*, the circle is always ultimately a broken one, as with the picture in Erskine's room.[94] In *The Unnamable* and *How it is* the pressure of details is so great and the narratorial consciousness so subject to change of direction, that the dominant feeling is one of painfully linear development into a future of unrelieved novelty.

This does not, however, mean that Beckett gets close to achieving a truly total history. It was possible for Joyce because he was 'omniscient' and 'omnipotent'; he was very much the God of his creation, however indifferent he pretended to be. Beckett longs to do the same but, as the voice of *How it is* says, 'of our total life it states only three-quarters'.[95] This recognition comes at the end of over twenty years' striving, the culmination of which, *The Unnamable*, represented nothing less than an attempt so to disorientate the reader's normal categories of perception that he can do nothing but accept the undifferentiated reality the Unnamable offers. Given that 'when all sequence comes to an end, time comes to an end',[96] the composition of fictional histories can only be reduced to arranging elements that are 'wholly present at every moment'.[97] This has meant, in practice, the removal of those moments of flashback and prophecy that enabled us to keep our bearings in *How it is*. In his most recent works Beckett has tried to achieve comprehensiveness and remain within the measurable world of the present. *Imagination Dead Imagine* and *The Lost Ones* portray worlds dominated by an intransigent, if fluctuating, light and 'the historian of a world . . . perpetually flooded with steady light, a world without day or night, month or season, would be able to describe only a more or less complete present'.[98] It is a far cry from Joyce's 'chaffering all-including most farraginous chronicle' *Ulysses*.[99] But it has the attraction of being part of the eminently human desire to situate oneself in a world of objects.

What is certain is that abstraction cannot, single-handed, provide the answer; the 'reality' of the writer (however uncertain it may be) will inevitably involve realism of a kind.[100] 'The natural compensation for an abyss of solipsism is a mountain of realism', wrote Herbert Read in 1936,[101] just before he was instrumental in getting *Murphy* accepted by Routledge. With certain modifications throughout his career, this has been Beckett's way. But he has always been careful to distinguish his own work from what he calls the 'literature of notations'; and this accounts for his dislike of the 'plane psychology'[102] of Balzac ('why call a distillation of Euclid and Perrault *Scenes from Life*? Why *human* comedy?')[103] and his relative indifference to the *nouveau roman* as epitomized by Alain Robbe-Grillet. The literature of notations has difficulty in accommodating the irrational, and its 'narratorial trajectory' is 'more like a respectable parabola [than] the chart of an ague'.[104] It also effectively postulates that man and object live different lives; while it is true that in both Balzac and Dickens people are characterized by the possessions among which they live (Sol Gills in *Dombey and Son* is a representative example and the best example of all is perhaps Madame Vauquer at the beginning of Balzac's *Old Goriot*), they remain in two separate worlds, cut off and unable to interpenetrate. Only in Gogol (whose importance the surrealists quickly realized) does this interpenetration occur. In Gogol, 'human beings are not so much characterized as usurped by their possessions';[105] and not simply by their possessions, but also by the phenomena of atmosphere, weather, etc., that surround them. Nineteenth-century fiction is constantly striving to attain what Beckett calls, in the appendix to *Watt*, a 'soul-landscape',[106] in which subject and object imperceptibly merge. Baudelaire's Paris, Dickens's fog, Whistler's seascapes – all these are part of a striving for what may ultimately be unattainable. Our puzzled responses to works like *The Trial* and *Watt* suggest that the 'soul-landscape' has at last been partly achieved. This is one reason why *Watt* is a distinct advance on *Murphy*; the World's End area of Chelsea (aptly named, but almost too aptly), Brewery Road and Murphy's garret move gradually away from 'soul-landscape' – despite (or because of) the notational realism. It is, as Mr Kelly would say, too 'beastly circumstantial'.[107] The opening scene of *Watt* takes place around Dublin's Harcourt Street Station, but it is never actually itemized as such, and it could be anywhere. The Unnamable's 'island' is doubtless Ireland, and the Paris abattoirs *are* in the rue Brançion, but they are more like fragmentary reminders of reality than realities established by the book. Text Six of the *Texts for Nothing* mentions London's Glass-house Street, Text Seven the South-Eastern Railway terminus (Victoria, from which one catches boat-trains to Paris?), Text Eight the place de la République and the rue d'Assas – but they are all less compelling than the courtrooms of the mind and the generalized countryside of bogs out of which they loom. The narrator of *How it is* speaks of a racecourse which is probably (as in *Watt*) the Leopardstown course Beckett's father often visited, but otherwise, in his desperate plight, he is content with other people's places, places he has read about (Klopstock's Altona, etc.). This abandonment of a known, shared, specified reality is part of the erosion of contour whose intellectual sources we have already examined. But the 'mountain of realism' remains: in Molloy's gallery of objects, in Malone's possessions (some inherited from Molloy), even in *How it is*, where a sardine tin and a sack assume extraordinary importance. We find this reflected in his other interests. It is Joyce's particularization that he particularly admired in *Finnegans Wake*.[108] It is the lack of particularization that he dislikes in the 'abstractors of quintessence' (a phrase from Rabelais applied to Moholy-Nagy, etc.)[109] and which makes him unable to swallow Kandinsky's 'liberation from the object'.[110] It is well worth reiterating that it is partly Proust's clear-sightedness that makes him attractive to Beckett: 'is it not precisely this conflict between intervention and quietism, only rarely to be resolved through the uncontrollable agency of unconscious memory, and its statement without the plausible frills, that constitute the essence of Proust's originality?'[111]

It is, perhaps, Beckett's own attention to detail which makes us think of Dickens. The influence of Dickens on Beckett is something that most readers feel but find difficult to analyse. As early as 1938 Dylan Thomas found a Dickensian tone in *Murphy*,[112] and there is clearly much to support this opinion. The pseudo-nineteenth-century narrative omnipotence – 'Let us take Time that old fornicator . . . by such few sad short hairs as he has'[113] – and the admission that some of the characters are 'puppets'[114] are perhaps the most striking. But Beckett also mocks the omniscience of David Copperfield in a story in *More Pricks than Kicks* by adding a trenchant phrase to David's leisurely meditations: 'This may be premature. We have set it down too soon perhaps. Still, let it bloody well stand.'[115] On the other hand, Beckett praises *Great Expectations* in his early essay on Joyce, and admitted to me that he once knew the passage in question, with its ominous and morose repetitive phrases, off by heart.[116] Certain elements in Dickens seem to coincide with Beckett's own obsessions: the interest in dens where one can withdraw from the cruel world, the acute sensitivity to cruelty in man's dealing with his fellow-men and in his exploitation of animals, the fascination with eccentricity and madness. Mr Dick has a kite like Mr Kelly, the conception of whom is clearly based on the Smallweeds in *Bleak House*; Captain Cuttle relies on his hat as much as Vladimir. The child Jo ('moving on, and moving on, ever since I was born')[117] and the narrator of 'From an Abandoned Work' ('I have never been on my way anywhere, but simply on my way')[118] have faced the essential randomness of existence and both are tormented by such unanswerable questions that they can only reply 'I don't know'. Consequently they live on a level not far removed from the animal, whether it be the blinking horn owl that presides over the unwisdom of Doctor's Commons (compare *The Unnamable*)[119] or Dora's little black dog that David fancies he is eating – surely the scene that lies behind the 'love-idyll' of *How it is* and *Krapp*. The transformation from human to animal is signalled by the application of bestial imagery: Pozzo persistently calls Lucky 'pig', an appellation also found in chapter 1 of *Little Dorrit*, a novel containing a man walking backwards (compare *Watt*) and a garrulous woman (compare Winnie in *Happy Days*). Dickens does not go so far as to suggest that the Book of Job exhibits a greater religious sense in man than in God,[120] but he prepares the way for a writer like Beckett to suggest precisely that. And it is easy to forget that Dickens, despite his affection for home and beauty, was afflicted with a specifically modern inability to understand existence: 'the greatest mystery in all the earth to me, is how or why the world was tolerated by its Creator, through the good old days, and wasn't dashed to fragments.'[121]

In practice, of course, realism, even 'romantic realism', has difficulty in dealing with the fantastic and the absurd. As its very name implies, it is at base alien to imagination. And the problem of being has always been squarely bound up with the question of imagination. Don Quixote, in his madness, claims to be able to be anyone he wishes. But Cervantes makes him an isolated figure, an eccentric who hovers above, but is eventually returned to, the world of the sane. By the time of Rimbaud, the imagination and the madman have become irrepressibly pre-eminent. 'To every being', says Rimbaud in *A Season in Hell*, 'several *other* lives seemed to me due.'[122] Valéry later took this idea a step further: 'if each man were not able to live a number of other lives besides his own, he would not be able to live his own life' ('Poetry and Abstract Thought').[123] Yeats's theory of masks partly derives from such a feeling; as Ellmann says, 'the masks include all the differences between one's own and other people's conception of one's personality. To be conscious of the discrepancy which makes a mask of this sort is to look at oneself as if one were somebody else.'[124] In Yeats's case, the mask idea was reinforced by acquaintance with the Japanese Noh tradition, and is an objectification, a reification, of Yeats's theory of the self and the anti-self. The actor is only an actor; the mask conceals the human identity beneath. At the same time the human identity is more fully revealed. As Artaud said: '[masks] mould their surroundings to their own image and make themselves a palace out of the space around them . . . the author has turned his characters inside out and put their soul on the outside: the soul is a tic.'[125] Pirandello does not need to resort to such a device because his situations are less minimal, his environments more bourgeois, his aims more to shock the audience into thinking rather than feeling. Beckett agrees with this line of thought, but seeks a different way of dealing with it.

In the growing uncertainty experienced in the early years of the century, the mask notion gets extended to cover the poetic text itself. 'Every word', wrote Valéry in his celebrated essay 'Man and the Sea Shell', 'covers and masks a well so bottomless that the questions you toss into it arouse no more than an echo.'[126] Artaud, in *The Theatre and its Double* (the very title of which suggests the relevance of the mask idea), generalizes this: 'True expression hides what it makes manifest.'[127] Some years before Maeterlinck had taken the idea to what might be considered its most extreme position:

> indeed the only words that count in the play are those that at
> first seemed useless, for it is therein that the essence lies. Side
> by side with the necessary dialogue will you almost always
> find another dialogue that seems superfluous; but examine it
> carefully, and it will be borne home to you that this is the
> only one that the soul can listen to profoundly, for here alone
> is it the soul that is being addressed.[128]

It is no surprise to find that in the same essay Maeterlinck explored the idea of a 'static' theatre which Yeats, and later Beckett, were to develop.

The self/anti-self, text/anti-text obsession was given greater range by Pound (*Personae*, 1909) and Eliot (*Prufrock and Other Observations*, 1917). The fool is no longer wise, as he had been in the Renaissance (in Erasmus, Shakespeare, etc.); the irony is no longer externally directed, reflecting back on outsiders. The irony now is self-reflexive, turned inwards, irony on irony, in a wilderness of mirrors. The absurd fool extended to the popular imagination in the 1920s through the new art form of cinema, and there was a resurgence of interest in clowns. Chaplin, Keaton and Langdon relied in their soundless world on the irreducible stand-by of the clown – gesture; the Russian pair Bim and Bom (whose names appear in *How it is*) and the Swiss clown Grock (whose tag, 'Nit m-ö-ö-öglich', used in *More Pricks*,[129] paradoxically asserted his essential seriousness) were at the height of their fame.

If there is something very French in finding pantomime so appealing,[130] there is something irrepressibly Irish in an attempt to make dramatic capital out of characters that do not move[131] or whose gestures are flagrantly at odds with what they say. Beckett's drama seems static partly because it is not simply tragic or comic, but rather constantly hovering, threatening to spill over one way, but constantly pulled up short by a contrary movement. There are good historical reasons for this. The nineteenth century, like the eighteenth, moved away from tragedy. But whereas the eighteenth-century laugh was (even in Swift) the laugh of reason,[132] the laughter of the nineteenth century was always close to unreason. Kierkegaard (in 1844, in *Either/Or*) put forward the view that 'the entire tendency of the age is in the direction of the comic'[133] and in *Repetition* recommended the genre of farce.[134] Mallarmé confirmed Kierkegaard's thesis: 'Every writer tends to be a humorist.'[135] Baudelaire, in his essay 'On the Essence of Laughter', unconsciously echoed a Kierkegaard title, when he spoke of the sage laughing, in 'fear and trembling', of laughter as a 'symptom of failing' betokening 'an infinite grandeur and infinite misery'.[136] Bergson wrote a lengthy essay on the subject which has often been used by Beckett commentators,[137] but it is in the scattered remarks of a thinker like Nietzsche that the increasing insecurity begins to be felt. 'I have consecrated laughter,' says Zarathustra, 'but not a single soul have I found strong enough to join me.'[138] As the century drew to a close, Strindberg, in *Inferno*, underlined the general tendency: 'Perhaps in the depth of our souls there lurks a shadowy consciousness that everything down here is all humbug, a masquerade, a mere pretence . . . nothing but a huge bad joke.'[139] 'Christ never laughed', Moran tells Father Ambrose, quoting Baudelaire. But the gods? What if they do? Strindberg is supported by Yeats in *The King's Threshold* when he speaks of 'God's laughter at the shattering world'.[140] In such a state of affairs, it is no surprise to find Mauthner, a philosopher, in a lengthy and fundamentally serious work, proposing that 'pure critique is logically but an articulated laughter'.[141]

Belacqua, prefers Democritus to Heraclitus,[142] the laughing philosopher to the weeping, as we learn from the story 'Yellow' in *More Pricks than Kicks*: 'At this crucial point the good God came to his assistance with a phrase from the paradox of Donne: Now among our wise men, I doubt not but many would be found, who would laugh at Heraclitus weeping, none which would weep at Democritus laughing.' Donne's paradox is hedged round with irony at the expense of optimists and sages, and Beckett's own development of the idea is fairly oblique:

> It is true that he did not care for these black and white
> alternatives as a rule. Indeed he even went so far as to hazard
> a little paradox on his own account, to the effect that between

F

contraries no alternation was possible [this, of course, strikes a blow against the mysticism of Bruno described in the essay on 'Work in Progress']. But was it the moment to be nice?[143]

Belacqua finally decides in Democritus' favour, but there are, of course, various ways of following Democritus. While Jarry explored the realms of farce (in the notorious *Ubu Roi*), Chekhov devoted himself to the minutiæ and tedium of country lives shattered by suicides and dominated by hopeless aspirations towards escape. *The Cherry Orchard*, a 'comedy', ends with a sick old man locked up and forgotten in an abandoned house. At such a moment one remembers that Gautier described comedy as a 'logic of the absurd'[144] and begins to understand why Chekhov's plays have increasingly come to be seen as an important precondition to the comprehension of the 'absurd'. Beckett is often close to Chekhov, but develops both the remorselessness and the frivolity and becomes, in Donne's words, 'a wise man that hee knowes at what to laugh, and a valiant man that he dares laugh'[145] – behind the second half of which lurks the figure of modern man, in fear and trembling, in search of a soul.

Joyce, in his Paris notebook, called comedy 'the perfect manner in art',[146] but he was a writer who tended to see things clearly and it is no surprise that the more querulous Beckett works in tragi-comedy. Unamuno's *Tragic Sense of Life* (1912) contains one of the classic accounts of the genre: 'the comic, the irrational tragedy is the tragedy of suffering caused by ridicule and contempt . . . the most tragic character would be that of a Morgutte of the inner man, who like the Morgutte of Pulci, should die of laughter, but of laughter at himself.'[147] Kierkegaard is suspicious even of this; and like him, like Belacqua indeed, Beckett is not attracted by elegant formulations: 'Let us', as he says to Duthuit, 'for once be foolish enough not to turn tail.'[148] 'All that matters', he told a company of actors, 'is the laugh and the tear',[149] and in writing his plays, he has realized Socrates' intuition at the end of *The Symposium* that, in the last analysis, they are the same. As Belacqua says, 'It came to the same thing in the end.'[150]

It is no surprise to find these ideas mirrored in the most challenging dramatic writing of the period, the theatre of Ibsen, Strindberg and Chekhov, and also in less important but still substantial writers like Maeterlinck and Pirandello. All, in their various ways, made important preliminary discoveries that enabled Beckett to write as he does. As a young man, he saw at the Abbey Theatre performances of *A Doll's House* and *An Enemy of the People*, but it was less these 'social' plays than the fantasy play *Peer Gynt* which made the deepest impression. Peer's importance resides in the fact that he is more unequivocally engaged on a quest for identity than, say, Raphael in Balzac's *Peau de Chagrin*; along with this goes an elemental landscape which was to influence the later expressionist drama. The expressionists felt drawn towards a representative characterization that would destroy the stereotypes of melodrama but which would still summon up quickly areas of experience when set against each other in dramatic juxtaposition. Beckett does not, like the expressionists, use labels like 'the Stranger', and he is at all times at pains to stress the individual sufferings of his characters. However, at the same time, as Vladimir says, 'all mankind is us, whether we like it or not'[151] – the actors on stage are surrogates, vicarious existers on our behalf. We are not all tramps, we are not all Peers, but when Peer meets the tramp in Act 5, they are the two sides of our predicament face to face. *Peer Gynt*, of course, combines seriousness and mockery in a way that is strongly prophetic of the modern condition as well as being part of the prevailing tendency in the nineteenth century towards tragi-comedy. Seriousness of theme seems to be constantly undermined by a capriciously fluid form, and when Peer recognizes that his fabular existence prevents him dying in the middle of Act 5, he is not far removed from Beckett's Clov who claims it is only the dialogue that keeps him where he is. Other Gyntian elements that Beckett employs are the sense of a gradually encroaching death, the anguished cry for a witness to selfhood, and Peer's persistent articulation of constriction and meaningless wandering ('Backward or forward, it's just as far. Out or in, it's just as narrow'). 'Being oneself means killing one's self', says the Boyg, and seems, from our perspective in time, to virtually supply the premise for the drama that followed. The Boyg presents the ways Peer can organize his experience: either he can accept resignedly the wisdom of the higher powers, or he can persist in fruitlessly peeling an onion which even at the centre reveals nothing but further layers.[152] Beckett's characters adopt the manner of the first option, without confidence in the matter that makes sense of it – they are resigned, but doubt the existence of the Higher Being that could soften their resignation. At the same time they reserve all their energies for pursuing the second way. As Beckett puts it in *Proust*: 'the heart of the cauliflower or the ideal core of the onion ... represent a more appropriate tribute to the labours of poetical excavation than the crown of bay.'[153] The excavation, in Ibsen, leads to a horrific awakening: we see the irreparable, we see that we have never lived. And Peer's assertion of self becomes in John Gabriel Borkman the preliminary to crime; being becomes the crime of crimes that only death can expiate. And even then the *pax vobiscum* echoes equivocally through the avalanche[154] in a dénouement that is barely stageable, which threatens to break the artistic form and suffocate us all.

Strindberg extends the dramatic territory thus mapped out, by altering the signposts and revealing a little more of the geological strata. From the unnamed Captain of *The Father* (1887) to the whole gallery of elemental figures that people the Damascus trilogy (1898) is the major step from Naturalism to Expressionism. As the 'real' personality gets reduced, so does the dramatic paraphernalia designed to create the illusion of life. Most importantly, perhaps, it is the dialogue that is affected. It becomes portentously formal, and 'wanders about, providing itself with material which is afterwards worked up, admitted, repeated, developed, and built up, like the theme in a musical composition';[155] Beckett has explicitly said that he is searching for 'the kind of form that you find in music, for example, where themes recur'.[156] Strindberg stresses other areas of particular interest to students of Beckett: the monologue, the mime and the ballet.

Strindberg explored the first of these in *The Stronger*, where, as in Beckett's *Not I*, or Cocteau's *Voix Humaine* (unforgettably reduced to the level of an 'unnecessary banality' by Beckett in his *Proust* essay)[157] only one character speaks throughout. Experience of the monodrama suggests that the irreducible amount of information that has got to be got across, despite the absence of dialogue, strains credibility; it is, in Donne's phrase, a 'dialogue of one'[158] in which we feel throughout the lack of a second speaker. The physical presence – the hooded figure in *Not I*, for example – softens the disjointedness, but at the expense of constantly suggesting a relationship that can never be properly articulated. The approach to monologue that stops short (*Happy Days*, for instance) seems to generalize the emotion more successfully.

Mime and ballet were used only sparingly by Strindberg, and with little success. Beckett, of course, experimented with mime fairly early in his dramatic career, and focused in *Godot* on the blasted ballet of Lucky, tottering round the stage like one of Yeats's Noh dancers crippled by suffering. Beckett has been careful to distinguish his mimes from the work of such artists as Marcel Marceau where the form is, in his opinion, being stretched to say things that language can say much better.

Of course, the light of potential salvation at the end of *Road to Damascus* is easier to bear than the harrowing light of Beckett's *Play*,[159] and there is a deadness and flatness about the dialogue of

Road to Damascus that makes it more moving to read than to see. Chekhov harnesses this deadness, and humanizes the resignation by creating tragi-comedy that is neither fantastic like *Peer Gynt* nor solemn like the Damascus trilogy. Increasingly, it has come to be realized that Chekhov's plays, punctuated by pauses and weighed down with the intolerable meaninglessness of existence, are as important to an understanding of the absurd drama as the extravaganzas of Jarry. Artaud's 'theatre of cruelty', aside from its experimental trappings, is, in fact, simply a writing large of the cruelty we find in Ibsen, Strindberg and Chekhov. In Chekhov, as later in Beckett, the cruelty is made bearable (without being sentimentalized) by generating an atmosphere that leaves one at the end of the play feeling as if the characters are merely one step farther along a course consigned to entropy.

The resigned tone of Beckettian exchanges may well, however, owe more to Maeterlinck than to Chekhov. Beckett has spoken very highly of Maeterlinck's *Les Aveugles* (1890), and *Intérieur* (1894; a chamber play much like those Strindberg was to write for the Intimate Theatre of Stockholm) was an important influence on Yeats's *Purgatory* which Beckett is known to admire. Another of Maeterlinck's symbolist dramas *L'Intruse* (1890) is a *drame d'attente* much as *Godot* is, with this difference: Godot arrives, in the form of Death.[160] The exchanges are often strikingly Beckettian in the curious disjointedness of monologue juxtaposed against monologue, uttered with the deadness of resignation in the futility of waiting:

The Uncle   What shall we do while we are waiting?
The Grandfather Waiting for what?
The Uncle   Waiting for our sister.[161]

Vitality only seems to enter the play when the characters speculate, in their isolated way, on general truths:

The Father He is like all blind people.
The Uncle They think too much.
The Father They have too much time to spare. . . .
The Uncle Not to know where one is, not to know where one
              has come from, not to know whither one is going,
              not to be able to distinguish midday from midnight,
              or summer from winter – and always darkness,
              darkness! I would rather not live.[162]

At one point in the play, the triviality of dialogue is set in sharp relief by a truly Beckettian ironic comment:

The Grandfather	She has come in?
The Father	Who?
The Grandfather	The servant.
The Father	No, she has gone downstairs.
The Grandfather	I thought that she was sitting at the table.
The Uncle	The servant.
The Grandfather	Yes.
The Uncle	That would complete one's happiness.[163]

At the climax of the play, the remorselessness of death, the inefficacy of action, the indifference of nature and the helplessness of aspiration come together in what Mario Praz has described as Maeterlinck's 'stammering mannerism',[164] a mannerism particularly dependent (as Beckett's is) on the adroit use of silences – one of the things in Maeterlinck that particularly impressed Yeats. It is as well to be aware, when estimating Beckett's dramatic achievement, that Maeterlinck's somewhat laboured solemnity and over-stylized weightiness petered out in fantasies, fairy tales and philosophizing. Beckett pursues a more refined course, but illustrates the acuteness of Arthur Symons's 1928 opinion, that 'The dramatist of the future will have more to learn from Maeterlinck than from any other playwright of our time'.[165]

Yeats certainly learnt from Maeterlinck, but he was always concerned not to detract from the Irishness of his subject-matter. His interest in Irish myth never waned (whereas Beckett's never began). 'Ireland', Yeats wrote, 'is not the home of buffoonery . . . but the home of an ancient idealism.'[166] Throughout his dramatic work, however, Yeats's analysis of heroism is qualified by his awareness of buffoonery. Blind Man and Fool (the simplicity is balladic rather than expressionist) begin and end in *On Baile's Strand*, the Old Man's sadness opens *The Death of Cuchulain*, and *Purgatory* and *The Cat and the Moon* concentrate almost exclusively on the more sordid aspects of reality. The fascination with eternal recurrence and crime in *Purgatory*, with disease, redemption and cruelty in *The Cat and the Moon* – these are themes that obsess Beckett also. 'Where there are no words there is less to spoil', says the Old Man at the beginning of *The Death of Cuchulain*. His strange mixture of serene remoteness and distracted proximity is curiously prophetic of such Beckett plays as *Krapp's Last Tape* and *Embers*. The formal, statuesque quality of Yeats's versions of Sophocles (which Beckett saw at the Abbey), together with the prevailing sadness of the plays, must have left a deep impression on him.

The second important figure in the Irish dramatic renaissance,

J. M. Synge, recognized, as Yeats did not, the primacy of buffoonery over idealism. Synge stresses this in the famous preface to *The Tinker's Wedding* and the subsequent play employs all the time-honoured tricks of irony and reversal of expectation. The elemental landscape of this play (announcing the even more severely reduced landscapes of Yeats and Beckett) reappears in *The Well of the Saints*, which concentrates on the themes of fantasy, imagination and freedom later to combine in *The Playboy*. In this play, as in Yeats's *Cat and the Moon*, blindness and suffering have an equivocal status: the ancient irony that the blind see more than us is qualified by the recovery of sight which leads directly to the recognition of ugliness. With the return of blindness, only death lies ahead for the protagonists.

Death – in its aspect of murder – dominates *The Playboy*, whose son-killing-the-father motif is the exact reverse of the father-killing-the-son idea that Yeats used in *Purgatory*. Though Beckett was impressed by Synge's play, the latter, exemplifying Yeats's idea of the 'curse of generation', is much closer to Beckett. Synge toyed with the idea of confronting Rabelais and Thomas à Kempis, but the play was never completed. He is perhaps closer to the first, whereas Beckett oscillates between the two.

Where O'Casey is concerned, it is clear that Beckett (as when he speaks about other artists) exaggerates the qualities which coincide with his own interests. In a 1934 review of O'Casey's one-act plays, Beckett praised O'Casey for discerning 'the principle of disintegration in even the most complacent solidities . . . mind and world come asunder in irreparable dissociation'.[167] There are indeed moments in O'Casey where disintegration is dominant – but these are moments only and can hardly be applied to the plays as wholes. O'Casey's fundamental position was revealed in his Communism, and in his dismissal of all modern dramatists because of their lack of optimism. He excepted Beckett from this judgment because of the 'poetry' in his plays, but the fact that he could isolate this quality at all is symptomatic of his whole position. The cyclic form of *Juno*, *The Plough and the Stars* and *The Silver Tassie* is far removed from the cyclic form of *Godot* or *Endgame*. For O'Casey ultimately puts his trust in history, and for Beckett that is simply one damned thing after another, repeating endlessly through eternity.

Beckett's attitude to Shaw was, as one might expect, lukewarm: 'I wouldn't suggest that G.B.S. is not a great playwright, whatever that is when it's at home. What I would do is give the whole unupsettable apple cart for a sup of the Hawk's Well or the Saints', or a whiff of Juno; to go no further.'[168] In all these plays, we find the 'hushed hate' of Irish melancholy.[169] Beckett inherits the melancholy, but the anatomy is distinctively his own.

Among present-day writers of stature, perhaps only Sartre approaches Beckett in learning and his work is a happy hunting ground for academics simply because his erudition seems to sanction influences from the most unlikely places. My intention has been to counter-balance, by clearly identifying and discussing all the crucial influences, readings of Beckett that are determined to find his 'people' dying gladiators, Rabelaisian abstractors of quintessence, picaresque saints, Kierkegaardian knights of infinite resignation. None of these descriptions is satisfactory on its own, and some of the parallels critics seek are forced and irresponsible; hopefully the account will also suggest, in a *volte face* worthy of the end of *How it is*, that rather than pursuing these lines, we should value his work for its idiosyncratic and individual approach to some of the most complex and unsolved problems of mankind. Although the most frequently invoked names in Beckett criticism are Kafka, Joyce and Proust, he has always been careful to explain how much his works differ from theirs; he is, ultimately, his own man, *sui generis*. He can say, disguised as the narrator of 'From an Abandoned Work', 'I was very quick as a boy, and picked up a lot of hard knowledge'.[170] He can occasionally, like Molloy, regard it as 'useful'.[171] But the most telling comment of all, for the critic as much as for the writer, is perhaps the Unnamable's: 'I'm a mine of useless knowledge.'[172]

7 Beckett's poetry

In the confessional you betray yourself.

('Le Monde et le pantalon')

De nobis ipsis silemus [Of myself I say nothing],
decidedly that should have been my motto.

(*The Unnamable*)[1]

Although Lawrence Harvey's important book[2] has revealed its
density, Beckett's poetry still seems to lack shape. There may,
ultimately, be something essentially shapeless about a poetic output
that is still rather scattered and inaccessible, but Beckett's work in
other genres suggests that it is indeed (as he told Israel Shenker) the
shape that matters. Any form that has led Beckett to cover his tracks
so carefully – while most of the poems are intimate, they are by and
large intimate at arm's length – deserves serious consideration as a
potential clarifier of his more serious work in other genres. Although,
as with Beckett's other works they benefit from being considered
chronologically, to follow this principle slavishly would put us in a
difficult position bibliographically, since Beckett is conscious, as any
poet must be, that when it comes to a collection of poems, particular
attention must be paid to their arrangement rather than their
provenance. Many poems remain uncollected, and can most easily
be dealt with as a group. But some poems which exist in French and
English versions are collected twice, once in the volume *Poems in
English* (1961) and again in *Poèmes* (1968). The English poems
discussed in the first part of this chapter are all to be found in the
earlier collection (as is 'Saint-Lô', Beckett's only post-war poem
composed originally in English); the French poems are easiest of
access in the later collection. In dealing with the collection-within-a-
collection, *Echo's Bones*, first published separately in 1935, and the
French poems of 1938–9, it would be absurd (and in some cases
impossible) to follow the poems strictly chronologically, and both
are treated as they would reveal themselves to a reader.

Perhaps *Whoroscope* would never have seen the light of day but
for Nancy Cunard's competition.[3] It is certainly one of Beckett's

least effective works in any medium, and Harvey's sixty-page account is as much extravaganza as exegesis. It is the poem of a scholar who requires more space than the hundred lines Nancy Cunard had stipulated to develop situations and insights that are fundamentally novelistic. The notes are as much (and as little) help as Eliot's to *The Waste Land* and were added, at Nancy Cunard's suggestion, presumably in the hope of catching the fag-end of the bandwagon.[4] They contain humorous moments rather more engaging than Eliot's unintentionally lugubrious pleasantries, but suffer from the same faults as the original they set out to parody. Descartes's consciousness (since it is he who speaks) is amusingly revealed to be rather more cluttered than his celebratedly lucid prose style would suggest: he is, by turns, irascible, peremptory, exclamatory, cringing, inquisitorial, self-congratulatory. It is no surprise to find that he shares most of Beckett's interests in the early years: the harmony of music, the distortion of perception by movement, the clash of metaphysical systems, the horror of the body, the quest for a moment of perfect understanding, the pull towards (or exerted by) the *femme fatale*. While one can, without too much difficulty, see these subjects as in some sense related one to another, the recording consciousness remains sublimely unaware of such connections, in a manner that must have appalled the narrator of *Murphy* five years later. Beckett has yet to make the necessary intellectual equations that will allow the carping and exhibitionist side of his mind to rest. The poems in *Echo's Bones*, and the 'jettisoned' poems published in magazines in the early 1930s, reveal how difficult the struggle was.

Of the jettisoned poems 'Yoke of Liberty' is clearly the best and one of Beckett's most successful poetic ventures. He used the paradoxical title (from Dante's *De Monarchia*, II, i) in his first published essay 'Dante . . . Bruno. Vico . . Joyce' to assist his articulation of 'a Necessity that is not Fate . . . a Liberty that is not Chance'.[5] The context here is altogether more intimate, and very delicately handled. There is a Chinese feel about the poem, with no sense of it degenerating into mere *chinoiserie*. Along with other poems of the period, it suggests he had more to learn from Pound than Eliot. The *femme fatale* may have a *fin-de-siècle* languorousness, but it cannot conceal her essentially predatory nature:

She preys wearily
on sensitive wild things
proud to be torn
by the grave couch of her beauty.

This last line makes us retrospectively aware of the physical horror that is lurking behind her compelling features:

> The lips of her desire are grey
> and parted like a silk loop
> threatening
> a slight wanton wound.

What strikes one as particularly impressive here is the lucidity of Beckett's vision, a quality which is in short supply in the early poems. But it is a clearness of vision that is enhanced by the momentary occultation of metaphor, to distance the intimacy, and to render oblique the uncertainty the poet feels. Although the eye is kept firmly on the object, no attempt is made to penetrate an alien psychology. In looking out, the poet reveals his own inner condition:

> But she will die and her snare
> tendered so patiently
> to my tamed watchful sorrow
> will break and hang
> in a pitiful crescent.[6]

The cold purity of a crescent moon above a beloved's grave is made to coalesce with the image of a bird winged by a trap so that it can never fly again, and can only eke out its existence with memories of how well it was 'tendered'. The bitterness coexists with the release of tension.

'From the only poet to a shining whore' is less successful, partly because the simplicity of the Rahab 'shining whore' / Beatrice 'fierce pale flame of doubt' contrast is spoiled by needless complexity at the beginning (giving the poem a sluggishness that the later fluidity makes all the more surprising), and partly by an exclamation that breaks the tone of the discourse, and spoils the sudden personal note sounded in the last line. The disgust at erotic satisfaction ('she foul with the victory / of the bloodless fingers') blends the *puttanina* with the spinelessness of the Saviour. Paralleling this, the satisfactions of the spirit are shown to be equivocal not only for Beatrice and Dante (and Beckett as Dante), but also for God, whose 'sorrow' doubtless derives from his inability to possess the beauty of Beatrice more carnally than even his penetration can guarantee.

Those with the patience to pursue Harvey's annotated texts of 'Hell Crane to Starling', 'Text', 'For Future Reference', and 'Casket of Pralinen for a daughter of a dissipated mandarin' will find that the tendency to equate the erotic with the religious experience[7] issues in a rather unhappy mixture of erudite allusion, hilarious bawdy, embarrassing self-exposure, and whimsical self-criticism. Occasional lines show a genuine lyrical gift:

> What is this that is more
> than the anguish of Beauty
> this gale of pain that was not prepared
> in the eaves of her eyes?
>
> ('Casket of Pralinen', 27–30)[8]

This gift is particularly in evidence at the end of a poem ('Text') where Beckett seems to have resolutely refused to do anything remotely poetic in the accepted sense. The main body of the poem is concerned with the disparity between God's justice and mercy, but the outraged and inflamed sexual imagination of the speaker seem softened as he moves to his climax and buries his being in a final lyrical ejaculation:[9]

> Presumptuous passionate fool come now
> to the sad maimed shades
> and stand cold
> on the cold moon.[10]

The landscape is no less surrealist than that of Shelley's 'Alastor', but unlike that poem, the *liebestod* here is entirely unheroic. The same is true of 'For Future Reference', where the lyricism is again saved for the end, and is very brief. This poem concentrates in a most instructive, but irritatingly allusive, way on the fantasies generated by the mindlessness of sex. The best lines of 'Return to the Vestry' again feature at the end, but this time in a context that is explicitly anti-erotic, as if to provide some solace for the fact that the erotic desire will return before long. The poem contains an allusion to 'Gentle Jesus, meek and mild' which is particularly trenchant:

> Gentle Anteros
> dark and dispassionate
> come a grave snake with peace to my quarry
> and choke my regret
> noble Anteros
> and coil at the door of my quarry tomb
> and span its rim with a luminous awning
> shallow and dim
> as a grey tilt of silk
> filtering sadly
> the weary triumph of morning.
>
> Or mock a duller impurity.[11]

At such moments Beckett's reworking of prose passages from 'Dream' (a technique from which Yeats partly derived his peculiar style) seems definitely worth while. At others it is difficult to see what Beckett is trying to achieve beyond the relief of what Wordsworth called 'a timely utterance'.[12]

Two parody poems deserve notice. The sonnet 'At last I find in my confused soul' reads like one of John Addington Symonds's translations from the sonnets of Michelangelo. Beckett is attracted by the Italian's neo-platonism which suggests to him that terrestrial separation may be replaced by the celestial mystical synthesis in which body and spirit are consumed. The 'syzygetic stars' may derive from Gnosticism.[13] The occasional infelicities of phrase and rhythm seem deliberate, yet there is a fatigue in rhymes and scansion that suggests no formal mode would ever have suited Beckett.

The other parody (of an 'aquatic manner' that we need not associate with any poet in particular) actually surfaced from 'Dream' in *More Pricks than Kicks*. It is recited by a pretentious poet at the party described in 'A Wet Night'.[14] Considered as a serious work, it perhaps requires the 'hitch' in the 'lyrical loinstring' Beckett needlessly applies in 'Casket of Pralinen'. But having said that, it is nevertheless an interesting intellectualization of the significance of the act of sex, carefully arranged to suggest the pattern of entry-tumescence-orgasm-detumescence. The flower imagery is based on that found in Navalis's *Heinrich von Ofterdingen* (also found at the climax of the short story 'Assumption') and like the sonnet discussed above, suggests how very much aware Beckett was of ways to fulfilment that had been found efficacious in the past. From this angle, these two poems seem less like simple parodies than experiments in a lyric mode to which he cannot give credence, despite his desire to do so.

The Goethean origin helps to make clear Beckett's aim in the concentrated poem 'The Vulture' that opens *Echo's Bones*.[15] The interpenetration of subject and object of which Beckett spoke in *Proust* seems here to have been established without too much difficulty. The crushing of 'I' and 'other' into one space has taken place before the poem begins and the theatre of action has become entirely internal. The voracious imagination of the poet stoops (like the Christ of 'Alba' but without his 'fingers of compassion') to disturb the blissfully 'prone' human beings who carry their lives as Jesus carried his cross (only permanently, making meaningless the Servant's suffering). They are 'mocked by a tissue that may not serve' until an apocalypse has translated them back into the chaos from which they came. At this point the poem stops, as if the poet had realized that from the chaos of the opening (where consciousness and world seemed to have been satisfactorily conflated) he can no longer derive solace. It is a conclusion which, standing at the beginning of *Echo's Bones*, casts its melancholy shadow across the volume as a whole, and beyond.

The two 'Enueg' poems cover a wider area. The form is a Provençal one, embodying a personal or general lament or complaint. The first poem traces the peregrinations of the poet after he has left the hospital where his beloved is dying of tuberculosis. The escape into nature is entirely without comfort; by a familiar poetic device the inner torment is projected on to the exterior world:

> [I] toil to the crest of the surge of the steep perilous bridge
> and lapse down blankly under the scream of the hoarding
> round the bright stiff banner of the hoarding
> into a black west
> throttled with clouds

Such is the pressure of the torment that conventional syntactic utterance goes by the board. The effect is to situate dramatically within the poem a fragmented structure analogous to the poet's perception of phenomena:

> Above the mansions the algum trees
> the mountains
> my skull sullenly
> clot of anger
> skewered aloft strangled in the cang of the wind
> bites like a dog against its chastisement.

The concentration on something beyond his own experience, the trivial acts of a gang of workmen, dissipate this tension, and are symptomatic of the mode the poet will ultimately adopt. But before he composes the central section (rather sentimentally portraying the camaraderie from which he is excluded) he swings back to focus, impressionistically, but with the precise skill of a pointillist, on the escape-route he is about to take:

> Then for miles only wind
> and the weals creeping alongside on the water
> and the world opening up to the south
> across a travesty of champaign to the mountains
> and the stillborn evening turning a filthy green

manuring the night fungus
and the mind annulled
wrecked in wind[16]

Here, as often, Beckett may have expected too much of his hypo-
tactic technique; we may feel he has adopted it too easily, even
granting the kind of inner complexity it generates. But it has the
attraction of particularity, following Eliot's 'Rhapsody on a Windy
Night' rather than Yeats's apocalyptic wind.[17]

The central section seems of a different order of particularity, a
particularity that is self-congratulatory in effect if not in aim, and
which has little commerce with the powerful resignation of the end
of the poem:

Blotches of doomed yellow in the pit of the Liffey;
the fingers of the ladders hooked over the parapet,
soliciting;
a slush of vigilant gulls in the grey spew of the sewer.[18]

The best of Beckett's early verse has this compulsive sonority, linked
to a fearless facing of the object. But the quotation from Rimbaud's
'Barbare' reminds us that he is far from the ecstasy of the French
poet, that the 'illumination' has been robbed of its colour. The
bright banner of the hoarding is a token of the persistence of reality
at a time of intense personal difficulty, and the arctic flowers that do
not exist, guaranteeing a super-reality for Rimbaud, only remind
Beckett of how intolerably rooted he is in the real.

'Enueg II' begins by reasserting fourfold that the real *is* real, but
makes more obvious the separation of subject and object. The
concentration of the opening is dissipated by a needlessly arcane
logic and a weak central section where the poet plays Judas. The
colloquial strain Beckett is always juxtaposing with the fundamentally lyrical impulse seems no more successful here than elsewhere,
and the initial conflation of face and world leaves him with nothing
to work on between the two crucial moments:

and the face crumbling shyly
too late to darken the sky . . .

the overtone the face
too late to brighten the sky[19]

Given that Beckett seems to have taken care to arrange the poems
for this collection, it is perhaps not too impressionistic to read this
poem as celebrating the independence of the individual object that

has cut itself off from its environment, liberating the poet and allowing him to go further, to the peak that is 'Alba'.

Harvey's account of this very beautiful poem (which I return to later) is one of his most successful *explications de texte*. It only needs to be reasserted that the remarkable synthesis of a Provençal form, a book on Chinese music, Dante and Beatrice, the woman taken in adultery, and Beckett's own meditation on the nature of art and mystical reality, is achieved without any of the strain we experience elsewhere. The flaccid qualities of other poems give way here to a directness and clarity that is unmistakably optimistic. The kind of integration achieved here (and achieved early, for it was written by 1929) proved difficult to repeat later, under the pressure of tensions that are hardly guessed at here. The 'sheet' is replaced by a world of objects unveiled by the perceiving consciousness under a pitiless sun; the 'bulk' is not apprehended again as 'dead' until a similar clarity returns in the late prose. The possibility of an aesthetic act that shall be 'a statement of itself drawn across the tempest of emblems' proves illusory. But it is only fair to say that the kinds of tensions that provoked Beckett to explore his dramatic and fictional worlds with such irresistible honesty necessitated the abandonment of what *Lessness* calls, nostalgically, 'the blue celeste of poesy', the 'blessed days of blue'.

'Dortmunder' immediately qualifies the optimism of 'Alba'. After claiming that the 'bulk' will be 'dead' and banished, the poet is faced by a prostitute who offers her very physical 'bulk' in opposition to the nullity he has so longed to achieve. Her physicality is especially ironic in view of the transfigured reality she inhabits, and sexual experience seems to involve an exact interchange of roles: 'the glory of her dissolution enlarged in me' involves him once more in the state of quotidian being he had escaped from in 'Alba'. The display of professional expertise ('the eyes black till the plagal[20] east / shall resolve the long night phrase') leaves him coldly aware of himself as the archetypal human representative, 'Habbakuk, mard of all sinners'. But the final gnomic utterance suggests that with the sex act completed, everything good has gone from the world, even if the lack of fuss and the death of the misogynous German philosopher keep the emotion in check:

> Schopenhauer is dead, the bawd
> puts her lute away.[21]

It is worth remembering that the music Beckett makes so much of in *Murphy*, the 'serenade, nocturne, albada' of the 'new life'[22] that one might be tempted to sentimentalize, is no more than copulation with an ex-professional.

The macaronic strain in the two 'Sanies' poems is not simply the result of reading Pound. The titles compare the poems to bloody discharges, and there is little worth salvaging from them. The first, set in the country around Dublin, covers a bicycle ride in which the poet remembers his birth and childhood before spying on lovers who so disgust him that he renounces his assignation with his own girl-friend. The colloquial tone is dominant throughout and the wry interest in the super-reality of the bicycle prepares us for the absurdly inflated 'dauntless nautch-girl' section, and the violent dismissal of her when he confronts her as real.

The second poem explores the Paris experience in a similarly ironic way. The happy land which Andrew Young's hymn locates 'far, far away' turns out to be very precise indeed, the American Bar in the rue Mouffetard that Hemingway later wrote about in *A Moveable Feast*.[23] The structure is less obviously connected with the mechanics of the sexual act, although the linguistic exuberance of the 'cavaletto' suggests some kind of forbidden pleasure that the poet will have to pay for in full. The Eliotic reminiscence, reminding us of how near *Ash Wednesday* is, does so at the cost of reminding us also how much more successful Eliot's organization of material is.

The three 'Serena' poems are, as their troubadour origins lead us to expect, evening poems. Numbers I and III are rooted in realities, the first encapsulating a London walk from the British Museum through London Zoo to Ken Wood, the latter, in keeping with its final injunction, 'keep on the move', follows no strict itinerary. Both are less successful and less imaginative than the central 'Serena II', but both are a product of that side of Beckett that has always wanted to state the simple occurrence of an elemental, isolated, irreducible fact. Hence his cry '[I] curse the day . . . / . . . / I was not born Defoe'; hence his admiration for the *Lettere volanti* of Aretino that are regarded as imperishable records of sixteenth-century reality; hence most of all his concern for Thales and his philosophy that allowed pluralism without denying deity ('all things full of gods'). Thales, according to Aristotle, believed that the soul was 'intermingled in the whole universe'[24] and this perfectly justifies his appearance in the mind of a poet who is seeking to experience the truth of that dictum at the same time as being continually thrust up against the barrier between self and world. The fragmented mode of the 'Enueg' poems and the 'Sanies' is again used, in the vain hope that the mere state-ment of fact, unadorned with metaphor, can somehow establish itself in the poem and rob it of its claim as 'literature'.

'Serena II' explains why there has to be change at all. This 'clonic earth' is 'worse than dream' because the recording poetic consciousness is compelled to articulate itself in metaphor even at the moment of actual perception. 'It is useless to close the eyes', however much reality seems like 'phantoms shuddering out of focus' or the broken chords of a woman pianist, because it is important for the creative artist to maintain a symbiosis, a relationship of relative balance between subject and object, and because the goddess that the poet has taken as his muse is the Earth Mother the ancients took as the source of all. As muse and temptress ('the light randy slut can't be easy') she provides the poet with a Pisgah-sight that he can only record by abandoning his own passivity:

> she took me up on to a watershed
> whence like the rubrics of a childhood
> behold Meath shining through a chink in the hills
> posses of larch there is no going back on
> a rout of tracks and streams fleeing to the sea
> kindergartens of steeples and then the harbour
> like a woman making to cover her breasts
> and left me[25]

Bereft of her presence, however, such lyricism dies. All Beckett can do is philosophize sadly, and give direct utterance to a position he will not supersede for thirty years. The certainty of tone must have struck him even then as ominous:

> with whatever trust of panic we went out
> with so much shall we return[26]

Even the engaging joke cannot hide the fact that the problematics of relationship are the only subject worth the candle:

> there shall be no loss of panic between a man and his dog
> bitch though he be

The conclusion enacts the withdrawal of the poetic mind as it is forced to rest on the bones of Echo, completing the circle that began with the aroused imagination slowly surfacing from the collisions of sleep. Given an aesthetic of balance like this, and a formal control as sensitive as this, it is no surprise that the concentration on reality in 'Serena III' is a failure.

The last three poems of the volume owe their increased resignation to the death of Beckett's father from a heart attack in 1933. None of them are entirely satisfactory, although 'Da tagte es' is Beckett's most accomplished rhyming poem in English. Given the critical effect the events described by the poem are known to have had on Beckett,[27] it is difficult not to find 'Malacoda' a distinct disappointment. The familiar stuttering mode seems no more highly charged than usual, and the simple triadic structure sets up no deep resonances. Beckett's inability at this stage of his poetic career to balance the frivolous and serious is nowhere more clear than here, and the hard-edged clarity is not sufficiently suffused with sadness to convince us that the 'nay' at the end represents any kind of definite rejection. We have only to compare the 'It is not' conclusion to 'Dante and the Lobster'[28] to see how flawed this device is here.

'Da tagte es' reinterprets the crucial awakening moment of Walther von der Vogelweide's[29] *alba*, 'Nemt, frowe disen kranz' in terms of death, where Walther's aim had been to show the perfection of love destroyed by contact with harsh reality. Beckett allows the idea of a lovers' parting to remain behind the image of his father laid in a winding sheet in an open coffin. The major work of dislocation is carried out by the third line, as can be seen by omitting it and rearranging the order of lines:

> the sheet astream in your hand
> and the glass unmisted above your eyes
> redeem the surrogate goodbyes[30]

The ultimate poetic dislocation of discussing and embodying the union of subject and object is resisted here, as in 'Malacoda', as inappropriate. The intense and unspeakable emotional shock wrings the neck of rhetoric without the poet experiencing any of the difficulty encountered in the poems of theorizing.

The final poem 'Echo's Bones' confirms this rejection of rhetoric. The poet has kept 'on the move' as 'Serena III' advised, walking on the earth that was a muse in 'Serena II' but which is now a grave. The decay of her flesh leaves Echo only her bones and her voice, but there is still the jocularity of 'muffled revels' and a breaking wind which sounds distinctly flatulent and which no longer needs to annul the mind (as in 'Enueg I'). The dry mock of the rejected lover of Narcissus is seen to be courageous in so far as it requires commitment on the very perilous ridge between 'sense and nonsense', but foolhardy in so far as the maggots have no problem telling them apart, and eat the bones as a matter of course. Echo's bones are turned to stone and she is left with only her voice. The idea surfaces again in *Embers* thirty years later: 'You will be quite alone with your voice', Ada tells Henry, 'there will be no other voice in the world but yours'.[31] And so the volume of what on first publication were called 'precipitates'[32] closes with a poem of muffled revelry that runs the gauntlet of sense and nonsense dispassionately, 'without fear or favour'. The serene tone of 'Da tagte es' has prepared us for a poem like this, and it is intended to balance the poem with which the volume began. But to say that the 'panic' of 'Serena II' has been surpassed is to indicate at one and the same moment what has been gained and what has been lost.

Two poems in English frame the twelve pre-war poems in French that followed *Echo's Bones*. Both, 'Cascando' especially, indicate that 'panic' could not be kept out for long. But 'Saint-Lô' seems to have brought a steadying influence that enabled Beckett to write the more thoughtful and philosophical French poems of 1946–8.

Coming to 'Cascando' from 'Echo's Bones' one observes how far it is the voice itself which is now being subjected to panic as the only 'trust'. This is announced in the first three lines, where the poet decides to allow the occasion of utterance to lead where it will: 'why not merely the despaired of / occasion of / wordshed'. One compensation is that the subject-matter can be squarely faced, with none of the obliqueness we associate with the more centrifugal poems in *Echo's Bones*. Part of the 'panic' is that the voice is conscious of the sentimentality it had failed to censor in *Echo's Bones*. Hence the devastating irony:

> the hours after you are gone are so leaden
> they will always start dragging too soon
> the grapples clawing blindly the bed of want
> bringing up the bones the old loves
> sockets filled once with eyes like yours[33]

Hence also the insistent attack on anything resembling a cliché, combined with the pained recognition that language is so painfully inadequate that it can only issue in such phrases:

> saying again nine days never floated the loved
> nor nine months
> nor nine lives . . .
>
> saying again there is a last
> even of last times . . .
>
> a last even of last times of saying
> if you do not love me I shall not be loved
> if I do not love you I shall not love[34]

The heart (and the sexual organ expressing the heart's affections) is now an 'old plunger' and it is not stopping like the bird in 'The

Vulture' but 'pestling the unalterable whey of words' in the prone womb of origin. This is the necessary preliminary to allowing the voice of panic to dominate the poem, at which point the title's reference to music ('cascando' means 'diminishing volume and decreasing tempo') is revealed, and the words behave like repeated notes in jagged combinations:

> terrified again
> of not loving
> of loving and not you
> of being loved and not by you
> of knowing not knowing pretending
> pretending

As this moment of perfect suspension is reached, the voice realizes it can go no further, and performs four increasingly dazzling distortions of focus. It begins by openly acknowledging for the first time that there is a personality behind it, and then immediately generalizes the relevance of what it has been saying. But the pressure of what it has been saying is so great that a qualification has to be made, and ultimately, after the kind of long pause that the drama more easily accommodates, the discussion is contextualized still further by an admission that true love is free of all such uncertainty. It is easy to over-dramatize this, but the last words do seem equivocally wrung from a recording apparatus finally silenced by the despair it speaks of at the beginning:

> I and all the others that will love you
> if they love you
>
> 3.
>
> unless they love you

The French poems of 1937–9 are free of this quavering uncertainty. It is important to remember that Beckett first became aware of the inadequacy of English in exploring the poetic medium, long before his problems in the novelistic medium confirmed this. The voice, aspiring (as Pater said all the arts must)[35] to the condition of music, but unable to sustain this condition without breaking the medium altogether, changes to a language more inherently musical, with more echoic power and a syntax that allows experiment without destroying form.

Beckett seems to have intended that the twelve poems should relate one to another, charting a spiritual crisis parallel to that of *Echo's Bones*. At the same time, though they vary considerably in quality, each poem should be considered individually. The first (one of the two with English equivalents) shows the voice of 'Echo's Bones' drowning the voice of 'Cascando' but adopting the latter's subject-matter. Beckett finds himself once more between the world of sexual satisfaction and the world of spiritual satisfaction. It is the problem of the Smeraldina versus the Alba all over again, but the profit has given rise to two types of loss:

> with each the absence of love is the same
> with each the absence of life is different[36]

The even tone and unhurried repetition convey the monotony that has succeeded the 'panic' of 'Cascando'. The blank statement of the beginning ('they come') hardly has time to take on its submerged sexual meaning before rhetoric strangles the voice into silence.

The second poem celebrates the Smeraldina way, and therefore necessarily loses the balance of the first. The 'calm act' of sex ('à elle l'acte calme'), untroubled by considerations of its spiritual value, seems the necessary precondition to genuine poetic utterance: 'l'absence / au service de la présence'. The 'quelques haillons d'azur dans la tête' ('few fragments of blue in the head') signal the first appearance of a metaphor for artistic creation that reaches particular prominence in *How it is*[37] and the late prose texts; 'toute la tardive grâce d'une pluie cessant / au tomber d'une nuit / d'août' ('all the late grace of a rain ceasing / to fall on an August / night') expresses a meteorological preference later given memorable expression at the beginning of 'From an Abandoned Work'.[38] The clarity of the last three lines derives from a feeling that he is at last above the storm, but there is an emotional chill about them:

> à elle vide
> lui pur
> d'amour[39]

> (with her empty
> him pure
> of love)

The third poem continues to explore this area, but Beckett deals more openly with the unsavoury aspects. Lying in bed, awaiting his satisfaction, the poet projects himself into the climax of the near future:

> être là sans mâchoires sans dents
> où s'en va le plaisir de perdre
> avec celui à peine inférieur
> de gagner[40]

(to be there jawless toothless
where the pleasure of loss is lost
together with the scarcely inferior
one of gain)

As before (in *Echo's Bones*), meditation on what precedes the moment
of bliss affects the coherence of the poem, and it is only when he
imagines himself at the heart of the mystery that the poem focuses
itself with precision. The continuous contact of love and death is
characteristic:

qu'elle mouille
tant qu'elle voudra jusqu'à l'élègie
des sabots ferrés encore loin des Halles
ou l'eau de la canaille pestant dans les tuyaux
ou plus rien
qu'elle mouille puisque c'est ainsi
parfasse tout le superflu
et vienne
à la bouche idiote à la main formicante
au bloc cave à l'oeil qui écoute
de lointains coups de ciseaux argentins

(let her moisten
as long as she likes till the elegy
of shod horses' hooves still far from Les Halles
or the riff-raff's water crumbles in the pipes
or nothing more
let her moisten
perfect the excess
and come
with her idiot mouth with her hand formicating
the hollow bulk the hollow eye listening
to far-off tinkling scissor snips)

The fourth poem is given a title, 'Ascension', that suggests the
Alba way. But, as the first poem had suggested, the two ways (like
Proust's) end at the same place, and the scene is as dispassionately
sexual as in the preceding poem. The poet has penetrated 'à travers
la mince cloison' ('across the thin bulkhead') as the first line semi-
mystically suggests, and in the moment of orgasm is reminded of the
dubious pleasures of childhood innocence. The final lines maintain
an ambiguous sense of attraction–repulsion as an unequivocally
human, sexual ascension takes place:

> de ses doits dégoûtants il ferma les paupières
> sur les grands yeux verts etonnés
>
> elle rode légère
> sur ma tombe d'air[41]
>
> (with his filthy fingers he closed the lids
> on her green eyes wide with surprise
> she delicately rides
> my tomb of air)

'To drink of the ashes of dead relations', wrote Sir Thomas Browne in *Urn Burial*, is 'a passionate prodigality'.[42] But the passions have changed, and this Prodigal Son ('un enfant prodigue') is faithful, both to Cynara and home, only 'à sa façon'.

The fifth poem, 'La Mouche' ('The Fly') is perhaps the most crucial, because it involves (or almost involves) the poet in a decisive act outside himself. The windowpane that cuts him off from the world has its purity and transparence disfigured by a fly, thrashing wildly about trying to escape. The poet's first impulse, to crush it, is superseded by the realization that only God would solve his problems thus. The description of the fly's plight reveals the poet's pity:

> ventre à terre
> sanglée dans ses boyaux noirs
> antennes affolées ailes liées
> pattes crochues bouche suçant à vide[43]
>
> (hell for leather
> girt in its black guts
> antennae frantic wings tied down
> legs hooked mouth sucking emptiness)

The suggestion that the solution actually lies within his power is not sentimental, since he is unable to carry out a decisive act, and the problem remains unsolved:

> sous mon pouce impuissant elle fait chavirer
> la mer et le ciel serein
>
> (beneath my powerless thumb it convulses
> the sea and the calm sky)

The sixth poem speaks of the 'musique d'indifférence' that we first experienced in 'Echo's Bones', as if the poet is well aware that indifference has been under threat in the preceding poem. The bones of Echo have now fragmented into essentials ('coeur temps air feu'; 'heart time air fire'), expressing the 'éboulement d'amours' ('atrophy of loves'). All he can do is break the pose of indifference and make a pitiful plea to the 'sable / du silence' ('sand / of silence'):

> couvre leur voix et que
> je ne m'entende plus
> me taire[44]

> (cover their voices so
> that I may hear no more
> me silent)

The true music, in other words, is beyond even bones as elemental as this.

The seventh poem does not progress much farther, but it does present the clearest account yet of the two entities in discord: 'il y a le vent / et l'état de veille' ('there is the wind / and wakefulness'), and it states pungently a familiar theme: 'les absents sont morts les présents puent' ('the absent ones are dead those still here stink'). It is more concentrated than the eighth poem only because it contains fewer lines; neither poem has a rigorous inner logic, and in neither is the absence of this logic compensated for by startling *aperçus*. Only the conclusion to the eighth, pointing out that passivity is no more a solution than the suspended violence of the fifth poem, adds much to the developing mosaic.

Beckett seems to have realized later that 'Dieppe', the ninth of the series, had an independent existence, and it is certainly a poem that takes on body from contiguity with the later French poems. The tenth poem, 'Rue de Vaugirard', describes in an amused tone the experience of the poet as he cycles through Paris. Treating himself as an Isherwood-like camera he 'expose la plaque aux lumières et aux ombres' ('expose[s] the plate to light and shade') by gaping innocently on reality, 'béant de candeur'. 'Fortifié', he starts off again ('on the move' as 'Serena III' has it), congratulating himself on having achieved 'un négatif irrécusable' ('one unimpeachable negative'). To consider the poem as an exceptionally oblique description of the sexual act, confusing everything and ultimately unsatisfying, would be a case of *honi soit qui mal y pense* worth savouring. The eleventh poem suggests nothing could be farther from his mind; but the twelfth has a different tale to tell.

'Arènes de Lutèce', the eleventh, is perhaps the most immediately accessible of the series,[45] delicately but not sentimentally describing the movements of an eye that perceives its owner as object with as much drama (and less fuss) as E and O in *Film* twenty years later. The Doppelgänger motif does not seem unduly schizophrenic,[46] partly because of the ease and fluidity of rhythm in the poem. Between the twin poles of 'indifference' and 'panic' lies a quiet zone in which careful notation suppresses behind the desire to record a profound engagement:

> De là où nous sommes assis plus haut que les gradins
> je nous voir entrer du côté de la Rue des Arènes,
> hésiter, regarder en l'air, puis pesamment
> venir vers nous à travers le sable sombre,
> de plus en plus laids, aussi laids que les autres,
> mais muets.

> (From where we are seated higher than the tiers
> I see us enter from the Rue des Arènes side,
> halt, look up, then ponderously
> come towards us across the dark sand,
> more and more ugly, ugly like the others,
> but silent.)

They separate for a moment, and the man makes his way to the position he is occupying in the first line of the poem. The woman hesitates, takes a step towards the exit, and then follows him. They meet face to face, as Murphy and Mr Endon had done, but without portentous significance being attributed to the moment. Beckett's sense of the drama of vision is nowhere more clear than here:

> J'ai un frisson, c'est moi qui me rejoins,
> c'est avec d'autres yeux que maintenant je regarde
> le sable, les flaques d'eau sous la bruine,
> une petite fille traînant derrière elle un cerceau,
> un couple, qui sait des amoureux, la main dans la main
> les gradins vides, les hautes maisons, le ciel
> qui nous éclaire trop tard.
> Je me retourne, je suis étonné
> de trouver là son triste visage.[47]

> (I shiver, it is I rejoining me,
> it is with other eyes that I now see
> the sand, the puddles underneath the drizzle,
> a little girl dragging her hoop behind her,
> a couple, lovers who knows, hand in hand,
> the empty tiers, the lofty houses, and the sky
> that lights us up too late.
> I return to myself, I am surprised
> to find her sad face there.)

In one sense, this is Beckett's most optimistic poem since 'Alba' in that it envisages the possibility of contentment from something outside the self, but it is at the same time one of his most depressing accounts of the persistence of memory and the passing of time. Only in art, the interpenetration of subject and object, can one catch a glimpse of paradise. And, with the same unerring logic of *Echo's Bones*, a glimpse of the paradise that has been lost entails a season in the depths of hell.

The twelfth poem maintains the clarity of the eleventh, but pursues the more philosophical problems first adumbrated in *Echo's Bones*. The tone is kept so resolutely neutral that it is easy to forget the hysteria generated in that volume, when similar problems came under review:

> jusque dans la caverne ciel et sol
> et une à une les vieilles voix
> d'outre-tombe
> et lentement la même lumière ...
>
> et les mêmes lois
> que naguère[48]
>
> (even in the cavern sky and earth
> and one by one the ancient voices
> from beyond the grave
> and slowly the same light ...
>
> and the same laws
> as not so long ago)

The 'ancient voices' go back beyond the 'outre-tombe' of Chateaubriand to the plains of Enna where Proserpine was ravished by Pluto. But the reassurance of invoking classical myth proves only a momentary bulwark for the microcosm. For the old dichotomies persist in the cavernous depths of the self; there is the same tension of sky and earth, the same light that consumes the darkness, the same laws of attraction and repulsion. Then, in a *ricorso* more daunting than that at the beginning of 'Dieppe', or the one in the central section of 'Cascando', there is always the 'bouche d'ombre':

> lentement au loin éteint
> Proserpine et Atropos[49]
>
> (slowly from far off extinguishing
> Proserpine and Atropos)

It is an even more uncertain void than the mouth of hell.

In this twelfth poem one finds precisely what Beckett himself finds in a painting by Geer van Velde. 'Here is a land', he writes in a post-war poem in French, 'in which oblivion leans gently on un-named worlds', in which there is 'nothing to cry about', in which the 'spiralling dust of instants' composes itself into an essential calm.[50] It is ironic that the poem from which this comes shows little but bluster and rage.

'Saint-Lô', an English poem of 1946, remains a comparative failure, for all its initial attractiveness. It is doubtful if Beckett could have written like this without the experiment of the French poems behind him, but the attempt to write as limpidly in his original as in his adopted tongue produces a great sense of strain here:

> Vire will wind in other shadows
> unborn through the bright ways tremble
> and the old mind ghost-forsaken
> sink into its havoc[51]

The careful management of sounds seems merely precious until we reach the characteristically equivocal emotions aroused in Beckett at the thought of mind dissolving. But Beckett's uncertainty becomes more strident in proportion as we feel the technical means to be inadequate. The fact that the river Vire will have to pass through shadows does nothing to mitigate the optimism of the opening, and prophecy is a mode Beckett is usually content to leave alone. The final two lines are too abrupt, if they are intended as a contrast, and if, as seems more likely, they are intended to predict the pleasurable destruction of mind in flux, the harshness of sound is overdone. Beckett is trapped in a public situation at Saint-Lô that cries out for utterance, but he is never at his best in 'occasional' poetry and in returning again to French, he also returned to more intimate subject-matter. John Fletcher thinks the poem is 'probably its author's verse masterpiece'[52] and Lawrence Harvey speaks of its 'unadorned perfection',[53] but it is difficult not to feel that its lyricism derives more from confusion than from the ambiguities so sensitively articulated in the French poems.

The *Quatre Poèmes* of 1948 ('Dieppe' is dated 1937) conclude the volume *Poems in English*. The poems are extremely direct in manner, with a pathos that occasionally, in English (as in the last of the four, in a mistranslated last line Beckett later corrected), strikes one as exquisite and sentimental. The French is more emotionally neutral, not only in the brief 'Dieppe' (where the translation allows too much specificity in the last line), but in all the moments of wordplay ('que mon amour meure'; 'qui me fuit me poursuit' – 'harrying fleeing' sounds much more desperate). 'Sans visage sans question' is less melodramatic than 'faceless incurious'; 'sans voix parmi les voix' is a purer kind of statement than 'among the voices voiceless'. The abstract philosophizing in particular travels badly.

The poet has meditated on 'a last even of last times' in 'Cascando'; the speculation becomes reality at Dieppe, as the ebb tide rolls in and out again. In the other three poems the named location disappears, but the 'threshold' situation ('these long shifting thresholds' as Beckett calls them) remains. The third poem envisages a transfer from a situation in which (as *Fin de Partie* puts it) 'quelque chose suit son cours' to one which can be apprehended and lived through as an 'instant'. But time cannot be divorced from space, as the translation of 'le temps d'une porte' ('the space of a door') obliquely admits, and as the fourth poem makes clear. The reiteration of a quotidian reality 'where to be lasts but an instant' is accompanied by a heavily rhetorical plea for external reality, general and par-ticular: 'what would I do without this world ... without this wave ... without this silence ... without this sky'. The rhetoric is suspiciously fulsome and is exploded by the bitterness of the second half of the poem. But the structure is not as simple as this; there is, in the first half, a gradual move away from the phenomenal towards the eternal. Wave and sky seem to be less a part of an externally perceived reality than a reality created by the recording conscious-ness. Only a world behind what the second poem calls 'ce rideau de brume qui recule', a world that only gives one back the image of oneself (because it can do no more) but which constantly asserts itself as outside oneself (because it can do no less), is desired by the poet. Without an apocalypse ('this wave where in the end / body and shadow are engulfed') life would be meaningless repetition, with an eye constantly seeking outside itself an image of solace that can only have been spun from inside itself. Thus the perception of space (and of objects in space) becomes 'convulsive'. As a corollary, the imagining of a figure/companion who might bring solace involves the poet in facing and giving oblique utterance to his essential loneliness. The minimal distortion of vision is better expressed in the French because a more neutral (though more rigid) syntax allows identities to remain shadowy, whereas in English the dislocations of subject and object are felt to be forced.

The fourth poem returns to the intimate tone of the first, as if the second and third had solved the more philosophical problems of perception and identity. The English version is probably the least satisfactory of the four, and the situation does not appear to have an irresistible connection with the earlier poems. The conditional mood is curiously direct and definite; in the French the rhyme (admittedly light) and the euphony consolidate this feeling. There are variants in both French and English and the poem gave him more trouble than any of the others. Ingenious attempts (such as Harvey's) to suggest that the streets of the fourth poem are in the lighted town of the first seem to me misguided.[54] The anti-erotic stance is characteristic, but little is added to the kind of complex responses to love already examined except, perhaps, a quietist pathos that is not Beckett's forte.

There is, to my mind, no point in pretending that Beckett is a great poet. But the poems examined in detail here do help to make clearer the essential features of his vision. They provide a useful commentary on Beckett's most intimate feelings and thoughts over twenty years. The late French poem 'Mort de A.D.' proves conclusively that his work is not entirely solipsistic and self-regarding. In this poem, he envisages the state of death in paradoxical terms more desperate even than those used to express physical pleasure:

> pressé contre ma vieille planche vérolée du noir
> des jours et nuits broyés aveuglement
> à être là à ne pas fuir et fuir et être là
> courbé vers l'aveu du temps mourant[55]

> (thrust up against my old plank pock-marked with the black
> of blindly mixed up days and nights
> in being there in fleeing not and fleeing being there
> bent towards the confession of expiring time)

This meaningful death-in-life is compared with the intolerable passivity of being able to do nothing but watch:

> buvant plus haut que l'orage
> la coulpe du temps irrémissible
> agrippé au vieux bois témoin des départs
> témoin des retours

> (drinking down above the storm
> the unpardonable crime of time
> gripping old wood the witness of departures
> witness of returns)

The concluding line, almost an afterthought, does nothing to compel us to regard it as optimistic; what Beckett found 'pernicious' in *Proust*[56] is still symptomatic of the earthly condition here. The world, as he was later to show in *Imagination Dead Imagine,* is 'still proof against enduring tumult', still undeniably there, however threatened by the feelings of the mind.

Perhaps this helps to explain why Beckett was fascinated by the poetic form for twenty years. It is important to remember that early in his career Beckett was roused by admiration for Joyce's *Finnegans Wake* to enunciate an aesthetic in which form and content were identical. There are no doubt philosophical difficulties in this position, and Beckett's development of it does not go much further than 'When the sense is sleep, the words go to sleep. . . . When the sense is dancing, the words dance.'[57] His first literary efforts were in the field of poetry because it seemed (after Apollinaire) the most likely medium in which form and content could be one.[58] That *Whoroscope* does not succeed is due to its 'occasional' nature: the poetry seeks its occasion outside itself. That 'Alba' does succeed is because form and content are one: the poetry has no occasion but itself. It is, as Mallarmé might have said, the occasion of itself, and it achieves this despite the title's admission that an ancient form is being given a modern content. This does not prevent two types of utterance coexisting in the poem, for while the crucial central section, describing a musical instrument, seems like music (in Beckett's terms, 'is that something itself'), the earlier section has the lightest possible external form ('before morning' acting as a frame at either end) and it situates itself in the mind almost as a physical object of contemplation:

> before morning you shall be here
> and Dante and the Logos and all strata and mysteries
> and the branded moon
> beyond the white plane of music
> that you shall establish here before morning
>
>> grave sauve singing silk
>> stoop to the black firmament of areca
>> rain on the bamboos flower of smoke
>>> alley of willows[59]

Belacqua tells the Alba in 'Dream of Fair to Middling Women' that he has achieved a new kind of poetic utterance, different from those he has employed in the past. His remarks are so appropriate to the 'Alba' poem we have here that it is difficult not to feel the two are one and the same:

> I have . . . achieved a statement more ample . . . more

temperate, less mannered, more banal (oh, Alba, a most
precious quality, that), nearer to the low-voiced Pushkinian
litotes.[60]

He immediately launches into a piece of poetic theory that helps us
to see what the real achievement of 'Alba' is:

> There is a shortness of poetic sight ... when the image of the
> emotion is focussed behind the verbal retina; and a longness
> of same, when it is focussed behind. There is an authentic
> trend from that short-sightedness to this long-sightedness.
> Poetry is not concerned with normal vision, when word and
> image coincide. ... Here the word is prolonged by the emotion
> instead of the emotion being gathered into and closed by the
> word. There are the two modes, say Marlowe and Chénier,
> keeping the order, and who shall choose between them.[61]

The fact that it is difficult to find either Marlowe or Chénier in
'Alba' is almost irrelevant when we have such a precise and capable
description of Beckett's manner. The two types of utterance are now
seen not as mutually exclusive but as complementary, and the
typographical sensitivity (later to reappear in such works as *How it
is*) helps to make content and form seem as indissoluble as they are in
a physical object. It is no surprise to find that Beckett's real poetic
affections are for such writers as Louise Labbé,[62] Malherbe[63] and
G. A. Bécquer.[64] The latter, indeed, was well aware of the two
kinds of poetry, one magnificent and sonorous, the other 'natural,
rapid, terse ... bare of artificiality, free in a free form',[65] and chose
the latter. What makes Beckett's situation so interesting is that he
understands the claims of the former as well. He greatly admires
Rimbaud, and Rimbaud's adoption of 'audibilities' that are 'no
more than punctuation in a statement of silences' helps him to situate
his own aims: 'I shall state silences more completely than even a
better man spangled the butterflies of vertigo'.[66] It is the same
impulse that enables him to distinguish between poetry conceived as
'prayer' and the 'great pharisee poems'.[67]

His poetry is, in fact, fundamentally lyric in impulse, as is perhaps
inevitable given the prevailingly romantic poets he studied at
Trinity. The lyric mode, however, requires a total commitment that
obstructs the self-reflexive gestures he could integrate into his fiction
and drama, and the satiric mode which he is also attracted to,
requires a total abandonment of the offending society as the prerequisite to holding up one's own clean hands, which he also cannot
do. Pound and Eliot brought the two modes together by force of

personality rather than careful integration. Both had a consistency of purpose that is denied to Beckett. There is a self-regarding quality in Beckett's work that derives from Prufrock having taken up a post as a university lecturer: an inner impulse gets inflated outwards.[68] Surrealism might have offered a way out,[69] and Beckett's fine translations of Éluard indicate how sensitive he could be to their work. But even this was commissioned work, and his later translations of Mexican poetry he dismissed as 'cette . . . foutaise alimentaire' ('this f–ing alimentary').[70] The superiority of Beckett's translations of Apollinaire and Éluard over his translations of Breton and Crével clearly derives from a sympathy with their aims, and an understanding of their achievement. Apollinaire and Éluard in their best work preserve an inner logic, where Breton and Crével wilfully sunder the relation between subject and object. Breton's 'pure psychic automatism' is the logical terminus of the ego of Hugo,[71] but Éluard has a hesitant quality that saves him from Breton's rant, and Apollinaire (notably in 'Zone')[72] hovers between subject and object without, as Beckett would say, taking sides. Beckett's early attraction to the poetry of Jules Romains was because of his 'concrete' style; his mystical Communism, like Jouve's Catholicism, he found less appetizing. In this latter instance, the disappointment Beckett felt on meeting Jouve doubtless played its part.[73] His defence of Denis Devlin in 1938 seems a similarly *ad hominem* act, however genuine his admiration for the poetry.[74] It is perhaps true of all these poets, including Beckett, that they have felt what Yeats called 'the fascination of what's difficult' but have tried (to quote Yeats again) 'to make it plain'.[75] The obscurity that remains is a direct result of honestly confronting the mess, 'without trying to say that it is other than it is'.[76]

8   Conclusion

Any conclusion to a book whose subject is still producing work of the first importance, is necessarily indecisive; it is certainly not the place for idle speculation about Beckett's future development. The main outlines of his concerns must have been obvious, if not to the reader of 'Assumption', at least by the time of *Murphy*. We need not expect any Victorian three-deckers, any *engagé* pamphleteering, any autobiography or any bourgeois melodramas from Paris this year; yet the uncompromisingly experimental products of Beckett's 'ontospeleology'[1] have become, with time, entirely unpredictable. The Nobel award came, as such prizes usually do, at the end of a career, at a point when comparative wealth only perhaps serves to situate how poor the beginnings were. The stamp of approval improves sales for a year or two, and academic incarceration (which some of Beckett's early work not only encourages, but deserves) begins. At the same time questions about where Beckett's total achievement leaves him in the literary stakes – which are difficult to answer and somehow alien to his work – begin to proliferate. If it is to Beckett's credit that he despises this kind of approach above all others, it would be untrue to say that Beckett is totally uninterested in his place in the Pantheon. But this interest is perfectly predictable in a writer so much involved in the difficulties of his craft, and so much more aware than most professional critics where short-comings are to be found. If a place on the ladder has to be found for Beckett, it seems perversely appropriate that the previous recipients of the Nobel Prize should provide us with the co-ordinates. He will never become the Kipling that everybody reads nor, by the same token, the Kipling nobody read. At the same time, it is difficult to see him commanding the reverence of Yeats, T. S. Eliot or Thomas

Mann. It would not be altogether irrelevant to think of him as of the same order as William Faulkner, occasionally given to simplifications and even sentimentalities, but in his best work going beyond the merely subjective to an exploration of the unacknowledged country we studiously suppress behind our public faces. He is not, like the Shakespeares and the Goethes and the Tolstoys, a writer one can unreservedly recommend as life-enhancing. But he has the same kind of honesty as they do. If, in his case, this gives his work a nervous quality, then we can find something similar in Proust, whom he so greatly admires, and whose stature is not in doubt. It would be utterly absurd to condemn his work to the ranks of the 'life-denying'. He offers us a salutary reminder of the genuine difficulty of being alive, but he is a writer who can provide for others the consolation he consistently refuses himself. If Beckett's study of what T. S. Eliot, in a famous phrase, called 'the boredom and the horror and the glory'[2] has done only a little to bring the third element of this triad into closer focus, he has at least made clearer the precise nature of the first and the second. And his own practice is as much a moral example to younger writers as Joyce's was for him.[3]

Beckett's corpus is not large by the standards of those writers who write a full-length work annually. This is primarily because of the difficulty he has with composition, but it is also because he is very selective about what sees the light of day. For many years he resisted the reprinting of *More Pricks than Kicks*, and *Mercier and Camier* and *First Love* were published fourteen years after they were written. It is difficult to see him allowing 'Dream of Fair to Middling Women' and 'Eleuthéria' to be published in his lifetime, and there are two stories and two critical articles that will probably suffer the same fate.[4] For years Beckett has scrupulously refused to allow anything he is dissatisfied with, or anything he has not been able to bring to some kind of conclusion, to be placed on public display. In recent years, however, he has relaxed this rigid rule to the extent of allowing a considerable amount of unpublished material – predominantly theatre – to be exhibited, and, more recently still, published, in the periodical of his French publishing house. One important feature of the exhibited material is that Beckett has continued to compose drama in French, since his apparent abandonment of the language, for the purposes of original theatrical composition, in 1956.[5] It also testifies to his continuing interest in mime,[6] and his remarkable versatility in 'lifting the old inert objects and changing their position, bringing them closer together and moving them further apart'.[7]

Of this new material released in France, it must be said that none of it greatly enhances our overall estimate of Beckett's achievement, but with the prose works particularly, especially those assigned to the otherwise almost barren 1950s, we get a tremendously invigorating sense of Beckett striving to once again find a tone of voice and a sense of landscape that would adequately encompass what he needed to utter.

The sketch for radio dated 1962–3?[8] bears obvious resemblances to *Words and Music* and *Cascando* and the presence of an inquisitorial female during the first half reminds one of Ada in *Embers*. Beckett's sense of the exquisite pain a noise inflicts on the listener is here developed in the context of a series of telephone calls that bring Proust to mind,[9] the noise of curtains being violently pulled back, and the apparently successful attempt to bring together Voice and Music, who otherwise remain parallel to one another, or reciprocally divergent. The tone of the voice of the man at the centre of affairs sounds rather like a trial run for Opener:

> *Elle* Ça vous plaît, à vous?
> (Un temps.)
> *Lui* J'en ai besoin.
> *Elle* Besoin? De ça?
> *Lui* C'est devenu un besoin.

> *Her* Does that please you?
> (Pause.)
> *Him* I have need of it.
> *Her* Need? Of that?
> *Him* It has become a need.[10]

This is particularly true of the final exchange before the woman leaves, or is caused to disappear:

> *Elle* Sont-ils . . . soumis aux mêmes . . . conditions?
> *Lui* Oui, madame.
> *Elle* Par exemple? (Un temps.) Par exemple?
> *Lui* On ne peut pas les décrire, madame.

> *Her* Are they . . . submitted to the same . . . conditions?
> *Him* Yes, madam.
> *Her* For example? (Pause.) For example?
> *Him* One cannot describe them, madam.[11]

The agitated voice of the conclusion is presumably of a different order, closer to *Cascando*'s Voice, but with less of a story to tell. The appeal to an outside agency for assistance gives birth to one fruitful union, but the mention of a death-rattle resounds gloomily over the winding-down at the end.

If the theatrical fragment[12] had not been dated '1960s?' one might have been forgiven for thinking that it was of the same provenance as *Endgame*; the blind street musician-cum-beggar and the crippled figure confined to a wheelchair seem almost like fragments of Hamm that have taken on independent life, except that actual physical violence is here closer to the surface and the tone is altogether less remorseless. The slacker quality of the exchanges allows Beckett to develop non-communication routines reminiscent of *Godot*, but it means that the cripple's prophecy of an endless series of changing incarnations for the blind man, with which the fragment ends, fails to strike with sufficient horror. The cripple's need for what Maddy Rooney would call 'a helping hand'[13] provokes exchanges of really painful drama, but the main satisfaction one takes from this uncompleted text resides in the beautifully judged modulations of voice:

> *A* Je ne suis pas assez malheureux. (Un temps.) Ça a toujours été mon malheur, malheureux, mais pas assez.[14]

> *A* I am not unhappy enough. (Pause.) That has always been my misfortune, unhappy but not unhappy enough.

and the crispness of the dialogue:

> *B* Il commençait à m'aimer et je l'ai
> frappé. Il va me quitter, je ne le
> reverrai plus. Je ne reverrai plus personne.
> Nous n'entendrons jamais plus la voix humaine.
> *A* Vous ne l'avez pas assez entendue?
> Toujours les mêmes gémissements, du berceau
> jusqu'au tombeau.[15]

> *B* He began to love me and I struck him. Now he is leaving me. I shall not see him again. I shall never see anyone again. We shall never again hear the human voice.
> *A* Have you not heard it often enough? Always the same groans, from cradle to tomb.

Of the prose *foirades* ('fizzles' in Beckett's forthcoming translation), the fifth[16] can comfortably be assigned to the period of *The Lost Ones*. Apart from clarifying some issues and concentrating on 'dans l'air noir des tours de pâle lumière' ('towers of pale light standing in the black air'),[17] it does not add much to our understanding of conditions in the cylinder, and most of the material is incorporated in the published text.

187

The other four *foirades* are all from the 1950s, two in the breathless manner of the *Texts for Nothing* and two, including the longest, in a more leisurely mode that has some affinities with 'From an Abandoned Work'. *Foirade ii*, like Text Five,[18] is an attempt to outline the relationship between the domain of real being and the world of false selves. The *foirade* is spoken by a voice which projects itself forward in time to the last days of the body it is inhabiting. The voice asserts that it will survive and be ultimately independent: 'c'est lui qui mourra, moi je ne mourrai pas' ('it will be him who dies, I shall not die').[19] At the same time it is forced to admit that its own existence, though unaffected, will not be able to be embodied in the same way: 'il n'y aura plus de je, il ne dira plus jamais je, il ne dira plus jamais rien' ('there will be no more I, he will never again say I, he will never again say anything').[20] It is what Malone hoped, and what the Unnamable almost achieved. The final words of the fragment look forward to *Cascando*, with the roles reversed, and the voice in command: 'il n'y a plus rien dans sa tête, j'y mettrai le nécessaire' ('there will be nothing in his head, I shall put in it all he needs').[21] The experience of the later texts only consolidates a manifestly impossible wish-fulfilment, to make it seem more melancholy still.

Foirade iv[22] involves a slightly less frenetic voice in similar, but even more hallucinatory, imaginings. While the voice in *Foirade ii* had decided not to speak 'de vers, d'os et de poussière' ('of termites, dust and bones'),[23] the voice in *Foirade iv*, identifying itself with the earth, is unavoidably aware of the minutiae of decay. Moving to and fro between house and garden with an alacrity not even the time-bound Moran could have achieved, the voice reiterates the longings of Victor Krap and Malone 'Ah . . . voir mourir' ('Ah . . . to see oneself die')[24] only to be brought to a halt by the recognition that in an instant the sky, and the eye gazing up at it, are irrevocably changed, with the death of one self and the inauguration of another.

In *Foirade iii*[25] the pleasure the protagonist derives from gazing at the ceiling is similarly short-lived. He is subject to visitations less physically painful than those of Malone, but equally inexplicable. The visitant, identified as Horn, troubles him not from the point of view of noise, but from the point of view of darkness and light. On the occasion Horn is asked to make his features more available for scrutiny, the light gets feebler and feebler until it is no more than a yellow gleam. This moment of disappearance just before darkness returns remains the most poignant of the protagonist's memories, because it allows him to exist, without being perceived, in a space other than that in which the images of exterior space organize themselves. The admission that it is his athleticism which has dished him, which is implicitly extended to include the act of memory which precedes creativity, is so alien, in its bizarre humour, to the serene tone of the rest of the text that it is not surprising Beckett could go no further.

Foirade i[26] is more concerned with movement than any other, allowing the protagonist only a brief moment of stasis in a 'tenue vaguement pénitentiaire' ('vaguely penitential position')[27] before getting on with the job of charting the obstacles and pitfalls, voluntary and involuntary, which make this boulder-less Sisyphus' life a misery. Continued acquaintance with the darkness makes it no less apprehensible, although the narrator is so much moved by hypothesizing a moment when all is 'inondé de lumière' ('drowned in light')[28] that he is led to consider this one of his hero's mistakes. In this text, however, it is much more a question of sound than of light, and the most careful analyses are devoted to the noise of the body moving forward which brings other noises in its train. This discursive treatment of what *Embers* and other plays dramatize so much more successfully, concludes with a consideration of a noise so minimal as to be almost imaginary. It is the final element in an attempt to describe exhaustively the occurrences which constitute reality for the protagonist, pointing forward to the much more appalling and inexorable world of *How it is*.

Trying to summarize the contents of a Beckett text runs quite counter to the spirit of Beckett's writing. It is, nevertheless, salutary to be reminded that, throughout this book, it has not always been possible to explore fully the ambiguities of a given situation. This need only be a serious shortcoming for those commentators who persist in regarding Beckett's work as a tissue of private concerns written in a dauntingly private language. He is, of course, as much a 'realist' as any other artist. The reality has changed in the most recent works, and words have become objects to be moved around, like chess pieces, by a remote and dispassionate hand. The field of operations has shifted (as far as literature ever can) from people to things, and become more rarefied in atmosphere. His writing has gained solidity at the expense of limpidity, and total clarity at the expense of basic lucidity. It is as if we see *with* Beckett now, whereas before we saw *through* his eyes. It is difficult to see where Beckett can go from here if only because the wrestling match has recently shown signs of producing a winner. For those who have seen all along who the eventual winner must be, the end product is bound to be unedifying, but there have been many more who have struggled without the comfort and complacency of foreknowledge. There has been, on the way, a growth in wisdom: he has added the *sagacitas* of Daedalus to the *sapientia* of Diogenes. It goes without saying that to read him at his best is a pleasure.

Notes and abbreviations

Abbreviations

The following are abbreviated throughout the Notes thus:

R.U.L.	Reading University Library Beckett Archive.
Our Exag.	*Our Exagmination Round his Factification for Incamination of Work in Progress,* London, 1935.
T.N.	*Three Novels (Molloy, Malone Dies, The Unnamable),* London, 1959.
Endgame	*Endgame* followed by *Act Without Words,* London, 1965.
Krapp	*Krapp's Last Tape and Embers,* London, 1965.
Eh Joe	*Eh Joe and Other Writings,* London, 1967.
N.K.	*No's Knife: Collected Shorter Prose 1945–1967,* London, 1967.
Play	*Play and Two Short Pieces for Radio,* London, 1968.
M.P.T.K.	*More Pricks than Kicks,* London, 1970.
Exhibition	*Samuel Beckett: an Exhibition,* catalogue by James Knowlson, London, 1971.
Film	*Film,* complete scenario, London, 1972.

The following are abbreviated after first citation thus:

Coe	Richard Coe, *Beckett,* London, 1964.
F. and F.	Raymond Federman and John Fletcher, *Samuel Beckett: his Works and his Critics,* London, 1970.
Fletcher	John Fletcher, *The Novels of Samuel Beckett,* London, 1964.
Harvey	Lawrence E. Harvey, *Samuel Beckett: Poet and Critic, 1929–1949,* Princeton, 1970.
Reid	Alec Reid, *All I can manage, more than I could,* Dublin, 1968.
Dream'	'Dream of Fair to Middling Women', unpublished, copy in R.U.L.

Notes

1 Biographical

1 The epigraphs are from *L'Express*, 8 February 1957, p. 26; *T.N.*, p. 197; *How it is*, London, 1964, p. 13.
2 Lawrence Harvey, *Samuel Beckett: Poet and Critic, 1929–1949*, Princeton, 1970, p. 154 (hereafter cited as Harvey).
3 *International Theatre Annual*, no. 1, London, 1956, p. 153.
4 *Exhibition*, p. 20.
5 Harvey, 'A Poet's Initiation' in *Samuel Beckett Now*, ed. M. Friedman, Chicago, 1970, p. 173; Huguette Delye, *Samuel Beckett, ou la philosophie de l'absurde*, Aix-en-Provence, 1960, p. 8; Harvey, p. 298. Much of *Malone Dies* is based on childhood memories of Beckett's, for example listening to dogs barking at night (*T.N.*, p. 207).
6 For fuller details, see 'A Poet's Initiation', p. 173.
7 One nevertheless regrets the loss of 'Some Home Truths about the Ancients' in the Portora Royal School magazine for Michaelmas 1922. He told Ruby Cohn ('Beckett for Comparatists', *Comparative Literature Studies*, 3, 1966, p. 451) that in the early years 'There was never any thought of becoming a writer'.
8 Stanislaus Joyce, *My Brother's Keeper*, London, 1959, p. 187. Vivian Mercier's *The Irish Comic Tradition*, London, 1962, is excellent on background.
9 *Beckett at Sixty*, London, 1967, p. 10. On his curious lecturing technique, see 'The Man Himself', *Trinity News*, 3, 7 June 1956, p. 5.
10 For a fictionalized account of student life at the École Normale, see Jules Romains's *Men of Good Will*, London, 1935–40.
11 Ernest Hemingway, *A Moveable Feast*, Harmondsworth, 1964.
12 Henry Miller, *Tropic of Cancer*, London, 1963, p. 209.
13 Samuel Putnam, *Paris Was our Mistress*, New York, 1947. Beckett is mentioned on p. 97.
14 Harry Crosby and his wife ran the Black Sun Press from Paris in the late 1920s.

15 Malcolm Cowley, *Exile's Return*, London, 1961, p. 135.
16 Gertrude Stein, *Paris France*, London, 1940, p. 1.
17 Irving Babbitt, *The New Laokoon*, Boston, 1910, p. xii.
18 See Roger Shattuck, *The Banquet Years*, London, 1969.
19 See Robert Baldick, *Dinner at Magny's*, London, 1971.
20 See also Gertrude Stein's account of the change, *Paris France*, p. 15.
21 Pierre-Jean Jouve, *An Idiom of Night*, London, 1968, p. 11.
22 'Ex Cathezra', *Bookman*, no. 87, 1934, p. 10.
23 *Exhibition*, p. 20.
24 Beckett spoke thus of Joyce to Vivian Mercier, *Tri-Quarterly*, 8, p. 207.
25 Richard Ellmann, *James Joyce*, London, 1959, p. 629.
26 Richard Aldington, *Life for Life's Sake*, London, 1968, p. 319.
27 Among those published in *transition* were Breton, Tzara, Éluard, Michaux, Hemingway, Hart Crane, Eizenstein and Artaud.
28 Hugh Kenner, *The Pound Era*, London, 1972, pp. 396, 556.
29 See Beckett's contribution to *Richard Aldington: an Intimate Portrait*, ed. Alister Kershaw and F. J. Temple, Carbondale, 1965, p. 3.
30 *Proust and Three Dialogues with Georges Duthuit*, London, 1965, p. 9 (hereafter cited as *Proust*). The copy Beckett used is now at R.U.L.
31 Concerning this period (for details of which see Ellmann, *James Joyce*, p. 661ff), Beckett told Peggy Guggenheim that 'he was dead and had no feelings that were human' (*Out of this Century*, New York, 1946, p. 205).
32 Ludovic Janvier, *Beckett par lui-même*, Paris, 1969, p. 12.
33 Cohn, 'Beckett for Comparatists', p. 452.
34 Richard Coe, *Beckett*, London, 1964, p. 12 (hereafter cited as Coe).
35 Alan Simpson, *Beckett and Behan and a Theatre in Dublin*, London, 1962, p. 69.
36 'A Poet's Initiation', p. 174. Harvey, p. 155, offers a slightly different translation.
37 John Fletcher, *The Novels of Samuel Beckett*, London, 1964, p. 38 (hereafter Fletcher).
38 Raymond Federman and John Fletcher, *Samuel Beckett: his Works and his Critics*, London, 1970, p. 21 (hereafter F. and F.).
39 Fletcher, p. 38.
40 Ellmann, *James Joyce*, p. 661.
41 Harvey, p. 183.
42 For fuller details, see Harvey, p. 170.
43 *Beckett at Sixty*, p. 9. See also Ulick O'Connor, *Oliver St. John Gogarty: a Poet and his Times*, London, 1964, p. 280ff.
44 *Our Exag.*, p. 15.
45 Yeats, *The Rose Leaf*, vol. 2, 1895, p. 166.
46 *Joseph Conrad; a Personal Remembrance*, London, 1924, pp. 213–14.
47 Quoted, from Vico's *De Constantia Philologiæ* by Sighle Kennedy, *Murphy's Bed*, Lewisburg, 1971, p. 76.
48 Coe, p. 14.
49 'Dream of Fair to Middling Women', R.U.L. copy, p. 42 (hereafter 'Dream').

50 Peggy Guggenheim, *Confessions of an Art Addict*, London, 1960, p. 197.
51 Martin Esslin, *The Theatre of the Absurd*, Harmondsworth, 1968, p. 36.
52 Alec Reid, *All I can manage, more than I could*, Dublin, 1968, p. 14 (hereafter cited as Reid).
53 Petrarch (in a letter of August 1347 to Cola di Rienzo) spoke of the Vaucluse in terms of 'a perpetual silence broken only by the murmur of the softly-flowing stream'.
54 A. de Say, 'Rousillon', *L'Arc*, 2, Spring 1958, p. 83.
55 Fletcher, p. 59.
56 *Beckett at Sixty*, pp. 17–18.
57 For fuller details, see *Exhibition*, pp. 63–4.
58 *T.N.*, p. 30.
59 Reid, p. 50.
60 *transition Forty-Eight*, 2, June 1948, pp. 146–7.
61 Letter of 11 January 1956 to Alan Schneider (one of fourteen published in *Village Voice*, 19 March 1958, pp. 8, 15).
62 Simpson, *Beckett and Behan and a Theatre in Dublin*, p. 64.
63 He told Gabriel d'Aubarède (*Nouvelles Littéraires*, 16 February 1961, pp. 1, 7) that the trilogy was written 'avec élan, dans une sorte d'enthousiasme'. Cp. Goethe writing *Wilhelm Meister* 'almost like a somnambulist'.
64 Letter of 27 December 1955 to Alan Schneider.
65 See the interview with Israel Shenker (*New York Times*, 6 May 1956, section 2, pp. x, 1, 3).

2 Writings on literature and art

1 *Proust*, p. 92. The *Proust* volume was among the first serious considerations of Proust's work in England. Beckett describes Mozart in the same terms at the end of the unpublished lecture 'Le Concentrisme' (R.U.L.).
2 John Fletcher, *Samuel Beckett's Art*, London, 1967, p. 20.
3 See the bibliography for details.
4 See the bibliography for details.
5 *Our Exag.*, pp. 3–4. Cp. 'You simplify and dramatize the whole thing with your literary mathematics' ('Dream', p. 91).
6 Ibid., p. 13.
7 That he genuinely wished to make Proust clearer is shown by his distaste for those critics who prized above all Proust's incomprehensibility ('Proust in Pieces', *Spectator*, no. 5530, 23 June 1934, pp. 975–6).
8 *Proust*, p. 11.
9 Ibid., p. 81. Cp. Jacques Rivière, 'Dostoevsky and the Creation of Character', *The Ideal Reader*, London, 1962, pp. 218–22; and Marcel Proust, *By Way of Sainte-Beuve*, London, 1958, p. 287.
10 *Proust*, p. 76. The Baudelaire quotation may be found in 'Philosophic Art', *Baudelaire as a Literary Critic*, ed. L. and F. Hyslop, Pennsylvania, 1964, p. 187. The Proust quotation may be found in *Time Regained*, trans. Stephen Hudson, p. 239.

11 *Proust*, p. 86.

12 Ibid., p. 83.

13 Ibid., p. 84. Cp. Baudelaire on the artist as translator in his 1861 essay on Victor Hugo. Both Rivière (*The Ideal Reader*, p. 120) and E. R. Curtius (*Marcel Proust*, tr. A. Pierhal, Paris, 1928, p. 24) stress this aspect. Cp. Breton's antagonism to the 'style of pure information' in the 1924 Surrealist Manifesto.

14 *Proust*, pp. 87–8. See *Time Regained*, p. 247, and Proust's letter to Antoine Bibesco in *Letters*, tr. Mina Curtis, London, 1950, pp. 189–90. 'Dream', p. 42, makes this clearer: 'You couldn't experience a margarita in d'Annunzio because he denies you the pebbles and flint that reveal it. The uniform, horizontal writing, flowing without accidence, of the man with a style, never gives you the margarita.'

15 *Proust*, pp. 64, 65–6.

16 Ibid., p. 13.

17 Ibid., p. 64.

18 'Dream', pp. 14–15.

19 Ibid., p. 142.

20 Ibid., p. 123.

21 Ibid., p. 24.

22 Ibid., p. 104.

23 Ibid., p. 154.

24 Ibid., p. 109.

25 Ibid., p. 91.

26 Ibid., p. 42.

27 Ibid., pp. 107–8.

28 Harvey, p. 434.

29 Ibid., pp. 433–4.

30 Ibid., p. 435. Beckett told Herbert Blau that French had 'the right weakening effect' (M. Esslin, *The Theatre of the Absurd*, Harmondsworth, 1968, p. 29).

31 Ibid., p. 434 and footnote. Cp. Balzac, *The Magic Skin*, Caxton edition, London, n.d., p. 90.

32 'Denis Devlin', *transition*, no. 27, April–May 1938, pp. 289, 293 (hereafter cited as 'Denis Devlin').

33 Ibid., p. 290.

34 Letter of 27 October 1888 to A. S. Souvorin, quoted by Miriam Allott, *Novelists on the Novel*, London, 1959, p. 99.

35 Quoted in *The Novelist as Philosopher*, ed. J. Cruickshank, London, 1962, p. 98.

36 *transition*, no. 21, p. 148.

37 'Le Monde', etc., p. 352 (my translation).

38 Ibid., p. 352.

39 Ibid., pp. 350–1.

40 Ibid., p. 354.

41 Ibid., p. 354.

42 Ibid., p. 349.

43 Ibid., p. 349.
44 Ibid., p. 352. Cp. Joyce's Aquinas-based aesthetic in *Stephen Hero* and *Portrait* (criticized by H.-J. Schulz, *This Hell of Stories*, The Hague, 1973, p. 82ff) and 'Dream', p. 31: 'There is only category, that furnished by your stases.'
45 'Peintres', etc., p. 4.
46 Ibid., p. 7. Cp. 'Dream', p. 112 (quoted earlier).
47 *Proust*, pp. 102–3.
48 Ibid., p. 101.
49 Ibid., p. 103.
50 Cp. Beckett's remark to Driver: 'The kind of work I do is one in which I'm not master of my material.' The interview with Driver is in *Columbia University Forum*, IV, Summer 1961, pp. 21–5.
51 *Proust*, p. 112.
52 Ibid., p. 110.
53 Ibid., p. 121.
54 Ibid., p. 119.
55 Ibid., p. 120.
56 Ibid., p. 125. In the view of Hegel (*Aesthetics*, tr. F. P. B. Osmanton, London, 1920, vol. 2, pp. 53–4) Romanticism was necessarily an art of failure.
57 See interview with Shenker (*New York Times*, 6 May 1956, section 2. pp. x, 1, 3).
58 P. Mélèse, *Beckett*, Paris, 1969, p. 10 (my translation).
59 'Le Monde', etc., p. 354.
60 See interview with Driver. Cp. 'Dream', p. 159: 'We were once upon a time inclined to fancy ourself as the Cézanne, shall we say, of the printed page, very strong on architecture.'
61 See interview with Driver.
62 Harvey, p. 435.
63 Ibid., p. 435.
64 See interview with Shenker.
65 'Recent Irish Poetry', *Lace Curtain*, no. 4, Summer 1971, p. 58.
66 Ibid., p. 58.
67 *Proust*, p. 110.
68 *Criterion*, vol. 13, July 1934, p. 706.
69 *Proust*, p. 31.
70 Ibid., p. 112. Cp. Leonardo da Vinci, *Treatise on Painting*, London, 1877, p. 142.
71 See interview with Driver.
72 'Recent Irish Poetry', p. 58.
73 'Le Monde', etc., p. 353. Lautréamont wrote: 'He is beautiful, like the chance meeting of a sewing-machine and an umbrella on an operating table' (*Les Chants de Maldoror*, canto 6, section 1).
74 'MacGreevy on Yeats', *Irish Times*, 4 August 1945, p. 2 (hereafter cited as 'MacGreevy on Yeats').
75 'Recent Irish Poetry', p. 58.

76 Beckett liked cubist painting, perhaps because 'the emphasis . . . is not placed on the problem of *space* itself but on the problem of the subjective dynamism existing between objects in space and the observer' (Christopher Gray, *Cubist Aesthetic Theories*, Baltimore, 1953, p. 85). Cp. Beckett on Proust's autosymbolism (*Proust*, p. 80).

77 *Baudelaire as a Literary Critic*, ed. E. and F. L. Hyslop, p. 88.

78 *Our Exag.* p. 15.

79 'Denis Devlin', p. 289.

80 Beckett indirectly criticizes Camus in *T.N.*, p. 133.

81 Leo Bersani, *Balzac to Beckett: Centre and Circumference in French Literature*, Oxford, 1970, p. 323. Cp. 'Dream', p. 10: 'The only perspective worth stating is the site of the unknotting that could be, landscape of a dream of integration.'

82 *Proust*, pp. 120–1.

3 The prose fiction

1 The epigraph is from 'Peintres', etc., p. 3.

2 Ernst Cassirer, *Language and Myth* (1925), quoted in *The Novelist as Philosopher*, ed. J. Cruickshank, London, 1962, p. 163.

3 Quoted by Edith Kern, *Existential Thought and Fictional Structure*, New Haven, 1970, p. 237.

4 *T.N.*, p. 418.

5 J. R. Harvey, 'La vieille voix faible', *Cambridge Quarterly*, 1, 1966, p. 394.

6 *N.K.*, p. 161.

7 Ibid., p. 163. Cp. 'never twice quite the same' ('Sounds', R.U.L.).

8 *M.P.T.K.*, p. 26.

9 *T.N.*, p. 17.

10 In interview with Driver (*Columbia University Forum*, IV, Summer 1961, pp. 21–5); cp. Rabelais' 'peut-être' and Leopardi's 'forse' (*Opere*, Mursia edition, Milan, 1967, p. 1012).

11 *T.N.*, p. 295.

12 Ibid., p. 293. See G. Puttenham, *Arte of English Poesie*, Arber reprint, London, 1895, p. 234. Diogenes Laertius, book 9, sections 69–70 (Loeb edition of the *Lives of the Philosophers*) seems an obvious source.

13 *Murphy*, London, 1963, p. 160.

14 Ibid., pp. 157, 44.

15 *T.N.*, p. 294.

16 *How it is*, London, 1964, pp. 126–8, 136.

17 Ibid., p. 41.

18 *N.K.*, p. 155.

19 See interview with Shenker (*New York Times*, 6 May 1956, section 2, pp. x, 1, 3).

20 *Proust*, p. 17.

21 *T.N.*, p. 315.

22 See, for a good discussion of this, James Knowlson, *Light and Dark in the Theatre of Samuel Beckett*, London, 1972, p. 18ff.

23 *Proust*, p. 26.

24 Beckett recognizes that the title, as usually translated, is misleading (ibid., p. 75). Cp. Germaine Brée, *The World of Marcel Proust*, London, 1967, p. 54.

25 Beckett was obviously attracted by Leibniz's strange conception of windowless nomads without accepting his complete system.

26 Samuel Johnson, 'Life of Pope' in the selection, ed. B. M. Bronson, New York, 1958, p. 327.

27 Marcel Proust, *Pastiches et Mélanges*, Paris, 1921, p. 239 n., quoted by Roger Shattuck, *Proust's Binoculars*, London, 1964, p. 79. For the complete article, see *Marcel Proust: a Selection of his Miscellaneous Writings*, trans. Gerard Hopkins, London, 1948. 'Dream', p. 128, reveals his fondness for the preterites and past subjunctives of Racine.

28 *T.N.*, p. 327 ('it's entirely a matter of voices, no other metaphor is appropriate'), p. 350 ('it is solely a question of voices, no other image is appropriate').

29 Ibid., p. 15.

30 Ibid., p. 62.

31 *Proust*, pp. 79–80. Beckett thus aligns himself with Schopenhauer, Yeats (see the essays on Spenser and Shelley), Diderot (*Jacques the Fatalist*, trans. J. R. Loy, New York, 1959, p. 22) and De Sanctis (*History of Italian Literature, passim*).

32 *T.N.*, p. 31; *Mercier and Camier*, London, 1974, p. 35.

33 *Murphy*, p. 146.

34 See, for example, chapter 1 of Mircea Eliade's *Myths, Dreams and Mysteries*, London, 1968.

35 *Murphy*, p. 43; Proverbs 30:15.

36 *Watt*, London, 1963, p. 245.

37 'Denis Devlin', p. 290.

38 An inferior form to the 'roman' in the opinion of Ramon Fernandez (see E. Muir, *The Structure of the Novel*, London, 1963, p. 119).

39 *T.N.*, p. 193.

40 Ibid., p. 150.

41 Beckett is dismissive of Gide in *Proust*, pp. 19–20, but quotes from him without disrelish in 'Dream', p. 40.

42 *T.N.*, p. 152. Cp. the Unnamable's 'possible deliverance by means of an encounter' (*T.N.*, p. 302).

43 *N.K.*, p. 144.

44 E.g. from *Purgatory*. Schopenhauer's attitude invites comparison.

45 *Endgame*, p. 44.

46 *Proust*, pp. 54, 63.

47 'Hommage à Jack Yeats', p. 620.

48 *N.K.*, p. 73.

49 'Ego Dominus Tuus', *Collected Poems*, London, 1971, p. 180.

50 *M.P.T.K.*, p. 39.

51 *Poetical Works*, Oxford edition, London, 1935, p. 903; note to *Don Juan*, canto 16, stanza 97. Cp. 'Sounds' (R.U.L.): 'worse than none the self's

when the whole body moves.'

52 *All That Fall*, London, 1965, p. 28.
53 *T.N.*, p. 32.
54 Ibid., pp. 98, 109.
55 *How it is*, p. 90.
56 'MacGreevy on Yeats', *Irish Times*, 4 August 1945, p. 2.
57 *Endgame*, pp. 50–1.
58 Paul Verlaine, *Oeuvres Poétiques*, Paris, 1969, p. 226.
59 *Proust*, p. 68, quoting Baudelaire's 'La Chevelure'.
60 See the essay on Mauriac in *Literary and Philosophical Essays*, trans. Annette Michelson, London, 1955.
61 *Northanger Abbey*, chapter 5; *Lady Chatterley's Lover*, chapter 9.
62 See Taylor Stoehr, *Dickens: the Dreamer's Stance*, Ithaca, 1965, p. 244ff.
63 *Watt*, p. 169.
64 Cp. Corporal Trim's story of the King of Bohemia and his seven castles, *Tristram Shandy*, volume 8, chapter 19.
65 See Theodore Baird, 'The Time Scheme of *Tristram Shandy* and a Source', *PMLA*, 51, 1936, pp. 803–20.
66 John Fletcher's Jungian interpretation of Molloy is in *Samuel Beckett Now*, ed. M. Friedman, Chicago, 1970, pp. 157–70. Other Jungian interpretations include Eva Metman's (in the 'Twentieth Century Views' collection) and Aldo Tagliaferri's (*Beckett e l'iperdeterminazione letteraria*, Feltrinelli, 1967, pp. 39ff, 63ff). G. C. Barnard (*Samuel Beckett; a New Approach*, London, 1970, pp. 5–8) discusses schizophrenia, which also interests Mayoux (see p. 79 of the 'Twentieth Century Views' collection).
67 *T.N.*, p. 170.
68 Ibid., p. 65.
69 Ibid., p. 115.
70 *First Love*, London, 1973, p. 33.
71 *T.N.*, pp. 344, 347.
72 Ibid., p. 107.
73 Ibid., p. 137.
74 Ibid., pp. 120, 121.
75 Ibid., p. 92.
76 See chapter 8 of H. Porter Abbott's *The Fiction of Samuel Beckett: Form and Effect*, London, 1973, based on an earlier article.
77 *How it is*, p. 142.
78 *N.K.*, p. 136.
79 This is an extension of Hugh Kenner's argument in *The Stoic Comedians*, Boston, 1962, pp. 37–42.
80 *How it is*, p. 20.
81 Ibid., p. 91.
82 Cp. Giacometti's wrestling with similar problems, as described by Sartre in *Essays in Aesthetics*, trans. Wade Baskin, London, 1964.
83 *T.N.*, pp. 158, 166–7. The rhetorical device of 'occultatio' (see Cicero, *Ad Herennium*, 4, 27) much used by Swift.

84 *T.N.*, pp. 101–2.
85 *Watt*, pp. 151–3.
86 *T.N.*, pp. 326, 330.
87 *Murphy*, p. 13.
88 *T.N.*, p. 197.
89 Ibid., p. 143.
90 *N.K.*, p. 161.
91 *M.P.T.K.*, p. 128, referring to line 16 of Donne's second 'Elegy'.
92 *M.P.T.K.*, pp. 128, 131.
93 Harvey is at present the best source for 'Dream' material.
94 Regarded as a model also in 'Dream' (p. 27), Toussaint is best known
     in literary circles as the subject of a sonnet by Wordsworth.
95 *T.N.*, pp. 293, 295, 329, 335. The last word (not in O.E.D. in this
     form) has a large entry by Diderot in the *Encyclopédie* and he discusses
     it in *D'Alembert's Dream* (Harmondsworth, 1966, pp. 227–8).
96 *How it is*, pp. 28, 32, 33, 20, 39, 63, 111.
97 *N.K.*, p. 163.
98 *The Lost Ones*, London, 1972, pp. 8–9.
99 Ibid., p. 16.
100 *How it is*, p. 42.
101 Ibid., p. 116.
102 Ibid., pp. 30, 61.
103 *N.K.*, p. 130.
104 Ibid., p. 129.
105 Ibid., pp. 135–6.
106 Introduction to his 1968 edition, p. xxi.
107 *T.N.*, p. 104.
108 Ibid., p. 95.
109 Ibid., p. 296.
110 *How it is*, p. 43.
111 *T.N.*, p. 295.
112 Ibid., p. 116.
113 *How it is*, p. 30.
114 *T.N.*, p. 300.
115 Ibid., p. 285.
116 Ibid., p. 297.
117 Ibid., p. 306.
118 Ibid., p. 182.
119 Ibid., p. 270.
120 Ibid., p. 297.
121 Ibid., pp. 114, 170.
122 Ibid., p. 295.
123 *How it is*, p. 83.
124 *N.K.*, p. 24.
125 Ibid., p. 71.
126 Ibid., p. 127.
127 *Murphy*, chapter 6.

128 Cp. *Malone, T.N.*, p. 222. Life as a fictional persona is life 'ashore' for him (*T.N.*, p. 194).
129 *Murphy*, p. 92.
130 Ibid., p. 191.
131 *T.N.*, pp. 220–1.
132 Ibid., p. 203.
133 Ibid., p. 213.
134 Ibid., p. 207. A reference to 'I will lift up mine eyes unto the hills, from whence cometh my help' is submerged here.
135 Ibid., pp. 95, 223.
136 Ibid., p. 221.
137 Ibid., p. 303.
138 *N.K.*, p. 164.
139 *Murphy*, p. 49.
140 Ibid., p. 147.
141 Ibid., p. 159. Cp. *Still*: 'even in the dark eyes closed not enough.'
142 Ibid., p. 171.
143 Ibid., p. 46; cp. James Joyce, *Ulysses*, London, 1960, p. 788.
144 *Murphy*, p. 161.
145 Ibid., p. 54.
146 Ibid., p. 47; obviously an ironic comment on Dante's *Vita Nuova*.
147 *Murphy*, p. 99.
148 Ibid., p. 83.
149 *M.P.T.K.*, p. 45.
150 *Murphy*, p. 106.
151 *M.P.T.K.*, p. 54.
152 Ibid., p. 55.
153 *T.N.*, p. 32. Cp. also Watt's mixed choir (*Watt*, p. 32) heard also by Camier (*Mercier and Camier*, p. 37) and Malone, whose account is of particular interest (*T.N.*, p. 208).
154 Ibid., p. 8.
155 Ibid., p. 8.
156 *N.K.*, p. 97.
157 'Peintres', etc., p. 7.
158 *Murphy*, p. 160; *T.N.*, p. 341.
159 All these arguments derive from Augustine, where Beckett probably first encountered it.
160 *T.N.*, p. 294.
161 Ibid., p. 302. Cp. 'I am Matthew and I am the angel' (ibid., p. 303).
162 Ibid., p. 233.
163 Ibid., p. 312.
164 *T.N.*, p. 337.
165 *Watt*, p. 74.
166 Ibid., p. 56.
167 Ibid., p. 130. The idea of to-and-fro movement has fascinated Beckett from Murphy's rocking-chair to *Come and Go*. Throughout the trilogy, 'come and go' is a phrase associated with existence in the real (i.e.

unreal) world. Mr Knott's house is particularly dangerous because it flatters to deceive. It seems like a paradise of stasis, but is as much a chaotic bustle as anywhere else.

168 *Watt*, p. 129.
169 Ibid., p. 129. Is the face described in the Addenda (p. 252) God's face?
170 Ibid., p. 145.
171 Ibid., p. 147.
172 *Proust*, p. 18.
173 *Watt*, p. 6.
174 Ibid., p. 202.
175 Ibid., p. 203.
176 *T.N.*, p. 207.
177 *Watt*, p. 181 (normal order restored).
178 Ibid., p. 74.
179 *Murphy*, pp. 66, 144.
180 *T.N.*, p. 106. The dog's funeral in part one of *Molloy* is equated by the hero with his own (ibid., p. 37).
181 Ibid., p. 323.
182 Ibid., p. 207.
183 See Philip Solomon's article in *French Review*, vol. 51, no. 1, 1968, pp. 84–91.
184 *Murphy*, p. 74.
185 *T.N.*, p. 396.
186 *Proust*, p. 24.
187 *T.N.*, p. 390.
188 Ibid., p. 346.
189 Ibid., p. 372.
190 Ibid., pp. 295, 305, 322, 317 (341, 354, 355), 353, 358.
191 *Murphy*, pp. 95, 69, 96, 82.
192 Cp. ibid., p. 43, and T. S. Eliot as 'Old Possum'.
193 *T.N.*, p. 69.
194 Ibid., p. 123.
195 Ibid., p. 281, quoting p. 171.
196 Ibid., pp. 84, 184.
197 Ibid., p. 184.
198 Ibid., p. 193; as James Knowlson pointed out to me.
199 Ibid., p. 236; cp. *Authors take sides on the Spanish War*, London, 1937, p. 6.
200 *T.N.*, p. 37.
201 *Sunday Times*, 20 December 1964, p. 15. Cp. R.U.L. MS. 1396/4/44, p.7.
202 *T.N.*, p. 39.
203 *Proust*, p. 17; *T.N.*, p. 53.
204 *T.N.*, p. 152.
205 Franz Kafka, *Diaries*, 6 December 1921, Harmondsworth, 1972, p. 398.
206 *T.N.*, p. 31.
207 Ibid., p. 83.
208 Ibid., p. 261.

209 Ibid., p. 111.
210 Ibid., p. 134.
211 Ibid., p. 133.
212 Ibid., p. 170.
213 Ibid., p. 173; cp. the end of 'The Expelled': 'Living souls, you will see how alike they are' (*N.K.*, p. 24).
214 *T.N.*, p. 84.
215 Ibid., pp. 92, 181.
216 Ibid., p. 235.
217 Ibid., p. 363.
218 Ibid., p. 375.
219 Ibid., p. 149.
220 Ibid., p. 203.
221 Ibid., p. 225; cp. p. 388.
222 Kafka, *Diaries*, 21 October 1921, p. 395.
223 *T.N.*, p. 31.
224 Ibid., p. 198.

4 Drama for stage, screen and radio

1 The Beckett epigraph is from interview with Driver (*Columbia University Forum*, IV, Summer 1961, pp. 21–5).
2 Yeats, 'The Man and the Echo', *Collected Poems*, London, 1971, p. 393. Auden, in 'In Memory of W. B. Yeats' ii, offers a diametrically opposed conclusion.
3 See 'Messenger of Gloom', *Observer*, 9 November 1958, and Jean-Marie Serreau's account in P. Mélèse, *Beckett*, Paris, 1969, pp. 150–1.
4 Letter of 29 December 1957 to Alan Schneider.
5 *Play*, p. 9.
6 See Colin Duckworth's edition of *En attendant Godot*, London, 1966, p. xlvi.
7 'Reality Is Not Enough', *Tulane Drama Review*, vol. 9, no. 3, Spring 1965, pp. 142–3.
8 F. and F., p. 30.
9 Ibid., p. 28.
10 *Exhibition*, pp. 22–3.
11 He told Ruby Cohn, 'It's just a game' ('Books about Beckett', *Southern Review*, 2, 1966, p. 718). Cp. Alan Simpson, *Beckett and Behan and a theatre in Dublin*, London, 1962, p. 71; and Reid, p. 20.
12 Quotations from 'Eleuthéria' are from the R.U.L. copy; my translation of this ('Eleuthéria', p. 62) and other quotations.
13 Ibid., pp. 38–9.
14 Ibid., p. 62.
15 Ibid., p. 63.
16 Ibid., p. 87.
17 Ibid., p. 91. One of Beckett's own dreams, as Harvey, p. 298, makes clear.

18 Ibid., p. 97; *Murphy*, London, 1963, p. 32. Its origin is in Proust (see John Fletcher, 'Beckett et Proust', *Caliban*, 1, 1964, pp. 89–100).
19 'Eleuthéria', p. 102.
20 Ibid., pp. 112–13.
21 Ibid., p. 114.
22 Ibid., p. 114.
23 Ibid., p. 115.
24 Ibid., p. 116.
25 Ibid., pp. 117–18.
26 Ibid., p. 133.
27 Ibid., p. 28.
28 Ibid., p. 33.
29 *Waiting for Godot*, London, 1965, p. 9.
30 Ibid., p. 10.
31 Ibid., p. 17.
32 Ibid., p. 10.
33 Ibid., p. 11.
34 Ibid., p. 12.
35 Ibid., p. 14.
36 *Proust*, p. 17.
37 *Waiting for Godot*, p. 14.
38 Ibid., p. 19.
39 Ibid., p. 12.
40 Ibid., p. 19; cp. 'Eleuthéria', p. 125. The title of one of Yeats's early volumes.
41 *Waiting for Godot*, p. 10.
42 Ibid., p. 21.
43 Ibid., p. 21. Cp. 'It's inevitable' (p. 25), twice by Estragon to once by Vladimir.
44 Ibid., pp. 21–2.
45 Ibid., p. 22.
46 Ibid., p. 29.
47 Ibid., p. 31.
48 Ibid., p. 36.
49 Ibid., p. 32.
50 Ibid., p. 43.
51 Ibid., pp. 50–1; *Watt*, London, 1963, p. 15ff.
52 *Waiting for Godot*, p. 59.
53 Ibid., p. 62.
54 Ibid., pp. 62–3.
55 Ibid., p. 69.
56 Ibid., pp. 69, 70, 74. According to Roger Blin (Mélèse, p. 148), Beckett sees *Godot* as a kind of Western.
57 Ibid., p. 75.
58 Ibid., p. 80.
59 Ibid., p. 83.
60 Ibid., p. 89.

61 Ibid., p. 91; cp. *Proust*, p. 18ff.
62 Ibid., p. 92. Roger Blin (Mélèse, p. 147) says the white beard was not in the first draft.
63 Letter of 21 June 1956 to Alan Schneider. The letter of 30 April 1957 states: 'My work is for the small theatre.'
64 Reid, p. 12. Cp. *Irish Times*, 18 August 1956, which stresses Beckett's belief in 'a world with no edges' ('Portrait Gallery' section).
65 See the Fletchers' edition of *Fin de partie*, London, 1970, p. 8.
66 *Endgame*, p. 12.
67 'Dialogue of Self and Soul', *Collected Poems*, London, 1971, pp. 265–7.
68 *Proust*, p. 21.
69 *Endgame*, pp. 15, 45. 'Beyond', says Hamm (p. 23), 'is the other hell.'
70 Ibid., p. 17; cp. Mother Pegg dying of darkness (p. 48).
71 Ibid., p. 19; cp. 'A drip' in *Embers* (*Krapp*, p. 24).
72 *Endgame*, p. 21.
73 Ibid., p. 27.
74 Ibid., p. 25.
75 Ibid., p. 28.
76 Ibid., p. 29.
77 Ibid., p. 31; *Waiting for Godot*, p. 87.
78 *Endgame*, p. 32; cp. Lucky teaching Pozzo, *Waiting for Godot*, p. 32.
79 *Endgame*, p. 35.
80 Ibid., p. 33; cp. Beckett: 'He wants Clov to see what he's going out into' (*Sunday Times Magazine*, 1 April 1964). Beckett sees Hamm as 'the remains of a monster' (ibid.).
81 *Endgame*, p. 37.
82 Ibid., p. 38. Beckett describes this speech as a 'malediction' (*Sunday Times Magazine*, 1 April 1964).
83 *Endgame*, p. 39.
84 Ibid., p. 42.
85 Ibid., pp. 43–4.
86 Ibid., p. 44.
87 Ibid., p. 45; cp. p. 12.
88 Ibid., p. 47.
89 Ibid., p. 47.
90 Ibid., p. 49.
91 Ibid., p. 50.
92 Ibid., p. 51.
93 Ibid., p. 52.
94 The notebook for *Film* (R.U.L.) shows Beckett again toying with this analogy (p. 17).
95 *Krapp*, p. 13.
96 Ibid., p. 12; cp. *Endgame*, pp. 12, 19, 45.
97 Ibid., p. 13, emphasis added.
98 Ibid., pp. 14, 15.
99 Cp. *N.K.*, pp. 23–4.
100 *Krapp*, p. 16.

101 Ibid., p. 15.
102 Ibid., pp. 16, 12. See James Knowlson, *Light and Dark in the Theatre of Samuel Beckett*, London, 1972, p. 19ff, for a detailed discussion of this aspect of the play. Cp. the 'light of the fire' in *Embers*.
103 Beckett first read Fontane's *Effi Briest* in the 1930s, in Germany; it is also referred to in *All That Fall*, London, 1965, p. 29.
104 *Happy Days*, p. 10.
105 Ibid., p. 12.
106 The 'sweet old style' (ibid., p. 19, etc.) is an ironic reference to the *dolce stil nuovo* poets to which Dante (*Purgatorio*, xxiv, 57) referred.
107 *Happy Days*, London, 1966, p. 16; cp. *T.N.*, pp. 201–2.
108 *Waiting for Godot*, p. 69.
109 *Happy Days*, p. 20.
110 Ibid., p. 22.
111 Ibid., pp. 22–3.
112 Ibid., p. 24.
113 Ibid., p. 26.
114 Ibid., p. 27.
115 Ibid., p. 28. For the earth as extinguisher, cp. *Endgame*, p. 42.
116 *Happy Days*, p. 29.
117 Ibid., p. 30.
118 Ibid., p. 31.
119 Ibid., p. 33.
120 Ibid., pp. 38, 39.
121 Ibid., p. 38.
122 Cp. Eliot's 'The Hollow Men' and 'Eyes that last I saw in tears'; cp. also the camera eye of the poem 'Rue de Vaugirard', and *Proust*, p. 27.
123 *Happy Days*, p. 43.
124 Ibid., p. 40.
125 Ibid., pp. 42, 43.
126 Ibid., p. 44. Rilke's line (*Sonnets to Orpheus*, I, iii) is: 'Ein Hauch um nichts. Ein Wehn im Gott. Ein Wind.'
127 *Happy Days*, p. 39.
128 Ibid., p. 45; *How it is*, p. 49.
129 *Happy Days*, p. 38.
130 His plans changed between the first production (1963) and the first French staging (1964); see *Exhibition*, p. 92: 'The inquirer (light) begins to emerge as no less a victim of his inquiry than they and as needing to be free.'
131 *Play*, p. 33.
132 *N.K.*, p. 164.
133 *Play*, p. 35.
134 Ibid., p. 15.
135 Ibid., pp. 21–2.
136 Ibid., pp. 18–19.
137 Ibid., p. 18.

138 Ibid., p. 21.
139 Ibid., pp. 20, 21.
140 Ibid., p. 16.
141 *Come and Go*, London, 1967, p. 7.
142 *T.N.*, p. 198.
143 R.U.L. notebook is marked: 'Begun 20.3.72; Finished 1.4.72; Addenda 21.4.72.'
144 Composed between December 1955 and October 1956 (Fletcher's edition, p. 6).
145 *Not I*, London, 1973, p. 9.
146 *Eh Joe*, p. 19.
147 *All That Fall*, p. 7.
148 'Dream', p. 213.
149 The factory in Henry James's *The Ambassadors*, for example.
150 *All That Fall*, p. 32.
151 Ibid., pp. 7, 10, 22.
152 Ibid., p. 7.
153 Ibid., p. 10.
154 Ibid., p. 31.
155 Ibid., p. 28.
156 Ibid., p. 29.
157 Ibid., p. 31.
158 Ibid., p. 33.
159 Cp. Beckett's interest in Geulincx's example of the man crawling along the deck (*T.N.*, p. 51; cp. p. 339).
160 *All That Fall*, p. 25.
161 Ibid., p. 34.
162 Ibid., p. 16.
163 Ibid., p. 13; *N.K.*, p. 144.
164 Ibid., p. 20.
165 Ibid., p. 21.
166 Ibid., p. 9; cp. footnote 96.
167 Ibid., pp. 23–4.
168 Ibid., p. 35.
169 Ibid., pp. 11, 17.
170 Ibid., p. 11.
171 *Krapp*, p. 21.
172 Ibid., p. 22.
173 Ibid., p. 22; *Endgame*, p. 45.
174 *Krapp*, pp. 22–3.
175 Ibid., pp. 23–4.
176 Ibid., p. 24.
177 Ibid., p. 38.
178 Ibid., p. 21.
179 Ibid., p. 39.
180 Ibid., pp. 32–3.
181 Ibid., p. 33.

182 Ibid., p. 35.
183 Ibid., p. 33.
184 Ibid., p. 35.
185 *N.K.*, p. 75.
186 *Watt*, p. 45.
187 *Krapp*, pp. 27–8; cp. p. 22.
188 The title of part of Yeats's 1933 collection.
189 *Play*, p. 29; the poem is an early Yeats work.
190 Ibid., p. 32.
191 Ibid., pp. 32–3.
192 Ibid., p. 34.
193 Ibid., pp. 34–5.
194 In *Evergreen Review*, no. 30, May–June 1963, p. 47.
195 *Play*, p. 46.
196 Ibid., p. 47.
197 Magazine version, p. 55; cp. *Play*, p. 36.
198 Ibid., p. 45.
199 Ibid., p. 47.
200 Ibid., p. 42.
201 Ibid., p. 43.
202 *N.K.*, p. 130.
203 *Play*, p. 41.
204 Ibid., p. 39.
205 Ibid., p. 41.
206 Ibid., p. 44.
207 Ibid., p. 45.
208 Magazine version, p. 55.
209 *Play*, p. 47.
210 *Film*, p. 77.
211 Ibid., p. 57.
212 Ibid., p. 85.
213 Ibid., p. 65.
214 *Eh Joe*, p. 17.
215 Ibid., p. 15.
216 In the review of Sean O'Casey's *Windfalls*, *Bookman*, 87, 1934, p. 111.
217 In the interview with Marowitz, *Village Voice*, 1 March 1962, pp. 1, 13.
218 *Bram van Velde*, London, 1960, p. 56.
219 Reid, p. 68.

5 The intellectual and cultural background to Beckett

1 The epigraphs are from *T.N.*, p. 39, and *How it is*, p. 41.
2 *Alone*, London, 1926, p. 170.
3 See Stravinsky and Robert Craft, *Dialogues and a Diary*, London, 1968, the diary entry for 16 May 1962.
4 *Murphy*, London, 1963, p. 159.

5 *M.P.T.K.*, p. 84.

6 The Israelite that Malone took advice from on the subject of conation is, of course, Spinoza; his friend Jackson's parrot quotes the same authority (*T.N.*, p. 218).

7 See W. van Leyden, *Seventeenth Century Metaphysics*, London, 1968, p. 75.

8 Descartes, *Discourse on Method*, ed. G. E. M. Anscombe and P. T. Geach, London, 1964, p. 21.

9 Introduction to *The Living Thoughts of Descartes*, London, 1948, pp. 31–2.

10 *The Birth of Tragedy*, New York, 1956, p. 80.

11 *Murphy*, p. 124.

12 On Geulincx, see Hugh Kenner, *Samuel Beckett: a Critical Study*, London, 1965, pp. 83–91. *N.K.*, p. 58, refers specifically to Geulincx's *Ethics*.

13 See 'Le Monde', etc., p. 356.

14 Cp. note 6 above.

15 Cp. Vico's theory that man cannot know what he does not do, i.e. has not made.

16 For good discussions of Geulincx, see van Leyden, *op. cit.*, and D. J. McCracken, *Thinking and Valuing*, London, 1951.

17 See *Dialogues on Metaphysics and Religion*, trans. Morris Ginsberg, London, 1923, p. 18.

18 *How it is*, London, 1964, p. 33.

19 *Murphy*, p. 76.

20 Ibid., p. 168.

21 Richard Ellmann, *James Joyce*, London, 1959, p. 661; reported to Ellmann by Beckett. If history is really the nightmare Stephen Dedalus says it is, Joyce would like to believe the idealists because he could then disregard it; Hume's history means he cannot.

22 See Jean Onimus, *Beckett*, Paris, 1968, p. 19ff.

23 See Ulick O'Connor, *Oliver St. John Gogarty: a Poet and his Times*, London, 1964, p. 28off.

24 James Joyce, *A Portrait of the Artist as a Young Man*, Harmondsworth, 1960, pp. 106–7.

25 Both quoted in the addenda to *Watt* (London, 1963).

26 Medieval historians referred to by Moran.

27 *T.N.*, p. 168.

28 *Our Exag.*, p. 14. Concerning Augustine and the two thieves, Beckett told Harold Hobson 'The Latin is even finer than the English'.

29 *The World as Will and Idea*, trans. R. B. Haldane and J. Kemp, London, 1896, volume 1, pp. 525–6.

30 *M.P.T.K.*, p. 156.

31 Beckett changed the characters A and B to A and C for the first publication of the complete *Molloy*, presumably to emphasize discontinuity and to allude to Cain and Abel. The Dante passage that begins 'Dante and the Lobster' concerns Cain. The influence of Byron's neglected drama *Cain* on the nineteenth century is discussed by George Steiner in *The Death of Tragedy* (London, 1968), and Honor

Matthews has discussed the use of the story in the theatre, in *The Primal Curse* (New York, 1967).

32 At the end of *Malone Dies* the character Lemuel (Samuel?) begins to kill off Malone's 'characters'. Lemuel means 'consecrated to God' and is Gulliver's name. Malone seems able to halt his cruelty in mid-stroke by an act of mind, which God is unable to do.

33 For Melville's use of the idea, see Leslie Fiedler, *Love and Death in the American Novel*, London, 1970, p. 360.

34 Whereas for Kierkegaard, the incarnation is confirmed by repetition, for Beckett every birth is only a repetition of sorts. Moran repeats Molloy with a difference; Malone's cyclical movements never, as far as the Unnamable can see, recur twice in the same way. And in the late texts the pressure of words from one repeated block prevents the perfect repetition of another. Malone's religious calendar is a succession of moveable feasts.

35 *M.P.T.K.*, p. 61.

36 *International Theatre Annual*, no. 1, London, 1956, p. 153.

37 See interview with Driver (*Columbia University Forum*, IV, Summer 1961, pp. 21–5).

38 *Murphy*, p. 125.

39 'Denis Devlin', p. 290.

40 See Baudelaire 'On the Essence of Laughter'. E. R. Curtius (*European Literature and the Latin Middle Ages*, Princeton, 1973, p. 420ff) traces the history of the idea.

41 See 'The Risen Lord' in *A Selection from 'Phoenix'*, ed. A. A. H. Inglis, Harmondsworth, 1971, pp. 553–60.

42 Cp. Moran on the Old Testament, *T.N.*, p. 119.

43 *Critique of Practical Reason*, trans. K. R. Abbott, London, 1959, p. 321.

44 *Proust*, p. 75. Beckett told Ellmann (*James Joyce*, p. 499) that the idea was originally Joyce's. Cp. Macmann: 'The ideas of guilt and punishment were confused together in his mind' (*T.N.*, p. 240).

45 See William James, *Varieties of Religious Experience*, London, 1971, pp. 302, 341.

46 *Our Exag.*, pp. 12–13. This is why Belacqua's *sursum corda* in 'Love and Lethe' is voyeurism and masturbation, later (*T.N.*, p. 111) equated with the artistically liberated imagination.

47 C. G. Jung, 'Answer to Job', *Collected Works*, volume 11, London, 1958.

48 *Hayden*, ed. J. Selz, Geneva, 1962, pp. 40–1.

49 In *transition*, nos 16 and 17 (June 1929), pp. 268–71. Cp. 'Dream', p. 37.

50 Harvey, p. 441.

51 Vega is mentioned again in 'Dream', pp. 14–15 and *Embers* (*Krapp*, p. 23); for its importance in Shintoism, see W. G. Aston, *Shinto*, London, 1905. The blue flower is mentioned again in the review of Rilke and comes from chapter 1 of *Heinrich von Ofterdingen*.

52 The woman is a madonna of sorts: Mary's colour is blue, and the star and sea imagery suggest the idea of Mary as 'star of the sea', *stella maris*.

53 See interview with Driver.

54 *M.P.T.K.*, p. 176.
55 Ibid., p. 176. Cp. 'Enueg I', quoting Robert Burton.
56 Harvey, p. 267. Malone quotes Democritus (*T.N.*, p. 193).
57 'Dream', p. 8.
58 The re-telling of the story of Hippasos reveals that Beckett's interest in philosophy is often anecdotal.
59 *Proust*, p. 125.
60 *Endgame*, p. 45.
61 'The Beckett Hero' (reprinted in the 'Twentieth Century Views' collection, ed. Esslin), p. 46.
62 See the entry 'Aristotle' in Lemprière's *Classical Dictionary*.
63 *Proust*, p. 112. In the unpublished lecture 'Le Concentrisme' Beckett stresses how wrong it is to 'make concrete Kant's thing-in-itself' where art is concerned; the first volume of his copy of Proust contains marginal notes referring to Kant (volume 1, p. 73).
64 The description of Sam and Watt (*Watt*, p. 153) feeding the rats shows Beckett parodying the idea.
65 *T.N.*, pp. 86–7; *Critique of Practical Reason, ed. cit.*, p. 33.
66 *World as Will and Idea*, volume 1, p. 531.
67 See the article on Schopenhauer in Edwards's *Encyclopaedia of Philosophy*.
68 See Martin Esslin, *Theatre of the Absurd*, London, 1962, p. 34, and Ellmann, *James Joyce*, p. 661.
69 See Gershon Weiler, *Mauthner's Critique of Language*, Cambridge, 1970, p. 9.
70 Ibid., p. 15.
71 Ibid., p. 32.
72 Ibid., p. 177. Cp. R.U.L. MS. 1396/4/44, p. 3.
73 Ibid., p. 274.
74 See the article on Mauthner in Edwards's *Encyclopaedia of Philosophy*.
75 Weiler, *Mauthner's Critique of Language*, p. 289.
76 John Fletcher was quite right to suspect that Beckett must have had 'some contact with logical positivism' (*Samuel Beckett's Art*, London, 1967, p. 136); Mauthner influenced Wittgenstein.
77 See Allan Janik and Stephen Toulmin's *Wittgenstein's Vienna*, London, 1973, pp. 130–1.
78 In the Driver interview; cp. 'Le Monde', etc., p. 349.
79 R. Heppenstall, *The Fourfold Tradition*, London, 1961, p. 257.
80 'Recent Irish Poetry', *Lace Curtain*, no. 4, Summer 1971, p. 58.
81 *T.N.*, pp. 162, 99. R. T. Riva's essay 'Beckett and Freud' (*Criticism*, 12, 1970, pp. 120–32) discusses parallels generally.
82 *Endgame*, p. 45.
83 Sigmund Freud, *Collected Works*, London, 1961, volume 21, p. 132. Cp. Schopenhauer, *World as Will and Idea*, trans. R. B. Haldane and J. Kemp, London, 1896, volume 1, pp. 457–8.
84 *Freud*, London, 1971, p. 186.
85 *N.K.*, p. 103.

6 The literary background to Beckett

1 The epigraph is from *Proust*, p. 29.
2 See E. R. Curtius, *European Literature and the Latin Middle Ages*, Princeton, 1973, chapter 17 *passim*, and p. 595ff.
3 *N.K.*, p. 117.
4 *T.N.*, p. 134.
5 *Endgame*, p. 39.
6 See John Fletcher, *Samuel Beckett's Art*, London, 1967, pp. 106–21.
7 *Our Exag.*, p. 22; but cp. Duckworth's edition of *Godot*, p. lix.
8 *Essays and Aphorisms*, trans. R. J. Hollingdale, Harmondsworth, 1970, p. 186.
9 *T.N.*, p. 362.
10 J. C. Powys, *The Enjoyment of Literature*, New York, 1938, p. 114.
11 *M.P.T.K.*, p. 18. Cp. Harvey, p. 295, n. 66. Translating *Inferno*, xx, 28.
12 'Fragments', *Collected Poems*, ed. T. D. Renshaw, Dublin, 1971, p. 45.
13 Powys, *Enjoyment of Literature*, pp. 132–3.
14 'Papini's Dante', *Bookman*, no. 87, 1934, p. 14.
15 *Our Exag.*, p. 18.
16 *Purgatorio*, xxiv, 57.
17 Quoted from Flaminio Nobile by J. C. Nelson, *The Renaissance Theory of Love*, New York, 1958, p. 154. Cp. Robert Briffault: 'The old troubadour conceit about love penetrating through the eyes . . . becomes (in the poets of the *stil nuovo*) invested with implications which soar into the rarefied atmosphere of transcendental metaphysics' (*The Troubadours*, Bloomington, 1965, p. 168).
18 'Ex Cathezra', *Bookman*, no. 87, 1934, p. 10.
19 Petrarch actually uses the phrase of Arnaut Daniel (in 'The Triumph of Love') which somewhat spoils Beckett's point.
20 Coleridge, *Notes and Lectures on Shakespeare and Other Literary Remains*, London, 1849, vol. 2, p. 23.
21 The poem 'Vive morte ma seule saison', as pointed out by Fletcher, reviewing Harvey, for *L'Esprit Créateur*, vol. 2, no. 3, 1971.
22 *M.P.T.K.*, p. 105. Ronsard is again referred to in the notebook for the German production of *Happy Days* (R.U.L., p. 44).
23 Cp. Denis de Rougemont, *Love in the Western World*, trans. Montgomery Belgion, New York, 1957, pp. 162–70.
24 *Stephen Hero*, London, 1966, p. 78. Stephen's Ballast Office (ibid., p. 216) reappears in *How it is*, London, 1964, p. 50.
25 By Benjamin Crémieux; see *TLS*, 13 April 1973, p. 424.
26 *Proust*, p. 81.
27 *Le Monde*, 19 January 1960.
28 'Dream', p. 42.
29 Ibid., p. 128.
30 In interview with Driver (*Columbia University Forum*, IV, Summer 1961, pp. 21–5).
31 T. E. Hulme, *Speculations*, London, 1924, p. 118.

32 'The Drunken Boat' in *Romanticism Reconsidered*, ed. Northrop Frye, New York, 1963, p. 23. See also chapter 7 of Frank Kermode's *The Romantic Image* (London, 1957).

33 *Proust*, p. 80. Cp. 'a petulant dribbling' (Constant's *Adolphe*) and Chateaubriand and Amiel as 'a pair of melancholy Pantheists dancing a fandango of death in the moonlight' (*Proust*, pp. 54, 82). 'For the intelligent Amiel there is only one landscape' (in the 1934 review of MacGreevy's *Poems*) is characteristically two-edged. 'Dream', p. 14, is very blunt: 'the gratuitous echolalia and claptrap rhapsodies that are palmed off as passion and lyricism and the high spots of the creative mystery.'

34 Quoted from the Italian critic De Sanctis, in *Proust*, p. 79.

35 *First Love*, London, 1973, p. 31.

36 *Hyperion*, trans. W. Trask, New York, 1965, p. 61.

37 *N.K.*, p. 56.

38 'Price Athanase', 1, 91; 'The Triumph of Life', 334; 'Hellas', 878–85.

39 *Confessions*, Harmondsworth, 1953, p. 263.

40 *Reveries of a Solitary*, trans. J. G. Fletcher, London, 1927, p. 40.

41 *Literary Essays*, London, 1963, p. 217.

42 *Leopardi: Selected Prose and Poetry*, Oxford, 1966, p. 297.

43 *Essays, Dialogues and Thoughts*, trans. James Thomson, London, n.d., p. 17.

44 Ibid., p. 63.

45 See Vico's poem 'Affetti d'un disperato', translated in H. P. Adams, *Life and Writings of Giambattista Vico*, London, 1935.

46 Beckett quotes Shelley in *Godot* and *Happy Days*; Baudelaire's 'Voyage à Cythère' and Phlebas the Phoenician in *The Waste Land* are parallels.

47 *Hyperion*, p. 154.

48 Translated from Poulet's article on 'Timelessness and Romanticism' in *Journal of the History of Ideas*, no. 15, 1954, p. 21.

49 Yeats.

50 Review of Rilke's *Poems*, *Criterion*, 13, 1934, pp. 705–6.

51 *An Evening with Monsieur Teste*, trans. Gould, London, 1936, p. 44.

52 In 'MacGreevy on Yeats', Beckett praises MacGreevy's translation of Valéry's *Introduction*.

53 *Introduction to the Method of Leonardo da Vinci*, trans. T. MacGreevy, London, 1929, p. 14.

54 Ibid., p. 22.

55 Ibid., p. 1.

56 *T.N.*, p. 305.

57 M. Cowley, *Exile's Return*, London, 1951, p. 147. Cp. Dostoevsky's *White Nights*, where 'the artist of his own life' desires nothing.

58 'MacGreevy on Yeats', p. 2.

59 '... let us submit to the disintegration of our body, since each new fragment which breaks away from it returns in a luminous and significant form to add itself to our work....' (Proust, *Time Regained*, trans. A. Mayor, London, 1970, p. 277.)

60 Quoted by Walter A. Strauss, *Descent and Return*, Cambridge, Mass., 1971, p. 86.
61 Cp. Valéry's quarrel with Pascal. Beckett has taken a keen interest in Valéry's *Notebooks*, as they have been published.
62 Rimbaud, *Collected Poems*, trans. O. Bernard, Harmondsworth, 1962, pp. 240, 316.
63 Ibid., p. 327.
64 See George Steiner, *Language and Silence*, Harmondsworth, 1969, p. 145.
65 *The Disinherited Mind*, Harmondsworth, 1961, p. 238.
66 'Where now? What now?' in *Evergreen Review*, 2, 7, 1959, p. 222. Cp. Schopenhauer's 'hollow globe from whose vacancy a voice speaks' (*World as Will and Idea*, trans. R. B. Haldane and J. Kemp, London, 1896, volume 1, p. 358). Roland Barthes' 'silence of the text as mimesis' seems a structuralist variant.
67 See *The Thoughts of Novalis*, trans. M. J. Hope, London, 1891, p. 217.
68 Soren Kierkegaard, *Concluding Unscientific Postscript*, chapter 3, section 1.
69 *T.N.*, pp. 370–1.
70 *First Love*, p. 31.
71 William York Tindall, *Samuel Beckett*, New York, 1964, p. 37.
72 John Fletcher, *Samuel Beckett's Art*, p. 89ff.
73 'Che Sciagura' is from chapter 11 of *Candide*.
74 Fielding is referred to in *M.P.T.K.* on p. 96.
75 *Don Quixote*, part 2, chapter 71, referred to in 'Le Monde', etc., p. 356.
76 See Germaine Brée, 'Beckett's Abstractors of Quintessence', *French Review*, 36, 1963, pp. 567–76.
77 Roger Shattuck, *The Banquet Years*, London, 1969, p. 238.
78 *Watt*, p. 245.
79 A. Schopenhauer, *The Art of Literature*, trans. T. B. Saunders, London, 1891, p. 77.
80 José Ortega y Gasset, *The Dehumanization of Art*, trans. M. Weyl, Princeton, 1948, p. 97. Cp. Diderot's respect for Richardson.
81 *Jacques the Fatalist*, p. 77.
82 Denis Diderot, *Oeuvres complètes*, ed. J. Assézat, Garnier, Paris, 1875–7, volume 6, p. 87.
83 *Watt*, p. 123.
84 *Oeuvres complètes*, volume 6, p. 180.
85 *T.N.*, p. 222.
86 *Jacques the Fatalist*, p. 210.
87 Ibid., p. 76.
88 The modern *picaro* is distinguished from the ancient by the fact that he is a truth-seeking quester, not merely a curious traveller. But cp. Grimmelshausen's *Simplicissimus*.
89 'The man who ridicules romance is the most romantic of men' (Keats, in a letter to George and Georgiana Keats of 19 February 1819).
90 In the interview with Shenker (*New York Times*, 6 May 1956, section 2, pp. x, 1, 3).

91 Arnold, *Poems 1840–1866*, London, 1908, p. 362.
92 *All That Fall*, London, 1965, p. 34.
93 See B. Kawin, *Telling it Again and Again*, Ithaca, 1972, pp. 131–45.
94 A nineteenth-century novelist, say Dickens, would have used this to reveal, rather than conceal, identity.
95 *How it is*, p. 142. Cp. Lévi-Strauss: 'a truly total history would cancel itself out' (*The Savage Mind*, London, 1966, p. 257). Cp. Zola: 'When I attack a subject, I would like to force the whole universe into it' (F. W. J. Hemmings, *Emile Zola*, Oxford, 1953, p. 30).
96 W. B. Yeats, *Mythologies*, London, 1959, p. 357.
97 Thomas Mann, 'The Making of *The Magic Mountain*', *Atlantic Monthly*, January 1953, p. 44.
98 Henri Focillon, *The Life of Forms in Art*, New Haven, 1942, p. 64.
99 *Ulysses*, p. 554.
100 Cp. Pound, *Literary Essays*, p. 420.
101 *Wordsworth*, London, 1936 (1965 edn.,) p. 124.
102 'Proust in Pieces', *Spectator*, no. 5530, 23 June 1934, p. 976.
103 'Dream', p. 107.
104 'Proust in Pieces', p. 976.
105 Donald Fanger, *Dostoevsky and Romantic Realism*, Cambridge, Mass., 1965, p. 119.
106 *Watt*, p. 249.
107 *Murphy*, London, 1963, p. 13. Cp. 'Such density of furniture defeats imagination' (*First Love*, p. 46).
108 *Our Exag.*, p. 14ff.
109 'Peintres', etc., p. 4.
110 Ibid., p. 4.
111 'Proust in Pieces', p. 976. This is why he is especially critical of his own 'handful of abstractions' (*Our Exag.*, p. 3) and why he liked the concreteness of Jules Romains's early poetry. Asking for 'facts, plenty of facts' in 'Dream' (p. 66) is not Gradgrindian; he wants to have 'music and whiteness facts in the fact of my mind' (ibid., p. 162).
112 *New English Weekly*, 17 March 1938, p. 455.
113 *Murphy*, p. 81.
114 Ibid., p. 86.
115 *M.P.T.K.*, p. 67.
116 *Our Exag.*, p. 15. *Great Expectations*, chapter 54 (Harmondsworth, 1965, p. 449) is the passage in question.
117 *Bleak House*, Harmondsworth, 1971, p. 319.
118 *N.K.*, p. 139.
119 *T.N.*, p. 295.
120 Soren Kierkegaard, *Repetition*, New York, 1942, p. 125; C. G. Jung, *Collected Works*, volume 11, London, 1958.
121 George Gissing, *Charles Dickens*, London, 1898, p. 197. Beckett refers repeatedly to Dickens in 'Dream' (pp. 90, 112, 117, 133, 141, 168).
122 Rimbaud, *Collected Poems*, trans. O. Bernard, Harmondsworth, 1962, p. 334.

123 Paul Valéry, 'Poetry and Abstract Thought', *The Art of Poetry, Collected Works*, volume 7, London, 1958, p. 58.

124 Richard Ellmann, *Yeats; the Man and the Masks*, London, 1961, pp. 175–6.

125 A. Artaud, *The Theatre and Its Double*, trans. Mary C. Richards, New York, 1958, p. 76.

126 Paul Valéry, *Aesthetics, Collected Works*, volume 13, New York, 1964, p. 4.

127 Artaud, *The Theatre and its Double*, p. 71.

128 'The Tragical in Daily Life', *The Treasure of the Humble*, London, 1908, pp. 105–6.

129 Bim and Bom are used for names of characters in *Murphy*; in *M.P.T.K.*, they appear with Grock (p. 176), the presiding genius of 'Dream' (pp. 7, 122, 183, 212). The tag means 'joking apart' and began as 'sans blague' as Grock's autobiography makes clear.

130 See, for example, Diderot's *Paradoxe sur le comédien*; the dramatic theory is not unlike Yeats's.

131 Cp. Diderot, quoted in Herbert Josephs's *Diderot's Dialogue of Language and Gesture*, Ohio, 1969, p. 68; and Tolstoy: 'It is consciousness of self which is static' (Journal for 15 January 1910).

132 'The Common saying of life being a farce is true in every sense but the most important one, for it is a ridiculous tragedy, which is the worst kind of composition', Jonathan Swift, *Correspondence*, ed. Sir H. Williams, Oxford, 1963–5, volume 4, p. 217.

133 *Either/Or*, New York, 1959, volume 1, p. 138.

134 *Repetition*, p. 48ff.

135 See Strauss, *Descent and Return*, p. 136.

136 *The Painter of Modern Life and Other Essays*, trans. and ed. J. Mayne, London, 1964, pp. 148, 152, 153.

137 Bergson's description of 'something mechanical encrusted upon the living' ('Laughter', in *Comedy*, ed. Wylie Sypher, New York, 1956, p. 84) is clearly relevant to such conceptions as Watt's walk, for instance.

138 Nietzsche, *Thus Spoke Zarathustra*, book 4, 'On the Higher Man', section 18. Cp. Beckett's review of 'Dante Vivo'.

139 *Inferno*, trans. C. Field, London, 1912, pp. 158, 176.

140 Cp. also Wyndham Lewis's *The Childermass* and Kipling's *The Light that Failed*.

141 Gershon Weiler, *Mauthner's Critique of Language*, Cambridge, 1970, p. 274.

142 Cp. Montaigne (*Essays*, book 1, chapter 50), Burton's 'Democritus to the Reader' (*Anatomy of Melancholy*), Leopardi (*Essays, Dialogues and Thoughts*, trans. James Thomson, London, n.d., p. 21).

143 *M.P.T.K.*, p. 175; Donne's tenth paradox is referred to.

144 Quoted by Bergson, 'Laughter', p. 177.

145 Donne's tenth paradox.

146 Hugh Kenner, *Dublin's Joyce*, London, 1955, p. 152.

147 M. de Unamuno, *The Tragic Sense of Life*, London, 1962, p. 311.

148 *Proust*, p. 122.

149 *Sunday Times*, 20 December 1964, p. 15.

150 *M.P.T.K.*, p. 175.

151 *Waiting for Godot*, London, 1965, p. 79.

152 See Rolf Fjelde, 'Peer Gynt, Naturalism and the Dissolving Self', *TDR*, volume 13, no. 2, 1968, p. 31ff.

153 *Proust*, p. 29.

154 Cp. Hölderlin's 'Hyperion's Song of Fate' and Baudelaire's 'Le Goût du Néant'.

155 Quoted by Raymond Williams, *Drama from Ibsen to Eliot*, Harmondsworth, 1964, p. 120.

156 Janvier, *Pour Samuel Beckett*, Paris, 1966, p. 254.

157 *Proust*, p. 26.

158 Donne, 'The Ecstasy', 74. Valéry calls *Monsieur Teste* a 'monodialogue'.

159 Parallels between Beckett and Strindberg (often very forced) are discussed by Anthony Swerling, *Strindberg's Impact in France 1920–60*, Cambridge, 1971, pp. 111–35. See also Rose-Marie G. Oster, 'Hamm and Hummel', in *Scandinavian Studies*, 41, 1969, pp. 330–45.

160 Cp. Pirandello's *As You Desire Me*, where the Unknown Lady also arrives eventually. Beckett toyed with the idea that Godot arrived in the form of Pozzo, see Duckworth's edition, pp. lx–lxi.

161 *The Intruder*, London, 1913, p. 13.

162 Ibid., pp. 22–3.

163 Ibid., p. 31.

164 Mario Praz, *The Romantic Agony*, London, 1960, p. 332.

165 'A Theory of the Stage', in *The Theory of the Modern Stage*, ed. E. Bentley, Harmondsworth, 1968, p. 342. Vladimir Nabokov has characteristically spoken of Beckett's 'wretched plays in the Maeterlinck tradition' (*Novel*, Spring 1971, p. 219).

166 Yeats in Lady Gregory, *Our Irish Theatre*, London, 1914, p. 9. Beckett mildly criticized Yeats in 1934 ('Recent Irish Poetry') but in 1962 (see chapter 5, n. 3) was convinced of his greatness. Katharine Worth's 'Yeats and the New French Drama' (*Modern Drama*, 8, 1966, pp. 382–91) is an excellent study; Marilyn Gaddis's 'Purgatory Metaphor of Yeats and Beckett' (*London Magazine*, 7, 1967, pp. 33–45) is more specialized.

167 'The Essential and the Incidental', p. 111.

168 *Exhibition*, p. 14.

169 Oliver St John Gogarty, *As I was Going Down Sackville Street*, London, 1968, p. 27.

170 *N.K.*, p. 141.

171 *T.N.*, p. 85.

172 Ibid., p. 319.

7 Beckett's poetry

1 The epigraphs are from 'Le Monde', etc., p. 349, and *T.N.*, p. 332

(quoting from the conclusion to Bacon's preface to the *Instauratio Magna*).

2 Harvey reprints Beckett's entire poetic output; cited for the uncollected poems as the most accessible source for most readers.

3 See Harvey, p. 33, for the circumstances surrounding its composition.

4 See Nancy Cunard, *These were the Hours*, Carbondale, 1969, pp. 109–22.

5 *Our Exag.*, p. 7.

6 Harvey, p. 314.

7 Beckett associates detumescence with the descent from the Cross ('assumption upside down', 'Dream', p. 162), a release from pain, bringing the 'hush and indolence of limbo'.

8 Harvey, pp. 280–1.

9 'Perhaps the most perfect form of Being would be an ejaculation', Harvey, p. 441.

10 Harvey, pp. 295–6.

11 Ibid., pp. 311–12.

12 Wordsworth, 'Ode: Intimations of Immortality', stanza 3.

13 O.E.D.'s sixth definition is given a gnostic context, but the biological (definition 3) or the mathematical (definition 5) may also have been in Beckett's mind.

14 Harvey, p. 275; *M.P.T.K.*, p. 65.

15 Goethe's 'Harzreise im Winter' was one of Eugène Jolas's favourite poems.

16 *Poems*, pp. 18–19.

17 T. S. Eliot, *Collected Poems*, London, 1963, p. 26; W. B. Yeats, 'Nineteen Hundred and Nineteen', *Collected Poems*, London, 1971, p. 237.

18 *Poems*, p. 20.

19 Ibid., pp. 21–2.

20 In 'Dream', p. 99, the phrase is used to describe the Alba's elevation above the Smeraldina's sexuality. Stanza 26 of 'Le Larron' in Apollinaire's *Alcools* (a collection Beckett admires greatly) contains the word 'plagale' and provides a useful background for 'Dortmunder'.

21 *Poems*, p. 24.

22 *Murphy*, London, 1963, pp. 47, 54.

23 Ernest Hemingway, *A Moveable Feast*, Harmondsworth, 1966, p. 9.

24 Quoted by Harvey, p. 89.

25 *Poems*, p. 32.

26 Ibid., p. 32.

27 Harvey, p. 155.

28 *M.P.T.K.*, p. 21.

29 Cp. also Heinrich von Morungen, *Penguin Book of German Verse*, Harmondsworth, 1969, p. 16.

30 *Poems*, p. 37 (rearranged).

31 *Krapp*, p. 35.

32 Beckett dropped this Eliotic addition for the 1961 edition, perhaps because it makes less sense when the poems comprise only part of a collection.

33 *Poems*, p. 41.
34 Ibid., pp. 41–2.
35 Walter Pater, *The Renaissance*, 'The School of Giorgione'.
36 See F. and F., p. 23.
37 *How it is*, London, 1964, p. 30ff.
38 *N.K.*, p. 139.
39 *Poèmes*, Paris, 1968, p. 10.
40 Ibid., p. 11; my translations.
41 Ibid., p. 12. The 'green eyes' suggest the Smeraldina (see Harvey, p. 122).
42 Sir Thomas Browne, *Religio Medici and Other Writings*, London, 1969, Everyman edition, p. 119.
43 *Poèmes*, p. 13.
44 Ibid., p. 14.
45 The title describes an ancient monument that might have appealed as a subject to Valéry; but the technique is very different.
46 Cp. John Fletcher and John Spurling, *Beckett: A Study of his Plays*, London, 1973, p. 94. Among Beckett's notes for *Film* is one saying: 'If music unavoidable Schubert's "Doppelgänger" with perhaps "Ich bin nicht wild, komme nicht zu strafen".' The quotation is from Mathias Claudius' poem 'Der Tod und das Madchen' which inspired Schubert's music.
47 *Poèmes*, p. 19.
48 Ibid., p. 20.
49 Beckett seems to have no particular account in mind, but he would know *Paradise Lost*, book 4, 1.269 and Ovid's *Metamorphoses*, book 5, ll.385–91.
50 See *Poèmes*, p. 21.
51 *Poems in English*, p. 43.
52 'The Private Pain and the Whey of Words' ('Twentieth Century Views', p. 31).
53 Harvey, p. 179.
54 Harvey, p. 229, makes clear that the poem has close connections with the death of Beckett's mother.
55 *Poèmes*, p. 22.
56 'Our pernicious and incurable optimism' (*Proust*, p. 15).
57 *Our Exag.*, p. 14.
58 H. Porter Abbott's discussion of the novels in the light of this remark seems misguided, in so far as it is doubtful if the aesthetic can be applied to novels, in the accepted sense, at all. The approach clearly works best with the late texts which, far as they are from Joyce, are perhaps the nearest Beckett comes to him.
59 *Poems*, p. 23.
60 'Dream', p. 151.
61 Ibid., pp. 151–2.
62 Ibid., p. 146.
63 Ibid., p. 42.

64 Ibid., p. 42. Not surprisingly, perhaps, he disliked Omar Khayyam (ibid., p. 176) and preferred Hafiz (ibid., p. 42).
65 *Obras*, Madrid, 1898, volume 3, pp. 112–13.
66 'Dream', p. 91. The reference is to the 'Délires II' section of *Une Saison en Enfer*.
67 'Humanistic Quietism', p. 70.
68 This is, admittedly, simplified literary history. The 'pure poetry' of Mallarmé was eventually undermined by the 'tribe' to whose language he had sought to give a pure sense. Perhaps only Yeats wrote successfully in both modes.
69 Sighle Kennedy (*Murphy's Bed*, Lewisburg, 1971, p. 220ff.) suggests Beckett was a verticalist. Verticalism was a Jolas-inspired development of Surrealism called into being when Jolas felt Surrealism had revealed its traditionalism.
70 *Beckett at Sixty*, London, 1967, p. 12.
71 Two authoritative books on Surrealism fail to make this clear: Anna Balakian's *Surrealism: the Road to the Absolute*, New York, 1959, and Mary Ann Caws's *The Poetry of Dada and Surrealism*, Princeton, 1970.
72 Translated by Beckett for *transition*. Bruce Morrissette's 'Narrative "You" in Contemporary Literature' (*Comparative Literature Studies*, volume 2, no. 1, 1965, pp. 1–24) discusses a distinctively Apollinairean device.
73 Margaret Callander's excellent account of *The Poetry of Pierre-Jean Jouve* (Manchester, 1965) does not discuss Beckett, but her discussion reveals many points of contact between the two writers. Beckett told me he particularly admired Jouve's novel *Le Monde désert* (1928).
74 Beckett was stung to reply to the review of his friend's work in *TLS*, 23 October 1937, p. 786.
75 Yeats, *Collected Poems*, London, 1971, pp. 100, 104.
76 See interview with Driver (*Columbia University Forum*, IV, Summer 1961, pp. 21–5).

8 Conclusion

1 A term used by Beckett in the *How it is* notes found in the ETE 56 notebook (R.U.L.).
2 Eliot, *The Use of Poetry and the Use of Criticism*, London, 1964, p. 106.
3 *Tri-Quarterly*, 8, p. 207.
4 'Les Bosquets de Bondy' and 'Echo's Bones'; 'Les Deux Besoins' and 'Censorship in the Saorstat'.
5 The most recent example dates from 1967–8 (*Exhibition*, p. 118).
6 See 'J. M. Mime' (*Exhibition*, p. 117) and 'Mime du Rêveur A' (R.U.L.).
7 *T.N.*, p. 202.
8 'Esquisse radiophonique', *Minuit* 5, September 1973, pp. 31–5.
9 Cp. *Proust*, p. 26ff.
10 *Minuit* 5, pp. 32–3.

11 Ibid., p. 33.
12 *Minuit 8*, March 1974, pp. 65–72.
13 *All That Fall*, London, 1965, p. 21.
14 *Minuit 8*, pp. 67–8.
15 Ibid., p. 69.
16 *Minuit 4*, May 1973, pp. 71–2.
17 Ibid., p. 72.
18 *Minuit 2*, January 1973, pp. 40–1.
19 Ibid., p. 40.
20 Ibid., p. 41.
21 Ibid., p. 41.
22 *Minuit 4*, p. 71.
23 *Minuit 2*, p. 40.
24 *Minuit 4*, p. 71.
25 *Minuit 2*, pp. 41–2.
26 *Minuit 1*, pp. 22–6.
27 Ibid., p. 22.
28 Ibid., p. 23.

Select bibliography

Select bibliography

Although in recent years the literature on Beckett has shown signs of swamping the writings which have called it into being, there is still, of course, no substitute for actually reading Beckett, and very little of his work, even the most minor items, is difficult of access. The stress in this bibliography therefore falls on his writing rather than his critics. At the same time, it would be foolish to deny oneself the benefit of a Virgil as guide through this 'inferno', and the second part of this bibliography is given over to the recommendation of important secondary material.

The chronological outline of Beckett's achievement offers the least distorting profile; juvenilia are omitted, but known unpublished works are included. Dates are predominantly those of publication, but known dates of composition are also used; this listing contents itself with first printing in book form and refers students to F. and F. for more complete details. Except in one case letters are omitted.

late 1920s
'Le Concentrisme' (paper read to Trinity College Modern Language Society), unpublished: R.U.L.

1928
Research essay on the 'Unanimistes' (submitted in accordance with the conditions attending the 1927 award, to Beckett, of the Moderatorship Prize).

1929
'Dante . . . Bruno. Vico. .Joyce' (essay on Joyce's *Finnegans Wake*); 'Assumption' (short story), uncollected; the first was published in *Our Exagmination round his Factification for Incamination of Work in Progress*, Paris, 1929, pp. [3]–22; the second in *transition*, nos 16 and 17, Paris, 1929, pp. 268–71 (pp. 242–53 of which contain a reprint of the Joyce essay).
'Che Sciagura' (satire), *T.C.D.: a College Miscellany*, vol. 36, p. 42; uncollected.

1930

'For Future Reference' (poem), *transition*, nos 19 and 20, Paris, 1930, pp. 342–3; uncollected.

Whoroscope (poem), Paris 1930; collected in *Poems in English*, London, 1961.

'From the only poet to a shining whore' (for Henry Crowder to sing) (poem), in *Henry-Music*, by Henry Crowder, Paris, 1930; uncollected.

Translations from the Italian in *This Quarter*, no. 2, 1930, pp. 630, 672, 675–83.

1931

'The Possessed' (parody), *T.C.D.*, vol. 37, p. 138; uncollected.

Proust (critical monograph), London, 1931; reprinted in *Proust and Three Dialogues with Georges Duthuit*, London, 1965.

'Hell Crane to Starling', 'Casket of Pralinen for a daughter of a dissipated mandarin', 'Text', 'Yoke of liberty' (poems), in *The European Caravan*, part 1, ed. Putnam and others, New York, 1931; uncollected.

'Return to the Vestry' (poem), *New Review*, no. 1, Paris, 1931, pp. [98]–9; uncollected.

'Alba' (poem), *Dublin Magazine*, vol. 6, Dublin, 1931, p. 4; collected in *Poems in English*.

Translation (with others) of *Anna Livia Plurabelle* for *Nouvelle Revue Française*, vol. 19, 1931, pp. 633–46.

1932

'Dream of Fair to Middling Women' (novel), unpublished; R.U.L. (Sections of it published in *transition*, no. 21, The Hague, 1932, pp. 13–20; *New Review*, no. 2, Paris, 1932, p. 57; and *New Durham*, Durham University, June 1965, pp. 10–11.)

'The Drunken Boat' (translation of Rimbaud's 'Le Bateau ivre'), unpublished; R.U.L.

'Home Olga' (poem), in *Contempo*, vol. 3, no. 13, Chapel Hill, 1934, p. 3; reprinted in Ruby Cohn's *Samuel Beckett: The Comic Gamut* and, most accessibly, in Ellmann's biography of Joyce; uncollected.

'Dante and the Lobster' (short story), in *This Quarter*, no. 5, Paris, 1932, pp. 222–36; collected in *More Pricks than Kicks* (*q.v.*).

'Poetry is Vertical' (manifesto, with others), *transition*, no. 21, pp. 148–9.

Translations of André Breton, Paul Éluard, and René Crevel, in *This Quarter*, no. 5, 1932 (see F. and F., pp. 92–3).

1934

More Pricks than Kicks (collection of ten short stories: 'Dante and the Lobster', 'Fingal', 'Ding-Dong', 'A Wet Night', 'Love and Lethe', 'Walking Out', 'What a Misfortune', 'The Smeraldina's Billet-Doux', 'Yellow', 'Draff'), London, 1934; reprinted, 1970.

'Schwabenstreich'; 'Proust in Pieces', in *Spectator*, no. 5517, 23 March 1934, p. 472; and ibid., no. 5530, 23 June 1934, pp. 975–6.

'Recent Irish Poetry' (book review), *Bookman*, vol. 86, London, August 1934, pp. 235–6 (under the pseudonym Andrew Belis); reprinted in *The Lace Curtain*, no. 4, Dublin, Summer 1971, pp. 58–63.

'*Poems*, by R. M. Rilke', 'Humanistic Quietism', 'Ex Cathezra', 'Papini's Dante', 'The Essential and the Incidental', (book reviews); the first is in *Criterion*, vol. 13, London, 1934, pp. 705–7; the second in *Dublin Magazine*, vol. 9, 1934, pp. 79–80; the last three in *Bookman*, vol. 87, Christmas 1934, pp. 10, 14, 111; all uncollected.

'A Case in a Thousand' (short story), *Bookman*, vol. 86, 1934, pp. 241–2; uncollected.

Translations for *Negro*, ed. Nancy Cunard, London, 1934.

1935
Echo's Bones and Other Precipitates (collection of poems: 'The Vulture', 'Enueg I', 'Enueg II', 'Alba', 'Dortmunder', 'Sanies I', 'Sanies II', 'Serena I', 'Serena II', 'Serena III', 'Malacoda', 'Da tagte es', 'Echo's Bones'), Paris, 1935; reprinted in *Poems in English*.

Murphy (novel), London, 1938.

'Echo's Bones' (short story); unpublished.

1936
'An Imaginative Work!' (book review, of Jack B. Yeats's *The Amaranthers*), *Dublin Magazine*, vol. 11, July–September 1936, pp. 80–1; uncollected.

'Cascando' (poem), *Dublin Magazine*, vol. 11, October–December 1936, pp. 3–4; collected in *Poems in English*.

1937
Contribution to *Authors take sides on the Spanish War*, London, 1937, p. 6.

1938
'Ooftish' (poem); 'Denis Devlin' (book review); both published in *transition*'s tenth anniversary number, no. 27, Paris, 1938, pp. 33, 289–94; uncollected.

'Les Deux Besoins' (criticism), unpublished; R.U.L.

Translation of a preface by Jean Cocteau to a catalogue for an exhibition at Guggenheim Jeune; see F. and F., p. 96.

Translations for the *London Bulletin* art magazine; see F. and F., pp. 96–7.

1937–9
Poèmes 37–39 (12 poems in French), in *Temps modernes*, vol. 2, 1946, pp. 288–93; collected in *Poèmes*, Paris, 1968.

1942–4
Watt (novel), Paris, 1953; reprinted, 1958, and London, 1963.

1945
'La Peinture des van Veldes, ou le monde et le pantalon' (art criticism), *Cahiers d'art*, nos 20 and 21, Paris, 1945–6, pp. 349–54, 356; uncollected.

'L'Expulsé', 'Le Calmant', 'La Fin', 'Premier Amour' (short stories); the first three published in book form as the *nouvelles* of *Nouvelles et textes pour rien*, Paris, 1955, the latter, Paris, 1970; English translations, by Beckett and others, are most accessible in *No's Knife; Collected Shorter Prose 1945–1966*, London, 1967, for the first three, and *First Love*, London, 1973.

Select bibliography

'Les Bosquets de Bondy' (short story); unpublished, University of Texas.
Mercier et Camier (novel), Paris, 1970; English translation, London, 1974.
'MacGreevy on Yeats' (book review), *Irish Times*, 4 August 1945, p. 2.

1946
'Saint-Lô' (poem), *Irish Times*, 24 June 1946, p. 5.

1947
Molloy (novel), Paris, 1951; English translation, Paris, 1955; London, 1959 (in *Three Novels*).
'Eleuthéria' (play), unpublished; R.U.L.

1948
Malone meurt (novel), Paris, 1951; English translation (*Malone Dies*), New York, 1956; London, 1958; and in *Three Novels*.
En attendant Godot (play), Paris, 1952; English translation New York, 1954; London, 1956; revised and unexpurgated translation London, 1965; first produced in 1953 (Paris); first London production 1955; critical edition (by Colin Duckworth), London, 1966.
'Trois poèmes' (poems in French, with facing English translation), *transition Forty-Eight*, no. 2, Paris, 1948, pp. 96–7; collected in *Poems in English* and *Poèmes*, which collects three other poems from this period.
'Peintres de l'empêchement' (art criticism), *Derrière le Miroir*, nos 11 and 12, Paris, 1948, pp. 3, 4, 7; uncollected.
Translations for *transition*, 1948–50; see F. and F., pp. 97–9.

1949
L'Innommable (novel), Paris, 1953; English translation (*The Unnamable*), New York, 1958; and in *Three Novels*.
'Three Dialogues with Georges Duthuit' (art criticism), *transition Forty-Nine*, no. 5, Paris, 1949, pp. 97–103; reprinted in *Proust and Three Dialogues with Georges Duthuit*, London, 1965.

1950
Textes pour rien (thirteen prose texts in French), published in *Nouvelles et textes pour rien*, Paris, 1955; and in English in *No's Knife*, London, 1967.

1951
Translations for *Anthology of Mexican Poetry*, Bloomington, 1958; London, 1959; reprinted, London, 1970.

1952
'Henri Hayden, homme-peintre' (art criticism), *Cahiers d'art – Documents*, no. 22, Paris, 1955, p. 2; reprinted in *Hayden*, ed. J. Selz, Geneva, 1962.

1955
'From an Abandoned Work' (short story), *Trinity News*, no. 3, 7 June 1956, p. 4; collected in *No's Knife*.

1956
Fin de partie (play, begun 1954), Paris, 1957; English translation (*Endgame*)

230

New York and London, 1958; first produced London, 1957 (French version) and New York 1958 (English version); critical edition of French text London, 1970. (For Beckett's fourteen letters to Alan Schneider see *Village Voice*, 19 March 1958, pp. 8, 15.)

Acte sans paroles I and II (mimes); the first published (with *Fin de partie*), Paris, 1957, and in the English translation; the second published (in English) in *New Directions*, New York, 1960 and (in French) in Frankfurt, 1963.

All That Fall (radio play), London, 1957; French translation, Paris, 1960; first broadcast, 1957.

1958
Krapp's Last Tape (play), London, 1959; French translation, Paris, 1960; first performance London, 1958.

1959
Embers (radio play), published (with *Krapp's Last Tape*), London, 1959; and (French translation) in *Comédie et actes diverses*, Paris, 1966.

1960
The Old Tune (translation of Robert Pinget's play *La Manivelle*), Paris, 1960; reprinted in Penguin *Traverse Plays*, ed. Haynes.
'Second Testament' (translation of poem by Alain Bosquet), in *Selected Poems of Alain Bosquet*, New York, 1963. See also Ohio, 1972, pp. 154–9.

1961
Comment c'est (novel, begun 1959), Paris, 1961; English translation (*How it is*), London, 1964.
Happy Days (play), published New York, 1961; London, 1963; (in French translation) Paris, 1963; first performance New York, 1961; London, 1962.

1962
Words and Music (radio play), published in *Play and Two Short Pieces for Radio*, London, 1964; and (in French translation) in *Comédie et actes diverses*; first broadcast, 1962.

1963
Play (play), London, 1964; (French translation) Paris, 1966; first performance Ulm-Donau, 1963; New York, London and Paris, 1964.
Cascando (radio play), Frankfurt, 1963 (in French); London, 1964 (in English translation); first broadcast in French 1963; in English 1964.

1964
Film, awarded *Prix Filmcritice* at Venice Film Festival, 1965; text in *Eh Joe and Other Writings*, London, 1967, and (with illustrations and production notes) London, 1972.

1965
Eh Joe (television play), London, 1967; French translation in *Comédie et actes diverses*; first televised, 1966.

Imagination morte imaginez (short prose piece), Paris, 1965; English translation (*Imagination Dead Imagine*) in *No's Knife*.
Le Dépeupleur (short prose text), Paris, 1971; English translation (*The Lost Ones*), London, 1972.
Come and Go ('dramaticule'), London, 1967; French translation in *Comédie et actes diverses*; first performed Berlin, 1965; Paris, 1966; Dublin, 1968.

1966
Assez (short prose text), Paris, 1966; English translation (*Enough*) in *No's Knife*.
Bing (short prose text), Paris, 1966; English translation (*Ping*) in *No's Knife*; see F. and F., Appendix II, pp. 325–43, prints the ten variant texts of this work.

1969
Sans (short prose text), Paris, 1969; English translation (*Lessness*), London, 1970.
Breath (play), in *Gambit*, vol. 4, no. 16, pp. 8–9; first produced, New York, 1969; Ms. of French translation (*Souffle*) at R.U.L.

1973
Not I (play), London, 1973.

1975
For details of *Foirades*, written at various times, see notes to chapter 8.

There are now a very large number of full-length studies of Beckett's work, and it begins to be obvious that two kinds of approach are at present popular. The first might without prejudice be called introductory studies, lucid and expository but largely consolidating the discoveries of others. The second might be thought of as basically scholarly, discovering sources, exploring hypotheses, adducing parallels. This latter approach demands respect, as likely to reveal matters of the most permanent interest; at the same time the intelligent general reader will not always want to consider only one area, and the best writing on Beckett is that which is written with enthusiasm as well as expertise. The subsequent bibliography includes work of both kinds.

John Fletcher's sound and unpretentious book, *The Novels of Samuel Beckett* (London, 1964), has not been superseded as a clear and sensible statement of what is central in Beckett's fiction; Eugene Webb's study of the same area (London, 1970) is also not without its merits, an honest and straightforward book. No single book on the plays can be unreservedly recommended; Alec Reid's attractive *All I can manage, more than I could* (Dublin, 1968) is little more than an essay, and the collaborative study of John Fletcher and John Spurling, *Beckett: a Study of his Plays* (London, 1973) is not consistently illuminating. The only book-length study of Beckett's poetry is Lawrence E. Harvey's *Samuel Beckett: Poet and Critic, 1929–1949* (Princeton, 1970), which is packed with interesting detail, but not always sufficiently focused to enable the reader to form a critical estimate. Of studies narrower in range, Raymond Federman's *Journey to Chaos: Samuel Beckett's Early Fiction* (Berkeley, 1965) should be mentioned, and Ruby Cohn's *Samuel Beckett: the Comic Gamut* (New Brunswick, 1962) contains much excellent analysis of Beckett's comic techniques. G. C. Barnard's 'new approach' in *Samuel Beckett: the Novels and Plays* (London, 1970) is largely psychoanalytical in orientation, and Jean Onimus's *Beckett* (Paris, 1968) pursues mainly the religious context. No one interested in style and stylistics can afford to ignore Olga Bernal's *Langage et Fiction dans les romans de Samuel Beckett* (Paris, 1970), and John Fletcher's *Samuel Beckett's Art* (London, 1967), collects his writings on Beckett's technique in each genre.

There is no completely satisfactory study of the intellectual and cultural background to Beckett; Nathan Scott's *Samuel Beckett* (Cambridge, 1965) emphasizes the tradition at the expense of the ostensible subject, and William York Tindall's essay *Samuel Beckett* (New York, 1964) is not long enough to permit detailed exploration. Richard Coe's essay in the 'Writers and Critics' series (London, 1964) is arguably the most capable broad exposition of Beckett's philosophical inheritance yet undertaken, despite David Hesla's *The Shape of Chaos: an Interpretation of the Art of Samuel Beckett* (Minneapolis, 1971). Hans-Joachim Schulz's monograph *This Hell of Stories* (The Hague, 1973) is, as its subtitle suggests, 'a Hegelian approach' of exceptional interest. Sighle Kennedy's *Murphy's Bed* (Lewisburg, 1971) covers a wider area, including the intellectual milieu of the 1920s and 1930s.

The most brilliant book in every sense, is still Hugh Kenner's pioneering *Samuel Beckett: a Critical Study* (London, 1965), which is consistently thought-provoking and imaginative. Ludovic Janvier's *Pour Samuel Beckett* (Paris, 1966), the first serious large-scale work in French, offers insights of a similarly refreshing kind.

There are a number of useful collections of essays on Beckett, including Ruby Cohn's *Casebook on Godot* (New York, 1967), and *Modern Drama*, vol. 9, no. 3, contains sixteen articles on Beckett's theatre, collected by the same editor. Her early collection for *Perspective*, vol. 11, no. 3, Autumn 1959, marks the first serious study of Beckett, and begins the drift of attention to Beckett's prose. Melvin Friedman's collection *Samuel Beckett Now* (Chicago, 1970), originally published in *Revue des Lettres Modernes*, no. 100, 1964, covers many aspects, but Martin Esslin's 'Twentieth Century Views' volume (Englewood Cliffs, 1965) is more comprehensive. Special collections on the novel trilogy (ed. J. D. O'Hara) and *Endgame* (ed. G. B. Chevigny) have been published in comparable series.

Of chapters in books, mention should be made of Kenner's *The Stoic Comedians: Flaubert, Joyce, and Beckett* (Boston, 1963), David Grossvogel's *Four Playwrights and a Postscript* (Ithaca, 1962), Leonard Pronko's *Avant-Garde: the Experimental Theatre in France* (Berkeley, 1962), Jacques Guichar-naud's *Modern French Theatre from Giradoux to Beckett* (New Haven, 1961) and

Select bibliography

Geoffrey Brereton's *Principles of Tragedy* (London, 1968). Kenneth Rexroth's *Bird in the Bush: Obvious Essays* (New York, 1959) is more engaging than Norman Mailer's *Advertisements for Myself* (London, 1970); Leo Bersani's *Balzac to Beckett: Centre and Circumference in French Literature* (Oxford, 1970) and Martin Esslin's *The Theatre of the Absurd* (Harmondsworth, 1968) have, in their different ways, much to offer.

Periodical articles of particular value are the following:

Blanchot, Maurice, 'Where now? Who now?', *Evergreen Review*, 2, Winter 1959, pp. 222–9.

Bonnefoi, Geneviève, 'Textes pour rien?', *Lettres Modernes*, no. 36, March 1956, pp. 424–30.

Chambers, Ross, 'Beckett and the padded cell', *Meanjin*, vol. 21, 1962, pp. 451–68.

Cmarada, Geraldine, '*Malone Dies*, a round of consciousness', *Symposium*, vol. 14, no. 3, Fall 1960, pp. 199–212.

Coe, Richard, 'God and Samuel Beckett', *Meanjin*, vol. 24, 1965, pp. 65–86.

Dreyfus, Dina, 'Vraies et fausses énigmes', *Mercure de France*, no. 1130, October 1957, pp. 268–85.

Erickson, John D., 'Objects and systems in the novels of Samuel Beckett', *L'Esprit Créateur*, vol. 7, no. 2, Summer 1967, pp. 113–22.

Fletcher, John, 'Beckett et Swift: vers une étude comparée', *Littératures X*, Toulouse, année XI, fasc. 1, pp. 81–117.

Gresset, Michel, 'Le parce que de Faulkner et le donc de Beckett', *Lettres Nouvelles*, no. 19, 1961, pp. 124–38.

Lodge, David, 'Some Ping understood', *Encounter*, vol. 30, no. 2, 1968, pp. 85–9.

Macksey, Richard, 'The artist in the labyrinth: design or *Dasein*?', *Modern Language Notes*, vol. 77, May 1962, pp. 239–56.

Montgomery, Niall, 'No symbols where none intended', *New World Writing*, no. 5, 1954, pp. 324–37.

Morse, Mitchell, 'The contemplative life according to Samuel Beckett', *Hudson Review*, vol. 15, pp. 512–24.

Ricks, Christopher, 'The roots of Samuel Beckett', *Listener*, vol. 72, 17 December 1964, pp. 963–4, 980.

Warhaft, Sidney, 'Threne and theme in *Watt*', *Wisconsin Studies in Contemporary Literature*, vol. 4, no. 3, Autumn 1963, pp. 261–78.

The memoirs of Sylvia Beach, Adrienne Monnier, Nancy Cunard, Peggy Guggenheim, Samuel Putman, Matthew Josephson, Malcolm Cowley, Ernest Hemingway, Richard Aldington and many others provide an image of the cultural milieu. The writings of Hans Jonas and R. McL. Wilson give indispensable help to anyone interested in Gnosticism. Works of literary history that provide interesting modern contexts for Beckett are: A. G. Lehmann's *The Symbolist Aesthetic in France 1885–1895* (Oxford, 1950), Michael Hamburger's *The Truth of Poetry* (London, 1970), Robert Martin Adams's *NIL* (New York, 1970), Morse Peckham's *Beyond the Tragic Vision*

(New York, 1962), Cyrus Hoy's *The Hyacinth Room* (New York, 1964) and Maurice Valency's *The Flower and the Castle* (London, 1962).

Interesting pre-romantic contexts are provided by Leonard Forster's *The Icy Fire* (Cambridge, 1969) (see esp. chapter 3), Erich Auerbach's book *Dante* (Chicago, 1961), Hiram Haydn's *The Counter-Renaissance* (Gloucester, Mass., 1950), Walter Kaiser's *Praisers of Folly* (Cambridge, Mass., 1963) and Martin Price's *To the Palace of Wisdom* (Urbana, 1971). On romantic contexts, Meyer Abrams's writings and Ernest Tuveson on *The Imagination as a Means of Grace* (New York, 1973), among well-known studies, and Irving Massey's *The Uncreating Word* (Bloomington, 1971), of the less well-known, should be consulted.

Index

Index